ARRESTING IMAGES:
CRIME AND POLICING IN FRONT
OF THE TELEVISION CAMERA

While most research on television examines its impact on viewers, *Arresting Images* asks instead how TV influences what is in front of the camera, and how it reshapes other institutions as it broadcasts their activities. Aaron Doyle develops his argument with four case studies of televised crime and policing: he examines the popular American 'reality TV' series *Cops*, the televising of surveillance footage and home videos of crime and policing, coverage of Vancouver's Stanley Cup riot, and the broadcast of publicity-grabbing demonstrations of the environmental group Greenpeace. Each of these studies is of significant interest in its own right, but Doyle also uses them to make a broader argument regarding television's impact. The four studies show how televised activities tend to become more institutionally important, tightly managed, dramatic, simplified, and fitted to society's dominant values. Powerful institutions, like the police, often harness television for their own legitimation and surveillance purposes, dictating which situations are televised and producing 'authorized definitions' of the situations, which allow them to control the consequences. While these institutions invoke the notion that 'seeing is believing' to reinforce their positions of dominance, the book argues that many observers and researchers have long overstated and misunderstood the role of TV's visual component in shaping its influences.

AARON DOYLE is an assistant professor of sociology at Carleton University.

Arresting Images

Crime and Policing in Front of the Television Camera

AARON DOYLE

UNIVERSITY OF TORONTO PRESS
Toronto Buffalo London

© University of Toronto Press Incorporated 2003
Toronto Buffalo London
Printed in Canada

ISBN 0-8020-3682-1 (cloth)
ISBN 0-8020-8504-0 (paper)

Printed on acid-free paper

National Library of Canada Cataloguing in Publication

Doyle, Aaron
    Arresting images : crime and policing in front of the televsion
    camera / Aaron Doyle.

    Includes bibliographical references and index.
    ISBN 0-8020-3682-1 (bound).   ISBN 0-8020-8504-0 (pbk.)

    1. Crime on television – Social aspects. 2. Reality television
    programs – Social aspects. 3. Mass media and criminal justice.
    I. Title.

    HM1206.D69 2003   302. 23'45   C2003-902939-5

An earlier shorter version of Chapter 3 appeared as '"Cops": Television
Policing as Policing Reality,' in M. Fishman and G. Cavender, eds., *Entertaining Crime: Television Reality Programs* (New York: Aldine de Gruyter, 1998).

This book has been published with the help of a grant from the Canadian
Federation for the Humanities and Social Sciences, through the Aid to
Scholarly Publications Program using funds provided by the Social Sciences
and Humanities Research Council of Canada.

University of Toronto Press acknowledges the financial assistance to its
publishing program of the Canada Council for the Arts and the Ontario
Arts Council.

University of Toronto Press acknowledges the financial support for its
publishing activities of the Government of Canada through the Book
Publishing Industry Development Program (BPIDP).

Contents

Acknowledgments

Many people helped me throughout the creation of this book. At the beginning, the late Kevin Carriere sparked my interest in reality TV. More importantly, I'll always remember the generous way in which he treated people. Barbara Alldritt was an early friend in graduate school and also an inspiration: one of the more courageous people I've known. Kevin Haggerty has been a tremendous friend. One of my chief coping strategies in academia for many years has been watching closely everything that Kevin does. I would like to thank other grad students and sessional friends at the University of British Columbia for making my time there a rich one, especially Brenda Beagan, Karyn Eisler, Laura Huey, Alice Lee, Mike Pollex, Eric Tompkins, Peter Urmetzer, Donna Vogel, and Nancy Wachowich. Key moral support also came from the folks at Sunday softball and the Nightcaps.

Neil Guppy deserves much gratitude for challenging me to make this a better piece of sociology, as I knew he would. I also owe thanks to Ken Stoddart, a model as a teacher and an ethnographer. I owe David Altheide a lot for his inspiration and assistance at various stages. Thanks also to Gray Cavender, Wes Pue, Bob Ratner, and two anonymous reviewers for University of Toronto Press for very helpful comments on earlier drafts of the book. And thanks to all those, too numerous to mention, who have commented on individual chapters or presentations drawn from this material. Special thanks to Liz Doyle for suggesting the title.

I am grateful to other faculty members for valued support and guidance during my time at UBC, especially Brian Elliott and David Tindall. Special thanks to Dorothy Chunn for her support during the time I was working on this book during my post-doctoral fellowship at the School of Criminology, Simon Fraser University.

I would also like to thank the people of the Department of Sociology and Anthropology, Carleton University, for their excellent support during the final stages of the project. Thank you to the Social Sciences and Humanities Research Council for their support during the research.

It is practically impossible to imagine a better mentor than Richard Ericson, not only in guiding the research that resulted in this book, but in contributing centrally to all aspects of my growth as a sociologist. I have been profoundly fortunate to be his student.

I am extremely grateful to University of Toronto Press and to Virgil Duff in particular for their support and patience with this project. Thanks very much to Terry Teskey, my copy editor. Thanks also to Debby Schryer for her help with the index.

I certainly could not have completed the book without the support of my extended family, especially Patrick, Kegan, Dany, and Meki. The fundamental influences of my parents, Doran and Mike Doyle, are clear to me in the book itself.

Finally, and most importantly, my deepest thanks to Liz for her wonderful, enduring love and support during these years, and to her and Genevieve and Charlie for making it all make sense.

ARRESTING IMAGES:
CRIME AND POLICING IN FRONT
OF THE TELEVISION CAMERA

CHAPTER ONE

Introduction

Since the birth of TV, a great many people have feared its possible influences. Hundreds of social scientists have researched TV's potential negative effects. Yet this huge body of research is often limited because it conceives of television's influences in too narrow a way. For all the worry about TV, much of its social impact is overlooked.

In this book I approach the influences of television in an alternative way. To do this, I investigate a trend that has previously been little researched. This trend is that TV is broadcasting more and more footage of 'real' incidents of crime and policing. Of course, TV programs have always been full of crime stories, but now, for various reasons, we are seeing a lot more criminal justice events that have been directly recorded on video, captured 'live' in front of the TV camera. I examine this trend through case studies of four kinds of situations from the front lines of criminal justice, each of which is increasingly broadcast to our living rooms.

These four studies – of the reality-TV show *Cops*, of TV's use of surveillance footage and home video of crime, of television's role in Vancouver's Stanley Cup riot, and of TV and Greenpeace – are each interesting in their own right, and can be read individually. However, I also use the four studies to make a broader argument, an argument about how we can think about the influences of television and other media more generally. To do so, I draw together and build on three somewhat unconventional strands of previous social scientific thinking about media. What makes these three earlier perspectives distinctive is that they can all be used to understand how TV influences, not individual audience members, but other *institutions*.

Analysing this kind of media influence – on other institutions – is still a new line of enquiry. It is a departure from most social science work on the media. Thus, these three somewhat similar recent perspectives have not yet been drawn together and treated comparatively. Yet these kinds of institutional analyses of media influence call out strongly for further attention and development. This is because they allow a way around key stumbling blocks that hold back a lot of mainstream social scientific research on TV and other media.

The potential influence of TV content on individual audience members has been the subject of literally thousands of studies in disciplines such as communications, sociology, psychology, and political science. The vast majority of this huge body of research literature conceives of the impact of TV quite narrowly: simply, that television content transmits messages to viewers, influencing their beliefs, attitudes, and behaviour. In fact, the term 'media effects' has become shorthand in much social scientific literature for this relatively narrow conception; with this choice of language, the point that media might have other effects beyond simply influencing audience members in these ways is brushed to one side. Ironically, critically oriented research on mass media most often features a mirror image of this limitation of mainstream work (Ericson 1991). This more critical research also tends to focus narrowly on the ideological influence of media content on individual audience members. Certainly it is essential to consider how TV might shape how people think about important social and political questions (and I am going to do so in this book). However, that is not the only form of TV's influence.

I began this research with the observation that TV does not simply stand back and record events to convey them to audiences. Instead, television, like other media, often shapes the things it records. In this book I investigate how television might actually alter or transform social situations when they are broadcast. Thus, my research asks a different type of question. Not the standard question: how does crime on TV affect television audiences? Instead, the alternative question: how is crime and policing itself altered as it is televised? Crime and punishment have always been staples of television news and TV fiction, just as they were central topics of print news and print fiction long before the birth of television (Kaminer 1995: 50–2). In turn, the social consequences of all these dramatic, disturbing portrayals of crime and punishment in the media have long preoccupied social scientists and cultural commentators (see, for example, Davis 1951; Gerbner and Gross 1976; Chibnall 1977; Hall et al. 1978; Graber 1980; Garofalo 1981; Ericson,

Baranek and Chan 1987, 1989, 1991; Sparks 1992; Acland 1995; Sacco 1995; Kaminer 1995; Surette 1997; Bok 1998; Goldstein 1998; Potter and Kappeler 1998; Best 1999; Lawrence 2000; Perlmutter 2000; Altheide 2002).

As TV has evolved, a newer development is that actual incidents of crime and policing are – more and more frequently – recorded directly by video cameras and broadcast on TV. Formerly, it was rare that television featured such 'real' footage. Instead, TV crime news was very much based on spoken story telling after the events by journalists on news programs (Ericson, Baranek, and Chan 1991; Ericson 1998). A reporter simply told the TV audience about incidents of crime and policing that had happened some time ago. TV might have used some related visual material – for example, the reporter might have used the crime scene as a backdrop as she or he recorded a spoken account of the crime. However, it was unusual to have footage of the actual crime and policing activities in question.

The trend now is that more and more 'real' video footage of various aspects of everyday life is broadcast on TV. The broadcasting industry term for such material is 'actuality' footage. It is most often not 'live' in the sense of being broadcast at the time it occurs, but it is 'live' in the sense of being an on-scene record of actual events. This trend towards more and more TV footage of actual events is apparent in many other situations far beyond the realm of criminal justice. There is more footage broadcast of 'real' events for several reasons: the increasing presence of video cameras, the use by TV news of various alternative sources of video, like home camcorders and surveillance cameras; and the advent of various reality-TV programs, from *Real TV* to *Trauma: Life in the ER* to *America's Funniest Home Videos*. These all interact with a culture in which, for many people, being visible in the media seems highly appealing. As TV merges more and more with the Internet and its web cameras, the broadcasting of everyday life will only increase.

One place where the increasing broadcast of such 'real' TV footage is most apparent is in the world of crime and its control, which has always been a central focus of public and media fascination. As TV has evolved, various kinds of criminal justice situations have more and more been captured by its cameras. For example, starting in the 1960s, an increasing number of political demonstrations and riots have occurred in front of TV cameras, resulting in often controversial news footage of police controlling crowds. Indeed, by the 1970s numerous activists had taken televised protest to the next step. They began to stage their own episodes of political lawbreaking for television – media stunts specifically tailored so that choreographed crime and its policing could be recorded by the cameras. As we moved into the 1980s and 1990s other 'real' and 'live' instances of crime and policing were captured for TV news by increasingly pervasive surveillance cameras and home camcorders. Finally, starting in 1989, 'real' policing was recorded for a whole new television format: reality-TV programs like *Cops* and its many imitators. The situations I have just described are four of the most common cases where crime and policing are recorded 'live,' and I will look at each one individually in the chapters that follow.

My research began with the speculation that the presence of TV cameras might alter these particular criminal justice situations. Furthermore, that in recording these situations TV might have various broader effects on criminal justice institutions. The potential for these types of TV influence may seem counterintuitive; people may have a commonsense view that the camera is a device that simply records things. Perhaps, then, all this might make more sense to the reader if I give a hypothetical example.

Consider a routine criminal justice situation that many of us have experienced: a roadside traffic stop by a police officer. Now consider how the social situation would be changed if such a police traffic stop were to be captured by a TV camera and broadcast to a wide television audience. The conventional social scientific way of thinking about television's role in this situation would be to analyse the content of the TV message about criminal justice that is given to audiences, and to research how this message might influence audience attitudes and behaviour. But television would likely also alter the traffic stop situation in other ways. The police officer's behaviour might be affected. The officer might start playing to the camera, for example, letting the driver go with a warning lecture that is also aimed at the TV audience, or, alternatively, deciding to 'throw the book' at the driver, given the high profile of the situation. As well, the experience would almost certainly be altered for the driver herself. For example, she might experience the traffic stop as much more punitive because of the shaming effect of TV.

Furthermore, if such police traffic stops were televised on a regular basis, this might lead to wider changes, changes beyond those particular situations that are broadcast. Indeed, the standard operating procedures for conducting traffic stops might well change, given that they would have become high-profile events. And the televising of traffic stops might also lead to wider changes in how traffic policing was institutionally organized. For example, more political attention, more resources, and more expertise might be committed to policing speeding drivers. Finally, the television audience might become players themselves in new ways in the new social situations that were created. For example, viewers might be able to phone a hotline to turn in speeders to a TV program.

In short, broadcasting this situation on TV would reshape this simple transaction in the criminal justice system. TV would make it something other than what it was; TV would essentially create a new social situation on the front lines of criminal justice. The resulting changes would extend beyond the immediate situation that was recorded, and also have wider ripple effects on the criminal justice system.

In fact, this example is not altogether hypothetical: some police traffic stops *are* now broadcast on TV – for example, on the reality-TV show *Cops*. And, while a *Cops* crew is not present at most traffic stops, many police cruisers are now mounted with surveillance cameras recording each and every such stop, and this surveillance footage increasingly finds its way onto TV news or reality TV. More generally, day-to-day episodes of contemporary institutional life that were not previously public events are increasingly broadcast on TV, episodes from within both the criminal justice system and many other social realms.

These types of influences of TV are quite different from those studied by most social scientists researching mass media. But such forms of TV influence would likely be predicted by a handful of scholars who have pioneered three alternative ways of thinking about media, which I will now introduce.

Three Perspectives on How Media Influence Other Institutions

This book builds on three theoretical perspectives that analyse this other direction of media influence. Each asks, in a somewhat different way, not 'How does TV affect who is in front of the set?' but instead 'How does TV affect what is in front of the camera?' As a consequence, each of these three alternative ways of thinking theorizes the influence of media in broader, more multifaceted, and more far-sighted ways than conventional models.

Following the lead of these three perspectives, the case studies I present here focus on how media influence life in other institutions. Contemporary social life increasingly occurs in major social institutions. Our identities are institutional identities; our careers are institutional careers. I look at institutionalized patterns of communication, and at the interaction between TV and other major institutions, mostly using the example of one key modern institution: the police (although the last study allows a comparison with another, more wholly media-driven institution, the environmental organization Greenpeace).

To say that some contemporary institutions (Greenpeace, for example) are largely 'creatures of the media' is far from a novel observation, either by social scientists or by anyone else. Yet media researchers have expended little effort in thinking systematically about such tendencies and their implications for how we theorize media influence. I have chosen these three perspectives to build on because they are the only three bodies of theory that deal directly with how media influence other institutions.

In the first of these alternative conceptions, thinkers such as Harold Innis, Marshall McLuhan, and Joshua Meyrowitz – 'medium theorists' – have examined how new forms of media such as the book, radio, and television reshape social life. For reasons I will discuss, I focus on the work of Meyrowitz (1985, 1994). An influential communications theorist, Meyrowitz argues that the advent of TV has broken down barriers between various social groups by including viewers in new 'information systems.' Thus, according to Meyrowitz, TV has had sweeping effects of social levelling, for example, between political authorities and everyday people.

A second, similar conception by other thinkers focuses more broadly on the influences of contemporary 'media culture' in general, rather than zeroing in on any specific medium such as TV. In this second conception, David Altheide and Robert Snow (1979, 1991) analyse the cultural logic of mass media, which they call 'media logic.' Altheide and Snow explore how media logic feeds back on and reshapes other key institutions that operate through the mass media, institutions such as electoral politics and organized religion. According to Altheide and Snow, the influences of media logic on these other institutions mean, for example, that various political and religious events become simplified and more spectacular and entertainment oriented, among other things.

A third, related way of thinking about media influence is the 'institutional perspective' of Richard Ericson, Patricia Baranek, and Janet Chan (1989). This perspective focuses on the news. It examines how media considerations come more and more to influence other institutions that are key sources of news. Ericson, Baranek, and Chan show how various institutions like the police, the courts, legislatures, and private companies are reshaped as they organize themselves to deal with the news media.

These three conceptions – Meyrowitz's medium theory, Altheide and Snow's media logic perspective, and Ericson, Baranek, and Chan's institutional perspective – have not previously been placed side by side and treated comparatively. They are not simply competing models: they each focus empirically on somewhat different targets, there is mutual influence between them, and they are often overlapping. Each of these three models is at least partly rooted intellectually in interpretive or interactionist sociology, although each links this to other types of sociological theory in different ways. If these three models are similar in important ways, there are also key points where they diverge. These points of disagreement must be addressed to build on this previous research.

Each of the three is, at least in part, a model of how media influence other institutions. This focus on the institutional level of influence offers a way around some of the deadlocks facing media audience research (Ericson 1991, 1994; Altheide and Snow 1991). Conventional social scientists continue to face tremendous difficulties in trying to show that the media actually *cause* particular views and behaviour in audiences, especially outside of experimental situations. Audiences may give a variety of interpretations to anything they see or hear in the media. It is very difficult to isolate the influence of media in particular from other interrelated factors, or to determine what comes first, particular audience attributes or particular patterns of watching TV or choosing reading material. These problems are clear in the large body of quantitative research attempting to link crime in the media with fear of crime or 'law and order' views among media audiences (for discussion of the difficulties here, see, for example, Gunter 1987; Ericson 1991; Sparks 1992; Sacco 1995; Heath and Gilbert 1996). There are similar problems in the massive bodies of work attempting to show a link between viewing of television violence, or pornography, and violent behaviour (see Cumberbatch and Howitt 1989; Ericson 1991; Lacombe 1994; Livingstone 1996; Freedman 2002). Those familiar with long-running debates within media audience research may feel frustrated by the relative lack of progress. Repetitive controversies have persisted for decades in the mainstream media literature about whether or not it is possible to quantify various 'media effects' on audience members

(Cumberbatch and Howitt 1989; Livingstone 1996). Meanwhile, critical researchers were mired in a long-running theoretical debate about whether media audiences should be understood as relatively 'active' or 'passive' (e.g., Fiske 1987; Seaman 1992; Morley 1996; Curran 1996). The different sides in the 'active versus passive audience' debate sometimes seemed entrenched in positions predetermined by their broader theoretical orientations. Of course, the question of media influence on individual audience members and its social and political consequences remains very important, but it is possible to step away from some of these knotty problems and come at these questions in a slightly different way.

Another difficulty with using the conventional model of media effects on individual audience members is the following. In attempting to isolate the influence of media, such research often tends to look at media effects abstracted from any social or political context. In order to zero in on and measure TV's influence, researchers take it out of the context in which it actually happens. Instead, this research attempts to measure media effects using various forms of 'public opinion' as operationalized and measured by social scientists. Of course, we all use notions or constructs like 'public opinion' to analyse society. Yet we have to be careful not to fall into the trap of assuming that survey responses that measure public opinion *automatically* translate into other tangible effects. Some research too often simply presumes that such public opinion as measured by researchers must necessarily have important social or political consequences. For example, researchers who study media 'agenda-setting' (e.g., Rogers and Dearing 1994) explore the relationship between which issues are high on the media agenda (get a lot of news coverage) and which issues are high on the 'public agenda' (are ranked as important in audience surveys). It has often been simply taken as given by such research that what is determined by surveys to be high on the 'public agenda' is socially and politically important, based on the assumption that public opinion naturally influences the 'policy agenda' (what policy makers actually do). Yet how this process of public influence on policy makers actually works is often simply left unexamined. Meanwhile, conventional audience research misses many other important kinds of media influence, other effects beyond simply how media impact individual audience members.

Thus, an alternative approach for researchers is to focus more on the media as a direct player in particular political and organizational contexts. This approach asks: What are the direct political consequences of what the media does? Concerns about media effects on audiences such as increased 'fear of crime' (Gunter 1987) or increased 'punitiveness' (Roberts and Doob 1990) are in any case often driven by the political implications of these kinds of public views. We care about fear of crime or punitiveness in audiences, at least in large part, because of how these public attitudes might feed back into the politics of the criminal justice system itself.

Ray Surette (1997) calls an alternative focus on the direct political and institutional consequences of media coverage an 'ecological approach.' As Surette notes, 'the media can directly affect what actors in the criminal justice system do without having to first change the public's attitudes and agendas' (1998: 216). For example, Mark Fishman (1978, 1981) analysed a New York media 'crime wave' of sensational reporting of alleged attacks against the elderly – even though there was no evidence that attacks against the elderly had actually increased. This 'crime wave' resulted in the allocation of more resources to police and the passing of tougher laws. Thus Fishman demonstrated important effects of the news media without needing to measure fear of crime in audiences.

A slightly different way of thinking about Surette's suggestion is for us to focus on media influence on other institutions. There are a number of studies of single examples of media influence on criminal justice institutions, studies such as Fishman's analysis of the 'crime wave,' or other research that suggests that the presence of television cameras has led to the rise of gentler kinds of policing at protests or demonstrations (Fillieule 1998). I will draw together the three strands of previous thinking that look beyond particular examples. These three develop what may be seen as more general conceptions of how media influence other institutions.[1]

If some ways of thinking about media influence are too narrow, in another way focusing on the institutional level also has advantages over the extremely broad conceptions of media influence of social theorists like Marshall McLuhan (1964), Mark Poster (1990, 1995), and Jean Baudrillard (1988). These theorists offer provocative visions of the transformations brought by the rise of electronic media like TV, but they are visions that are so general, sweeping, abstract, and sometimes cryptic as to defy much by way of empirical exploration. (For example, Poster describes the destabilization of the subject; Baudrillard discusses the implosion of reality.)

The institutional analysis I am arguing for here represents a middle ground between these various other ways of thinking about media. It is a middle ground that captures the general and pervasive sweep of various possible media influences, and yet is sufficiently down to earth to be open to detailed evaluation through empirical research.

In the next chapter I will discuss in more detail each of these three alternative perspectives that have led the way in looking at media influence on other institutions. Laying out these perspectives in depth and comparing them raised a number of questions for me, and I discuss how those questions led to my case studies. In chapters 3 through 6 I present the four case studies. In the conclusion, I analyse the implications for how best to think about the influences of TV. Finally, in a brief postscript I discuss how all of this also has implications for how we might theorize the evolution of contemporary criminal justice.

CHAPTER TWO

Three Alternative Ways of Thinking about Television's Influences

This chapter places side by side the three innovative ways of thinking about television's influence that I have just introduced, and analyses them in depth. Comparing these key works raises a series of questions about how best to understand TV's influences. I conclude by laying out how I will try to answer these questions in my case studies.

Meyrowitz's Medium Theory

First I will consider 'medium theory.' This looks at the social influence of the rise of particular communications technologies – particular forms of medium – such as television, radio, or the book. According to Joshua Meyrowitz, its key current proponent, medium theory

> focuses on the particular characteristics of each individual medium or each particular type of media. Broadly speaking, medium theorists ask: What are the relatively fixed features of each means of communicating and how do these features make the medium physically, psychologically, and socially different from the other media and from face-to-face interaction?
>
> Medium theory examines such variables as the senses that are required to attend to the medium, whether the communication is bi-directional or unidirectional, how quickly messages can be disseminated, whether learning how to encode or decode in the medium is difficult or simple, how many people can attend to the same message at the same moment, and so forth. Medium theorists argue that such variables influence the medium's use and its social, political and psychological impact. (1994: 50)

Marshall McLuhan is by far the best known of medium theorists, due in part to his unique place in popular culture, especially during the 1960s and 1970s, as a media icon himself. But McLuhan's work did not engage much with other social science, and McLuhan was often elliptical and cryptic as he speculated about the influence of television and other electronic media on individual consciousness (see, for example, McLuhan 1964). Nevertheless, in focusing attention on the social importance of the properties of particular media like TV, McLuhan paved the way for the work of Meyrowitz (1985, 1994). Other social theorists such as Harold Innis (1950, 1951), whose work on media was the key influence on McLuhan, and more recently, Mark Poster (1990, 1995), John Thompson (1990, 1994, 1995), and Jean Baudrillard (1988) have made broad, society-wide arguments about the importance for social theory of historical shifts in the predominant media of communication. But Meyrowitz has developed the most coherent, specific, and systematic body of arguments that explain how TV and other electronic media might influence other institutions, so I focus on his work here.

It was Meyrowitz who first defined medium theory as a unified perspective. He built on the work of McLuhan and Innis, along with others he had identified as early medium theorists in other disciplines such as English literature, history, and political economy. Contemporary medium theory received its most important expression in Meyrowitz's much-celebrated book *No Sense of Place* (1985). In contrast to McLuhan and other early medium theorists, Meyrowitz turned to the discipline of sociology to help understand what he found about media. He seized on and extended the brilliant analysis of the sociologist Erving Goffman concerning interpersonal interactions (see especially Goffman 1959). Meyrowitz sought to apply Goffman's analysis to a new realm. Instead of face-to-face interactions, he applied the analysis to social relations occurring through electronic media, centrally television. He did so by creating a bold new theory of how such media reshape social situations. Meyrowitz reconceptualized Goffman's situationist analysis of face-to-face interactions so that it was based on 'information systems' rather than on geographical place. Media like television are understood by Meyrowitz to create particular types of social settings, settings that include or exclude people in particular ways. Compared to print media, Meyrowitz argues, the medium of television tends to include very diverse kinds of people in the same information systems. Television is more of a 'shared arena' (Meyrowitz 1990) than various print outlets because it reaches wider and more diverse audiences, and because, compared to print media,

TV requires less specialized skill from audiences in 'decoding' or understanding.

Much of Meyrowitz's case hinges on his point that, as opposed to print communication, the particular kinds of information conveyed by TV tend to reduce social distance. As he argues, 'while written and printed words emphasize ideas, most electronic media [he refers centrally to television] emphasize feeling, appearance, mood ... There is a retreat from distant analysis and a dive into emotional and sensory involvement' (1994: 58). He sees this type of social information as demystifying the distinctions between different social groups: TV emphasizes what is common to us all. Adopting Goffman's terminology, Meyrowitz suggests the shift from print to television meant a move from conveying formal 'front region' information – what people want you to see – to informal, behind-the-scenes 'backstage' information. TV and other electronic media therefore 'merge formerly distinct public spheres, blur the dividing line between public and private behaviours, and sever the traditional link between physical place and social "place"' (1985: 8).

Thus, for Meyrowitz, a key way TV brings about institutional change is to show audiences what was previously unseen. It should be pointed out here that, like many other analysts, Meyrowitz greatly emphasizes the visual aspect of television in determining the meanings of what is broadcast. He argues that TV 'exposes' (1994: 67) the situations it records, that television 'shows us ... close up ... in living colour' previously hidden social realms (1994: 68). This heavy emphasis on the visual is also demonstrated in a key analogy: 'watching television is somewhat like watching people through a one way mirror in a situation where people know they are being watched by millions of people' (1985: 39). Similarly, he argues, 'television has lifted many of the old veils of secrecy' (1994: 68), allowing us to 'peek behind the curtain' (1985: 60) and so on. Do Meyrowitz – and many others – overstate the extent to which TV is actually a visual medium? I will come back to this point.

Meyrowitz is much too sophisticated to argue that TV just presents reality, unfiltered and unbiased. Indeed, he specifically states that media like TV are 'filters.' Yet he does base much of his arguments about the sweeping social changes brought by the rise of TV on the point that television simply makes 'visible' new things that were previously invisible. Thus, he argues that TV news is more revealing than newspapers: 'The speed of encoding in television, combined with its wide spectrum of non-verbal information, leads to a new degree of exposure of the many details, fluctuations, and uncertainties that were traditionally filtered out in newspaper reports. What was once part of the backstage area of life is now presented as "news"' (1985: 112).

Meyrowitz used empirical material from the period 1954 to 1984 to illustrate his points. Television sets were first manufactured in 1946. By 1950 only 10 per cent of American households featured one; by 1955 this figure had risen to 67 per cent (Baker and Dessart 1998: 18). Meyrowitz argued that reconfigured information systems – most centrally as a result of the rise of TV – helped create a 'new social landscape' during the years 1954–84. He was careful to qualify these claims: he suggested that the rise of television simply had an 'important contributing influence' on many social trends that characterized the 1960s and 1970s, trends in which different social groups began to demand equality. Meyrowitz suggested that the social consequences of the rise of electronic media, centrally TV, included the following: a merging of different stages of socialization, a diffusion of group identities, and a flattening of hierarchies; he believed that conceptions of childhood and adulthood have blurred, notions of masculinity and femininity have merged, and politicians have been lowered in stature more to the level of everyday people. Wider-reaching 'social information systems' also led to a blending or homogenization of other traditional group identities; electronic media altered one's 'generalized other.' To put it more simply, TV expanded the set of people one saw as similar to oneself, and emphasized commonality rather than differences between groups.

These changes occurred in part because the meaning of particular social situations changed as a result of electronic media. For example, the 'housewife' (or, increasingly, househusband) was no longer someone as totally isolated in the home. According to Meyrowitz, these broad cultural shifts as a result of TV and other electronic media also brought about change in another way: they led to political pressure from audiences, 'pressure to integrate roles and rights' (1994: 67). Thus, as TV broke down social barriers, members of isolated and distinct groups began more and more to demand equality. The greatest impact was on groups defined by physical isolation: those confined by kitchens, playgrounds, prisons, convents, and so on.

The prison is one of many institutional settings that Meyrowitz argued was altered by TV (although he does not investigate any of these settings in much depth). The prison offers an example of the institutional changes described. TV and other electronic media altered the social meaning and experience of the prison directly: prisoners were no longer segregated from the outside world in terms of receiving information (1985: 117–18). As well, receiving this knowledge of the outside world increased minority consciousness and caused minority groups such as prisoners to demand equality in further ways (1985: 132).

More generally, according to Meyrowitz, TV and other electronic media bypassed old channels and undermined a system of graded hierarchy based on segregation of knowledge. Meyrowitz argued that the old segregated, hierarchical system was undermined both directly, by making available new social information, and indirectly, through creating political pressure for change. TV thus resulted in various types of social levelling.

Meyrowitz's argument combines tremendous breadth and lucidity. It raises important new points about the televising of criminal justice. In particular, it led me to think about how TV creates new social situations when it introduces audiences into new information systems on the front lines of criminal justice. Meyrowitz draws attention to the neglected sociological importance of the formal properties of television as a medium. How do these formal properties affect the redefined social situations that TV creates?

No Sense of Place (Meyrowitz 1985) is essentially an argument about how the rise of new media, centrally TV, brings about social change. However, television is certainly no longer a new medium: it has been on the scene now for more than fifty years. Do his arguments still hold? Even though TV itself is not new, the arguments still seemed to apply to my research for this book. This is because I study new types of social situations that have appeared quite recently with the introduction of television into new realms. The key point is that the specific traits of TV and all other media are not static: they continually evolve as media technology and the social relations around that technology evolve. This technological development includes the evolution not just of television itself, but also of supporting technologies that interact with TV. To give an analogy, the social role of the newspaper was fundamentally changed by the emergence of the telegraph and its rapid diffusion of news, as James Carey (1989) has argued. In the case of television, one key factor is the evolving video camera technology that TV can draw footage from, as I discuss in the next two chapters. There is also usually a lag between the time a new media technology such as TV appears and the time at which various institutions adapt to it. For these reasons, new social situations continue to be created by the medium of TV, even though TV has been on the scene for more than half a century.

Reviewing Meyrowitz's analysis raised a number of questions for me. His analysis transposed a way of thinking based on face-to-face interaction (drawn from Goffman's work) into situations that are mass mediated. I began to ponder whether, in making this shift, it was possible that Meyrowitz neglected to consider the power relations that would now shape the social information that viewers receive through TV, and the resulting potential biases in that information. A televised interaction is a much more complex social event than a face-to-face interaction between two individuals. Broadcasting requires large re-sources and necessarily involves at least one major institution (the television broadcaster) and often other major 'source' institutions (i.e., the institution whose activities are being broadcast, for example the police). Once such potent institutions are involved, the power imbal-ances among the different players may be much more pronounced than in a case of simple face-to-face interaction. These power relations may lead to biases in how the situation is presented on TV. Of course, in contrast to Meyrowitz's work, there is a large body of other research that shows there are indeed biases in favour of powerful institutions and social groups in television content, and particularly in TV news (e.g., Gerbner and Gross 1976; Gerbner et al. 1994; Tuchman 1978; Fiske and Hartley 1978; Fiske 1987, 1996; Gans 1979; Ericson, Baranek, and Chan 1987, 1989, 1991; Shanahan and Morgan 1999). Meyrowitz argues, however, that all this other research has missed something. It focuses too narrowly on media content (Meyrowitz 1985: 14–15). He argues that this other research thus neglects different types of key influences, influ-ences stemming from the properties of TV itself that are consequences of how TV changes types and patterns of information flow. In his view these alternative kinds of influences may have a levelling effect, essen-tially working in the opposite direction from all the biases in TV content that previous researchers found.

The situations I chose to look at in this book – situations where, more and more, television directly records the events in question – seemed to me to be a good test of Meyrowitz's arguments. In the cases I study, his arguments about how TV makes visible new social situations would seem to be the most applicable. Thus my research asked: To what extent does television actually 'lift veils of secrecy' and let audiences see into new kinds of situations? What biases might there be in the selection of particular situations that are shown, and in how TV presents them?

Meyrowitz zeroes in on the formal properties of television as a medium – the fact that it is visual, a one-way medium, and so on. He makes some key leaps in his reasoning, from examining the kinds of information that TV communicates to what TV's influences will be on viewers. However, he does little to investigate how TV programming is actually made. He bases his arguments mostly on who is viewing televised situations under what circumstances, rather than examining who is actually in front of and behind the TV camera.

For example, Meyrowitz (1985) refers numerous times to the fact that prisoners can now watch television, decreasing their isolation. However, he never mentions that, even so, it remains rare that television cameras are allowed to record and broadcast events from inside prisons themselves (Doyle and Ericson 1996). As previous research has shown, prisoners can now watch TV, but the backstage regions inside prison walls are certainly not shown on TV very much. More generally, although TV has properties that *could* allow it to convey more revealing types of 'back region' information, the question still remains whether or not TV cameras will be allowed to *record* that back-region information, and if so, who will control the circumstances in which that occurs.

In using my four case studies to assess Meyrowitz's medium theory, I thus ask the following question: To what extent does TV simply 'make visible' these new social situations, or reveal new kinds of back region information from them? On the other hand, what biases might there be in the social information conveyed by TV, and why?

Meyrowitz argues that television operates to help tear down old hierarchies and level social distinctions. He sometimes tends to speak of these hierarchies in an abstract way, as occurring among different 'groups,' like men and women or children and adults. But hierarchies actually occur in specific social contexts, such as in various institutions, and in some places Meyrowitz does speculate about specific changes in social institutions like the school or prison, changes he argues are a result of TV's breaking down social barriers.

It seemed to me that a good way to test Meyrowitz's arguments would be to explore in depth how introducing TV affects inequality in places where it is well known that unequal power relations exist. The criminal justice system seemed an obvious place to start. There is a great deal of research showing how the justice system treats different social groups unequally, varying along dimensions such as ethnicity, class, and gender (for a variety of examples, see Brogden, Jefferson, and Walklate 1988; Norris et al. 1992; Ontario 1995; Young 1999; Neugebauer

2000; Hannah-Moffat 2001). There is also a definite hierarchy among the various players, such as police and civilians, in interactions on the front lines of criminal justice (see, for example, Ericson 1982, 1993). How will such imbalances be affected by the introduction of TV into these situations?

Meyrowitz's theory focuses in part on how TV changes social situations by influencing viewers. These viewers, exposed to new social information by TV, start to push for social justice and equality. However, Meyrowitz does not specify the actual processes through which TV audiences come to apply this pressure for change. This raised further questions for my research. When TV introduces audiences into these new social situations, how much do they actually begin to push for equality and fairness, as Meyrowitz predicts? How and why do they do it?

There is a key difference between the work of Meyrowitz and the two other conceptions that I will examine now. The other two explore more directly the contexts in which media content is made, the actual situations where TV footage is recorded. As well, these perspectives also examine other institutions that are key sources of media content, like legislatures, courts, and the police.

Altheide and Snow's Media Logic

A second way of thinking about media influence on other institutions was pioneered by the media sociologists David Altheide and Robert Snow (1979). Altheide and Snow's underrecognized work argued that what they call 'the cultural logic of mass media,' or simply 'media logic,' had massive influences on the social landscape. These included reshaping practices in other institutions, for example, in the realms of politics, religion, or sport (1979: chaps. 4–7). Thus, 'all social institutions are media institutions' (1991: ix).

Altheide and Snow state that media logic consists of 'how material is organized, the style in which it is presented, the focus or emphasis on particular characteristics of behaviour, and the grammar of media communication ... when a media logic is employed to present and interpret institutional phenomena, the form and content of those institutions are altered' (Altheide and Snow 1979: 10–11). Thus, 'media logic' is a broader way of conceptualizing media influence than that of Meyrowitz. It includes, but also looks beyond, the formal properties of particular media like TV. Media logic also includes the dictates of formats such as news. Altheide and Snow examine both the technical needs and the commercial requirements of mass media. This includes broad imperatives that are equally true for different types of media like TV or popular magazines, such as the commercial need to entertain audiences.

In contrast to Meyrowitz's work, media logic focused much more directly on how institutions took the inititative and actively reshaped themselves to fit media needs. Meyrowitz zeroed in on one particular theme, his optimistic notion that TV had a liberating effect by breaking down social barriers. Altheide and Snow instead described a myriad of diverse, sometimes insidious influences. These were occasionally trivial, for example, altering the tempo and rules of televised sporting events, but could involve much more fundamental changes, such as the recasting of the entire political campaigning process into a series of media events. Media logic placed much more emphasis on unequal power relations. In the world of media logic, media institutions and considerations dominated these relations.

The following are key properties of media logic that shape other institutions:

1 Media logic gives particular institutional events that are in the media spotlight a great deal of added importance. Mass-mediated events thus become 'bigger than life' both for audiences and for institutional players (1979: 51). This may happen even if the particular events draw media attention for somewhat arbitrary reasons. For example, the fallout of a political scandal like the Bert Lance affair during the Jimmy Carter presidency was much greater because the story broke in a slow news month and so was given extensive media attention.
2 Media can act both to legitimate and to delegitimate, for example, highlighting particular topics and experts as important or 'controversial.'
3 The entertainment imperative of mass media also feeds back on other institutions. Mass media thus encourage dramatic or spectacular behaviour in other institutions.
4 Media communication calls for simplicity. Entertainment very often takes the form of story telling, and media logic also encourages other institutions to present and interpret themselves in simple storylines.
5 Catering to a huge and diverse TV audience prompts what Altheide and Snow call an 'ideal norm' orientation in TV programming. TV

producers have to produce bland, innocuous programming that fits with traditional values, such as promoting and celebrating the conventional family. Producers aim to produce the 'least objectionable program' in order to maintain the mass audience. This 'ideal norm format' then plays back on institutions that rely on TV exposure, for example, certain religious organizations, causing these institutions to be similarly 'middle of the road.' Generally, Altheide and Snow argue, fitting media needs makes other institutions try to shape what they do to be uncontroversial, in order to keep a broad and diverse audience happy.

To sum up, then, according to Altheide and Snow, 'media logic' means that particular phenomena in other institutions that are mass-mediated will have tendencies to be more important, dramatic, spectacular, entertaining, simplified, presented in the form of a story, and shaped to fit with conventional values. The pivotal point is that such phenomena are not simply *portrayed* that way by the media – they also *become* that way, as other institutions strive to fit media needs.

Altheide and Snow's conception captures, in a way that many others do not, just how pervasive media considerations are today. Fitting the needs of media has become ingrained and essential to many aspects of contemporary institutional life. This is so much so that these media considerations can more or less be taken for granted. In many situations, for example, the political campaign trail, the requirement to fit media needs is so fundamental as to be invisible, something like the air we breathe.[1]

Making a case for their new approach, Altheide and Snow emphasize very strongly how pervasive media logic is in all aspects of contemporary life. Because their conception is so broad and diverse, they open up a considerable challenge for those of us who want to build on their work. Reviewing that work left me with a number of questions. If they are correct in their arguments, how much might the notion of media logic apply to various institutions beyond those that they studied? If so, what are its specific influences in different places, and what are its limits? Are all institutions equally influenced by it? How powerful are media considerations, and media institutions, in relation to other institutions?

Altheide and Snow state repeatedly that the mass media have become a 'dominant' institution (e.g., 1979: 236, 1991: 3). Yet it is sometimes unclear exactly what this 'dominance' means. In a later book that updates their arguments (1991), they suggest we are entering an era of 'post-journalism.' They highlight how the news media, especially TV news, depend heavily on prepackaged material such as news releases from source institutions like the political arena. Key news sources like politicians and their spin-doctors largely 'produce' news themselves, making journalists increasingly redundant. Thus, the question arises: Is it the media outlets themselves that are dominating, or is it instead the 'cultural logic of media' that increasingly shapes organizational life, so that even media organizations themselves are secondary?

The source institutions on which Altheide and Snow (1979) initially focused their research (politics, religion, professional sport) all depend heavily on mass audience approval. In the twenty-plus years since *Media Logic* was published, TV has penetrated ever deeper into the fine grain of various other key institutions. TV is more and more turning some front line day-to-day institutional operations that were formerly relatively private into more public media events. A good example is the day-to-day policing activities now recorded for the reality-TV program *Cops*.

Could media logic really come to shape an activity like policing, which, on the face of it, seems driven by much more pressing consider-ations like public safety? A case study by Altheide (1993) offered one highly suggestive example of just how much media logic might shape a police operation. He described how Arizona police organized a particu-lar sting operation, Azscam, that targeted state politicians. This police operation was a very novel one: its primary aim seemed to be to produce incriminating TV footage of politicians for immediate release to the news media, rather than producing criminal evidence for the courts. Indeed, the resulting trial by media largely bypassed the need for the formal criminal process. Arizona police thus essentially created a new police tactic by harnessing media logic to their own purposes. This raised the question of whether this example might reflect a more general trend in how media influence policing operations.

As Altheide and Snow point out, media logic will be more influential within institutions that are more reliant on media (1979: 103). Certainly police more and more strive for a favourable media image (Ericson, Baranek, and Chan 1989, Schlesinger and Tumber 1994). Yet compared to other institutions, police are not so dependent on whether or not they can 'score points' in the media. Police do not need to achieve media audience support as measured through votes (politics), financial dona-tions (politics and religion), or TV ratings and attendance (sports). This raises the question of whether police will be less prone to the influences of media logic than these other institutions. What will happen when the needs of media conflict with the interests of another powerful institution like the police? Who holds the balance of power then? The case studies presented in chapters 3–6 allow me to test the concept of media logic, and its limits, in four new contexts.

The Sociology of News Production and the Institutional Perspective of Ericson, Baranek, and Chan

Thirdly, my research also builds on a large body of previous research on the sociology of news production. This body of work on how the news is made led to the 'institutional perspective' of Richard Ericson, Patricia Baranek, and Janet Chan (see, especially, Ericson, Baranek, and Chan 1989; Ericson, 1991, 1994), which is a third way of thinking about how media influence other institutions.

In the studies in the following chapters, I examine both TV news coverage of criminal justice and reality-TV crime programs, which are in some ways analogous to news. Looking at previous research on the news has been helpful because what is distinctive about reality-TV can be thrown into relief by using the news for comparison. Much earlier research has shown that the normal processes by which news is produced tend to support the status quo. For various organizational and cultural reasons, the ways news is made – both on TV and in other media – tend to favour the powerful and to preserve their place in society, as shown by various classic studies (e.g., Tuchman 1978; Hall et al. 1978; Gans 1979; Fishman 1980). The news is often dominated by an official perspective, because of a routinized overreliance by reporters on official sources. In particular, journalists depend a great deal on the police as a daily news source (Chibnall 1977; Hall et al. 1978; Fishman 1978, 1980, 1981; Ericson, Baranek, and Chan, 1987, 1989, 1991; Schlesinger and Tumber 1994).

This research on news production differs in a key way from the first two perspectives we have considered. The medium theory and media logic approaches argue that media cause dramatic social transformations. The third approach suggests, to the contrary, that players from other institutions – like government officials and police – most often control the content and influences of the news media, and the result is not social transformation, but maintenance of the status quo.

At this point I should say a little more about the particular source institution I focus on for much of this book: the police. This book adds to a body of research showing the central role of police in shaping media content. First I should point out a few things about the place of the police in society more generally. Despite what some crude conspiracy theories say, police are not simply an all-powerful arm of the state. Instead, social scientific research details how police are a semi-autonomous institution. They face political constraints and are vulnerable, but also wield considerable influence (for an excellent history see Reiner 2000). Although relatively independent, the police have a strong tendency towards working to protect the existing hierarchy. In maintaining order, they reproduce the current order (see, for example, Ericson 1982, 1993). Police also occupy a central place in contemporary culture as a symbol of authority and the state (Loader 1997).

According to the 'dominant ideology model' as described by Stuart Hall and his colleagues (1978), the news media most often treat official accounts – in particular, those of police – as simply 'the facts.' Police sources dominate the news, not because of a conspiracy among the media and the authorities, but simply as a result of the routines on the police news beat. The way crime reporters' working lives are organized, there are few other accessible sources of news.

Mark Fishman's (1978, 1980, 1981) research has shown that a key factor in this dominance is the media's demand for a steady quantity of news items. He described how deadlines and financial pressure caused an overreliance on readily available and easily legitimated information from official sources, especially police.

Research by Ericson, Baranek, and Chan (1989: chap. 2) offered a somewhat more complex and nuanced insight into police–media relations. Their ethnography of the 'police beat' in Toronto revealed that there was an inner circle and outer circle of police reporters. Inner circle reporters are very friendly with police sources and reflect police ideology to a large extent. They have access to more information, but also self-censor to maintain close ties with police sources. Outer circle reporters place more emphasis on reporting police and organizational wrongdoing; their relationship is more like a running battle.

In sum, though, previous research suggests a general tendency towards police ability to manage and control the content of the news (Sacco 1995). A recent trend in a handful of works is to look at a different direction of media influence: on the source institutions themselves. This small number of works have examined what researchers call the 'mediatization' of other institutions (Schlesinger and Tumber 1994). This term refers to how institutions like police are reshaped as they become more professional with the news media (see, e.g., Blumler and Gurevitch, 1995, on the mediatization of electoral politics).

Mediatization has occurred in an era when TV has in many ways become the most influential news medium (Fiske 1987; Ericson, Baranek, and Chan, 1991: 24; Baker and Dessart 1998). Being oriented to news most often means TV news, and many aspects of mediatization are geared specifically to TV.

Mediatization is very marked in the police institution in particular. Police increasingly take the initiative in self-promotion through the news media (Ericson, Baranek, and Chan 1989: chap. 3; Schlesinger and Tumber 1994: chap. 4). This helps police achieve political ends and is also a way of closing off areas of vulnerability. The police version of a story is much more effective in heading off journalists' enquiries than no version at all (Fishman 1980; Ericson et al. 1989). Police self-promotion sometimes includes promoting the notion of an ever-growing crime problem. For example, in early 1995, when Statistics Canada released a report suggesting that violent crime in Canada was not increasing, the RCMP immediately countered with a statement to the news media reinterpreting the crime figures to suggest violent crime was indeed worsening (*Vancouver Sun*, 7 February 1995). Many police departments now have large centralized public affairs units featuring civilian public relations experts.

These kinds of influences are typical of those described by the institutional perspective of Ericson, Baranek, and Chan (1989). These researchers have shown myriad ways in which news media organizations help shape and in turn are shaped by criminal justice institutions. They detailed a range of diverse consequences for police of news media coverage, among them interfering with investigations; harming crime victims, their relatives, or accused criminals prior to trial; promoting or hurting the image of the force; creating workload pressures or pressures to solve particular cases; influencing individual police careers; distributing emergency information; helping solve crimes; deterring potential criminals; and pressuring the police administration for various political reasons (Ericson et al. 1989: 156–69). Generally, these researchers found that police had considerable ability to manage and control the media. The police were at least as important in determining media influence as were the media themselves.

Like Meyrowitz, these researchers applied a version of the notion of 'front regions' and 'back regions' (Goffman 1959) to analyse what was revealed by the news media.[2] Meyrowitz had argued that because TV was a visual medium, it opened up various back regions for scrutiny. Unlike Meyrowitz, though, Ericson and company actually conducted a direct investigation into how the news was made, and they came to quite different conclusions. These researchers found that, in practice, police were most often able to limit severely media access to their back regions.

The research of Ericson et al. was grounded in a theory of the 'knowledge society' (see also Stehr and Ericson 1992), in which powerful media and source institutions and high-level players in these institutions dominate in a society defined by hierarchy based on knowledge. Methodologically, the research of Ericson and company reflected this theory of the knowledge society, as the researchers mostly investigated the activities and perspectives of these powerful institutions. They concentrated on observing and interviewing these potent institutional actors, and gave little attention to the experiences of ordinary people without any official role (apart from a case study of letters to the editor). This made me wonder: did these researchers find that powerful institutional players dominated news making simply because, in their research, they neglected to talk to the ordinary people who were involved in making the news, for example, crime victims and witnesses? By observing how TV was made in a variety of further situations, I could address this potential limitation of their research. Were those without affiliations to powerful institutions really as marginal as this previous work indicated?

Each of these three perspectives offers a somewhat different view of the relationship between TV and the broader culture. Meyrowitz argued that TV and other electronic media helped bring about a huge, mostly liberating cultural transformation. Thus, TV influenced the broader culture more than vice versa. Altheide and Snow saw the reverse: the broader culture constrained TV. This led to a blandness and conventionality of TV content, because producers attempted not to offend the sensibilities of a mass audience. Altheide and Snow argued that this led to a similar 'middle of the road' quality in other institutions, which likewise had to make what they do fit with TV's requirements for broad but bland appeal. Ericson et al. also saw the broader culture explicitly as a factor reproducing the status quo. They found that media and news sources were often compelled to make what they said and did fit with dominant cultural beliefs. Thus, media and sources reproduced the dominance of those beliefs (Ericson, Baranek, and Chan 1989: 204–8). My case studies would also allow me to explore these contrasting visions of the relationship between TV and the broader culture.

The police news sources studied by Ericson and company were often far from the front lines, passing on information that had come to them through channels rather than witnessing the events personally. Similarly, the various influences on the police that these researchers described were distanced from the front lines, mostly involving the restructuring of bureaucracies or various after-the-fact consequences of news stories. Ericson and company did not look at situations where the media were present at the front lines of policing, directly recording the events.

In fact, a massive content analysis by Ericson et al. showed that most TV news has not involved directly recording the events in question (Ericson, Baranek, and Chan 1991). Thus Richard Ericson argues that 'even in television news ... journalists and their sources mainly give talking head accounts of the facts rather than being everywhere as an eyewitness to reality as it happens' (1998: 85).

However, this book looks at exceptions: situations when the camera is directly on scene, both in TV news and in reality television. I ask if the influences of TV might take distinctive forms in these situations. We know there is a general tendency towards control of the news by police. But does this hold even when crime and policing is directly recorded on TV and broadcast on television? Secondly, will media considerations feed into the criminal justice situation and reshape it in more direct and fundamental ways when the situation occurs immediately in view of TV cameras?

These questions all fit under one broader umbrella: How is the making of crime news different when the events in question occur directly before the TV camera?

Summary of Research Questions

To summarize, my big, overarching question for empirical research was: How much, how, and why are these particular criminal justice situations changed as they are broadcast on television? More specific questions I would use to evaluate and build on previous theorizing were:

1 How much does TV 'make visible' new social situations or reveal back region information from the world of crime and policing?

2 What biases might there be in the 'social information' TV conveys about these criminal justice situations, and why?

3 How much does televising these situations bring about the kind of breakdown of hierarchies and levelling of the playing field between social groups that Meyrowitz describes? Does televising these situations lead to audience pressure for social change to reduce inequality and social injustice? Through what processes or mechanisms is this political pressure by audiences applied?

4 Is there something about the properties of TV as a medium that makes it a social leveller?

5 How do the activities of the institutions under study come to be shaped by media considerations or media logic?

6 What difference does it make how dependent the source institution is on the mass media? Are some institutions more influenced by media logic than others?

7 What is the balance of power between media institutions and media considerations on the one hand, and various source institutions on the other? What are the limits of the influence of media logic?

8 Do particular situations of crime and policing that occur directly before the cameras create more vulnerability for police than those reported in standard police news?

9 Do these situations – where crime and policing are televised live – show distinctive types of TV influence on the situations themselves?

10 What role does the broader cultural context play in the media's influences?

It soon became evident that the relatively new and unconventional type of question I am asking – how does television reshape the criminal justice situations it records? – was bound up with more conventional questions – what is conveyed on TV, and who and what factors shape TV content? The path to answering my new research question thus led me back through some older, more conventional ones.

I will demonstrate the connection between these newer and older types of questions with a simple example. If the reality-TV show *Cops* conveyed an actual, uncensored, back region account of policing, this might force police officers who were recorded for the program to censor their own behaviour quite substantially. On the other hand, if the officers who were recorded knew police had final say over what was aired, they would feel little pressure to moderate their behaviour as it was videotaped.

In short, it began to be clear even at this stage that how TV influences the situations it records is bound up with who controls the content of what is televised. This may seem an obvious point, but it has been ignored by some key earlier accounts.

Selection of Case Studies and Research Methods

Like the key works I have just discussed, my research contrasts a range of examples from different institutional situations. Producing four separate case studies would allow me to draw broader conclusions.

I have three reasons for studying instances where TV directly captures institutional behaviour. First, these situations – immediately in front of the cameras – seemed likely to provide microcosms where the nature of TV's influence on other institutions would be most evident. The idea that TV makes visible new situations seemed to apply best to such cases. Secondly, because they are newly televised, these situations are revealing contexts in which to investigate possible changes created by TV. Finally, there has been little previous research on this general trend towards broadcasting live crime and policing.

The world of criminal justice is one realm where the trend towards live TV is very apparent. I am interested in how the broader culture interacts with TV's influences, and the cultural place of crime has been the subject of insightful previous research I can draw on, as I discuss in more detail in chapter 3 (see, for example, Garland 1990, 2001; Sparks 1992; Simon and Feeley 1995; Sasson 1995; Kaminer 1995; Scheingold 1984, 1995; Loader 1997).

I also look at how television affects patterns of inequality, so I can draw as well on all the previous research that has documented inequality in police practices, along dimensions like ethnicity and class (for assorted examples, see Brogden, Jefferson, and Walklate 1988: chap. 6; Norris et al. 1992; Reiner 2000; Neugebauer 2000), as well as hierarchical power relations depending on institutional roles, such as police versus suspects (e.g., Ericson 1982, 1993).

I chose four particular cases for study. Together they exemplify many of the key situations in which crime and policing is now captured 'live' for TV.

The first centres on reality television. I examine the reality-TV program *Cops*, the earliest, most popular and most imitated program to feature actual footage of 'real' crime and policing. *Cops* was an obvious choice.

A second looks at new technologies that offer alternative sources of video, allowing television news and reality TV to cast a wider net for 'real' footage. I compare the increasing use by TV of both surveillance camera footage and home video. Neither has previously been studied by social scientists. I suspected there might be an interesting contrast between the treatment of surveillance footage from police sources and that of home video coming from ordinary people with no institutional authority.

While TV news cameras infrequently record events in the normal course of day-to-day crime and policing, one exception is the policing of riots or demonstrations. These are highly visible, large-scale events, often of a lengthy duration, in public locations. Especially in the case of planned demonstrations, or riots coinciding with major sports events, they may be anticipated by the news media. Riots are also interesting because the combination of high visibility and violent chaos makes it much more difficult for police to maintain control of their public image. For my third case study, I investigate one highly controversial, televised, and bloody episode of riot policing that was close at hand: the policing of Vancouver's Stanley Cup riot.

The fourth study was selected as a counterpoint to the first three. It examines what happens when the media initiative is in the hands of the 'criminals,' situations where TV news cameras capture law breaking because protesters seek it out, notifying the media in advance. This fourth study looks at the media stunts of the environmental organization Greenpeace. It explores how making these TV stunts their central tactic has actually fed back on and shaped Greenpeace more broadly.

My four studies would use a diverse range of qualitative research methods and ethnographic data. How I set out to answer these questions, and what I found, is the focus of the next four chapters.

CHAPTER THREE

Reality Television and Policing: The Case of *Cops*

Cops was not only instantly popular but also groundbreaking when it appeared in 1989. It was the first reality-TV program about crime to use actual video footage as opposed to re-enactments.

To make *Cops*, a video and sound team accompany police officers in action. The program has been recorded in dozens of American cities, as well as Britain, Hong Kong, Russia, and Bolivia. Suspects and other civilians shown on *Cops* sign releases giving permission for the program to show them. If they will not sign, their faces are digitized to blur them and conceal the civilians' identities. The raw footage is edited down to three vignettes in each half-hour episode. *Cops* thus put a new spin on the *cinéma-verité* documentary form (Corner 1996).

Three factors combined to lead to the development of *Cops*: technological advances meant video cameras were smaller and more portable; executives at the new Fox network sought innovative and inexpensive programming that attracted their target audience; and police forces offered massive co-operation, part of the trend towards increasing police self-promotion in the media (Ericson, Baranek, and Chan 1989; Schlesinger and Tumber 1994: chap. 4).

Cops was created and brought to the new Fox network by producers John Langley and Malcolm Barbour. The two made a deal with the sheriff's department in Broward County, Florida, to send video crews carrying mobile shoulder-held cameras out with police on duty in 'one of the highest-crime areas in the nation, where drugs and the constant influx of new people created one hot situation after another' (Block, 1990: 279). Fox aired some pilot shows in early 1989 in Los Angeles, and 'the ratings went through the roof. During a five-night run in Los Angeles, *Cops* finished second in the time-period, beating two of the three [established] networks' (Block, 1990: 279). In particular, *Cops* proved very popular with Fox's target audience: young, low-income earners who had not previously been targeted by the three major networks (Fishman 1998: 66). The new reality program's visions of 'real' crime were part of a broader Fox move toward 'tabloid TV,' apparently influenced by network owner Rupert Murdoch's earlier background as a highly successful owner of salacious print tabloids.

Cops has often been the highest-rated reality-TV program (Coe 1996). A further advantage of programs like *Cops* and its imitators is that they are cheap to make, one reason for their rapid spread. Part of the commercial strategy of the fledgling Fox network, which put *Cops* in prime time, was to offer inexpensive programming. *Cops* producers found they could make an episode for around $200 thousand – about a third of the cost of a typical half-hour of situation comedy (S.C. Smith 1993).

Another key commercial element in the success of *Cops* was this: television executives quickly discovered, that unlike news-magazines, which dated quickly, *Cops* had a timeless quality. Episodes of *Cops* retained immediacy for years after they were produced. This made *Cops* highly suitable for countless syndicated reruns of its now five hundred plus episodes, even as new episodes continue to air on the Fox network in Saturday night prime time. Thus, *Cops* became one of the most frequently aired North American television programs devoted exclusively to crime, showing twelve times a week in some areas. It brought 'real crime' to new places on the television schedule and to new moments in viewers' daily rhythms. Numerous other shows have copied or adapted its approach, including *American Detective, LAPD: Life on the Beat, To Serve and Protect*, and Britain's *Blues and Twos*.

Before the advent of *Cops*, there had been isolated instances of *cinéma-verité* or fly-on-the-wall documentaries recording police in action, not always offering favourable visions. For example, documentarian Roger Graef's controversial and award-winning BBC *Police* series led to calls for reform of how British police handled rape cases.[1] While some police forces in major American cities were initially reluctant to co-operate with *Cops*, it soon became clear that appearing on the new reality show would, for reasons I will shortly discuss, prove a much safer bet in protecting police image.

For the purposes of this analysis, thirty episodes of *Cops* aired between 1991 and 1997 were reviewed in depth. Other data were obtained from a copy of the *Too Hot for TV* video marketed by *Cops* producers, featuring outtakes from *Cops*. Some anecdotal data about *Cops* audiences were drawn from informal discussions with a handful of regular viewers. Information about *Cops* was drawn from the official *Cops* website. This included transcripts of self-interviews by two *Cops* producers and of an interview with a police officer who had appeared on *Cops* a number of times. Unless otherwise indicated, the unattributed quotations that follow are from these interviews.

The Realities of Reality TV

To understand how television influences the situations shown on *Cops*, it is first necessary to examine how *Cops* presents these situations. Joshua Meyrowitz's (1985) arguments raise the question of what happens when viewers of *Cops* are introduced into the social situation of front-line policing. Does television bring about social changes because it 'exposes' the reality of policing in new ways, as Meyrowitz might speculate? Certainly, its producers call the reality-TV show 'unfiltered' television (Katz 1993: 25). Alternatively, are police able to control the televised portrait of themselves, even with cameras on scene, and thus control the consequences of this new form of publicity?

According to *Cops* creator and executive producer John Langley, the program was conceived as a television version of the standard 'ride-along' in which a curious civilian tags along in a police cruiser for a shift. Langley describes *Cops* as simply a slice of 'raw reality.'

However, my research reveals that *Cops* is far from simply unfiltered reality: it offers a very particular and selective vision of policing. I argue that *Cops* is instead best seen as 'reality fiction,' to use a term one celebrated *vérité* documentary filmmaker adopted to describe his work (Benton and Anderson 1989). Executive producer Langley notes that 'reality is often ironically difficult to capture because it is unstructured, unpredictable and unscripted.' However, the 'raw reality' of the video footage undergoes considerable processing before it hits the airwaves. As Langley states:

> The process begins with production in the field with producer Bert Van Munster and his staff of cameramen and soundmen and support staff; and then it comes back to post-production with supervising producer Murray Jordan and his editorial staff. All the material comes back to Los Angeles, with the field staff tagging what looks like potential *stories* [italics added]. Then our editorial staff cuts together the most interesting material, whereupon I determine what goes in the shows after recutting or refinessing if

needed. Basically we try to put together interesting combinations. For example, an action piece (which hooks the audience), a lyrical piece (which develops more emotion), and a think piece (which provokes thought on the part of the audience).

One may note the movement in Langley's description from 'unpredictable and unscripted' reality to ready-to-air 'stories' with thematic unity. The description 'reality fiction' is useful because it throws into direct juxtaposition *Cops*' distinctive claim to be 'reality based' or 'raw reality' and this story-telling quality. The expression 'reality fiction' conveys the somewhat obvious point that *Cops* is a constructed version of reality with its own biases, rather than a neutral record. Beyond this, the word 'fiction' also highlights that, because of a need to turn 'reality' into entertaining narratives for television, the producers of *Cops* rely on a number of story-telling devices. While the appeal of *Cops* is in part that it seems to present raw reality, it also offers narrative qualities, such as heroes for audiences to identify with, unambiguous storylines concluding with resolution or closure, and, often, a moral or theme. *Cops* producers very skillfully combine these story-telling devices with other mechanisms suggesting 'raw reality.'

Thus, while the requirements of television and desires of police affect which events are selected to be shown on *Cops*, television story telling also affects *how* these events are portrayed.

First, I will discuss how the program naturalizes the material it airs. A voice-over during the opening credit sequence of *Cops* quickly establishes the reality-based nature of the programming: '*Cops* is filmed on location with the men and women of law enforcement.' One distinctive feature of *Cops* is that there is no *formal* narration, apart from this initial announcement, nor any other artifice that suggests journalism. Nor is there a musical soundtrack as in other reality-based programs, such as *LAPD: Life on the Beat*; instead there is simply what seems to be actuality sound. As Langley puts it, 'We were certainly the first, and we are still the only reality show that has no actors, no script and no host. That's as pure as you can get in documentary film-making.'

Various modernist factual and fictional forms of story telling use different strategies to construct realism. News deploys truth-claims largely rooted in appeal to legitimate authorities and their authorized forms of discourse, such as science and law. Visual evidence has usually played more of a supporting role, even on television news, which has not tended to feature actual footage of the news events in question

(Ericson, Baranek, and Chan 1987, 1989, 1991; Ericson 1998). In contrast, the claim to realism of *Cops* is based more fully in the visual: in the pervasive cultural understanding that 'seeing is believing' and in the emotional authenticity of 'live' incidents. News purportedly seeks to provide audiences with the five Ws (who, what, when, where, why); *Cops* ignores some of these questions entirely (who the civilians present are, when the events occurred) and is more concerned with offering the illusion that the viewer is on-scene. However, if it relies on the visual, *Cops* also derives authenticity from its first-hand oral accounts 'straight from the horse's mouth.'

Cops creator Langley states that the program allows the viewer 'to share a cop's point of view *in real time* during the course of his or her duties.' While clearly the footage often condenses into seven- or eight-minute vignettes action that takes place over a much longer period of time, most of the action does unfold in a linear sequence that simulates real time. This is one key way in which naturalization occurs. Real time is also suggested by a lone subtitle flashed once in most vignettes indicating the time that a particular piece of action commences, for example, 'burglary call, 6:23 p.m.' There is the suggestion that the action flows continuously from the time that was flashed, as if a stop-watch had been started.

Although events on *Cops* are presented as though the visuals and soundtrack are both captured simultaneously in the raw, often the sound that is aired has actually been recorded at other times from the visuals. This allows for a subtle, frequently used device the casual viewer may not notice, that simulates the continuing flow of real time: continuity in sound is edited to overlap cuts in the visuals, and vice versa. For example, the continuous sound of a police officer talking, police radio calls, or a helicopter overhead will overlap a cut between two different visuals. The continuous sound suggests continuity in time, as if the viewer has simply looked in a different direction during continuous action (although in fact an hour's worth of action and dialogue could have been omitted between the cuts). Real time thus suggests continuous time; however, it does not attempt to inform the viewer how far back in time the incident actually occurred by giving the calendar date (for example, 6:23 p.m., 22 June 1995). Thus, real time also means the programs do not date easily and are suitable for reruns in syndication. *Cops* does not recede into history; instead, cops chase, wrestle, and handcuff criminals in an eternal present. While presenting the 'action highlights' of a particular incident in real time provides a fictive immediacy or 'nowness' that may make *Cops* more exciting to viewers, it also naturalizes the footage, at least somewhat. Events unfold in an edgy, fast-forward procession that seems disconcertingly paced, yet naturalization occurs in that the actual cuts are concealed.

Although the program attempts to construct real time, the executive producer acknowledges that the vignettes are edited down from much longer stretches of videotape. *Cops* originally recorded about 100 hours of videotape for each hour of airtime. As the producers grew more experienced they reduced the ratio to fifty or sixty to one.

Any indicators of the presence of the *Cops* camera crew during encounters between police and civilians are nearly always edited out. As the *Too Hot For TV* video reveals, this entails considerable cutting of footage of civilians reacting to the camera, often with verbal hostility. Outtakes from the program include, for example, numerous episodes of individuals cursing at the camera.

Each half hour episode of *Cops* consists of three vignettes separated by sets of advertisements. Individual vignettes usually centre on one officer who sets the scene, an officer whom I will call the 'host cop.' The identity of the host varies from episode to episode, but his or her role is the same. At certain points before and after the 'action,' the host cop will talk directly to the camera. (Sometimes more than one cop will talk to the camera in a particular vignette, so there is more than one host.) The host cop addresses the camera most often while she or he is driving the camera crew to and from an incident that forms the focus of the vignette. Even in this context, the presence of the camera crew is not acknowledged. In this way *Cops* offers the illusion that the viewer is in the car with the officer on the way to and from the action.

While naturalizing its depictions of criminal justice, *Cops* simultaneously incorporates story-telling devices that promote a particular vision of policing. This vision resonates with a prominent system of meaning in the broader culture, a particular way of thinking about crime that supports a 'law and order' approach to criminal justice. In the previous chapter I raised the question of the role of the broader cultural context in shaping the nature of television's influences. I will now examine the wider cultural backdrop against which '*Cops*' is produced by its makers and seen by TV audiences.

The Broader Cultural Context of *Cops*

In describing the place of crime and criminal justice in contemporary culture, I am synthesizing various previous accounts (Scheingold 1984, 1995; Sparks 1992; Garland 1990, 2001; Kaminer 1995; Simon and Feeley 1995; Sasson, 1995; Loader 1997) leavened with my own ideas.

Clearly, there is no one 'public view' of criminal justice – this is much too monolithic and static a model. Nevertheless, previous research highlights one wider system of meaning about criminal justice that is prominent, and sometimes dominant, in the public, media, and political cultures. I will call this broader system of meaning 'law-and-order ideology.'

While law-and-order ideology has been chronically present in public, media, and political discourse, it may have assumed an even larger role in recent years (Simon and Feeley 1995). Particular media portrayals of criminal justice interact with and help to shape, reinforce, and evolve this broader system of meaning, even as they are in turn shaped by it. The relationship is thus a dynamic and circular one. Similarly, this broader system of meaning also shapes and is shaped by the views of particular members of the public, by the police institution, and by politicians who promote a 'law and order' approach to crime.

In this system of meaning, society is seen to be in a state of decline or crisis because of the ever-increasing threat of crime, specifically violent street crime of the underclasses. The answer is tougher, more punitive crime control. One key cause of the crime problem is thought to be a failure of politicians and the criminal justice system to get tough with street crime. Due process and other 'softnesses' of the justice system are part of the problem, because all right-thinking people know criminals are guilty. Interestingly, the police themselves are not seen as too soft, but as being held back by other elements of the system. This system of meaning strongly emphasizes the role of police as 'crime fighters' (Manning 1978), as opposed to various other ways of understanding their function, for example, order maintenance and emergency service. The capacity of police to control crime is considerably exaggerated. Thus, the answer to the crime problem is partly more police, and police who are allowed to get tougher.

Intertwined with the notion of a soft system is an Us-and-Them mentality: crime is seen as a problem of evil or pathological individuals who are a Them less human than Us. Criminals are strangers, not our family members. Police are the thin blue line between Them and Us. An overt claim that crime control is utilitarian is bound up with less conscious, more affectively charged undercurrents of fear and anger, identification with powerful authority, and punitiveness and retribution.

Various analysts argue that this punitiveness involves the displacement of anxieties and angers from other sources (Garland 1990; Sparks 1992; Scheingold 1995). Law-and-order ideology is seen to touch a chord with audiences who are looking for a focus for their anger. Certainly, audiences are often fascinated with deviance. Tied up with the anger it invokes may be audiences' anxieties and ambivalences about their own identification, at least to some extent, with the criminal (Sparks 1992).

Ian Loader argues that the police in particular have, beyond their instrumental roles, a very important symbolic place in contemporary culture, one that fits with law-and-order ideology:

> Within prevailing ... 'structures of feeling' the police figure is central to the production and reproduction of order and security ... the degree and sheer intensity of much public interest in the policing phenomenon suggests that something else is at stake here other than a reasoned calculation of what police can accomplish by way of social protection. Popular sentiment toward policing is marked by a high 'fantasy content' regarding what police can and should do ... It is attracted to the idea of an omnipotent source of order and authority that is able to face up to the criminal Other ... In this respect popular attachment to policing is principally affective in character, something which people evince a deep emotional commitment to and which is closely integrated with their sense of self. Policing, it seems, can provide an interpretive lens through which people make sense of and give order to their world; the source of a set of plausible stories about that world which help people sustain 'ontological security' ... It is against this backdrop that one might refer to the police as having, not only coercive power, but also symbolic power. (1997: 3)

Another facet of the broader cultural context is the place of violence. Audiences are often fascinated by violence, especially when it is condoned and employed by authorities like police with whom they can identify. Part of the police's symbolic or cultural power can thus be traced to their mandate for the legitimate use of violence. Police violence is an extremely potent act of communication.

Identification with authority and authorized violence gives one a sense of power. This may be one part of the audience experience with representations of crime and policing in the media. Another facet of the television audience's experience of power with *Cops* in particular may be the power of seeing or watching, whether this occurs as 'voyeurism' – watching private incidents against the will of others – or 'surveillance' – watching others for the purpose of control action. Other analyses have theorized 'the gaze' as a form of power (Goffman 1972; Norris and Armstrong 1998). More broadly than any of these particular instances, simply being the watcher rather than watched puts one in a position of power.

While it contrasts with the recent trend in criminal justice system discourse towards more rational and technical approaches to crime (Feeley and Simon 1994), law-and-order ideology fits traditional media templates well, because of its simplicity, drama, emotiveness, violence, and easily identifiable villains. Because law-and-order ideology is media friendly, and because it seems to touch a chord with some audiences, it has been a key tool of politicians across the partisan political spectrum: not only the Republicans but the Clinton Democrats in the U.S.; not only the Conservatives but the Blair 'New Labour' government in Britain; not only the right-wing Alliance party but even some nominally social-democratic NDP provincial governments in Canada.

Ideology is meaning that fosters relations of domination (Thompson 1990). Law-and-order ideology is implicated in power relations along some broader social dimensions and thus helps reproduce inequality along those dimensions. It displaces a different set of meanings that links crime with social structural causes such as poverty and unemployment. Law-and-order ideology thus has political implications far beyond its influence on the justice system itself. It may become connected with different systems of meaning that also construct people as Us and Them, for example, race. Stories about crime and control – about deviance and how it is punished – have always been a central tool through which people make sense of and dramatize other cultural anxieties (Sparks 1992; Scheingold 1995; Loader 1997), such as concerns about ethnic differences, about the city and urban life, about government and the state, or, more broadly, about modern life or modernity itself. For example, Scheingold speculates that 'the public's obsession with street crime may actually be fueled by a much broader and more amorphous social malaise ... a focus on street crime allows both the public and the politicians to evade more intractable and more unwelcome problems' (1995: 165).

In particular, law-and-order ideology may speak most clearly to white audiences. Crime narratives often become a way of telling stories about race. Reactions to the O.J. Simpson case, for example, dramatized stark differences between white and African American concerns and perceptions regarding law and order, differences that are repeatedly confirmed by survey research (e.g., Flanagan and Longmire 1996). Fear and loathing of criminals often means nonwhite criminals. For politicians, playing the 'crime' card may be a slightly more subtle way of playing the 'race' card. As Gamson (1995: xi) notes, 'the image of the enemy – the violent criminal – has the additional advantage of providing a hidden image of the "black" violent criminal whose content can be decoded in this way by the intended audience while providing the users of the image with plausible deniability of any racial intent' (1995: xi). The 'war on drugs' in the U.S., for example, may be read by some observers as a 'war on blacks' (Fiske 1996; Andersen 1996). A review of social scientific research on fear of crime suggests it is closely linked, not only with fear of strangers, but also with fear of other social groups (Hale 1996).

Class is another key dimension along which law-and-order ideology works. This is shown, for example, in the focus on street crimes of the lower classes, while less attention is given to other types of criminal activity, such as white-collar and corporate crime.

Because law-and-order ideology is bound up with these wider dimensions of inequality, if portrayals on *Cops* resonate with that ideology they will tend to have the opposite effect from that hypothesized by Meyrowitz. Rather than creating pressure for social equality, they will help reproduce an ideology that justifies and reinforces social inequality.

How *Cops* Tells Its Stories

While naturalizing its depictions as 'reality' in the ways I have just discussed, *Cops* simultaneously presents a very particular vision of criminal justice through various story-telling devices. This is a vision that articulates very well with law-and-order ideology.

Identification

Firstly, *Cops* promotes audience identification with police and a simultaneous distancing of the viewer from suspects. Much audience research on crime and the media does not use very complex psychological models of the ways people interact with media texts. Such research instead suggests a rather passive, linear process whereby media consumers absorb faulty information or scary representations, making them misinformed or fearful. However, consumers also interact with media texts partially by identifying with particular characters (Livingstone 1994). *Vérité* documentary makers sometimes deliberately promote certain meanings in their 'reality fictions' by structuring their documentaries to encourage identification with particular individuals in those films (Anderson and Benton 1991: 49). Good story-telling requires such protagonists.

Cops similarly encourages the viewer to identify with police, while distancing the viewer from other individuals who are portrayed. This creates an Us-Them dichotomy that fits with prominent cultural understandings of criminality: crime is a problem of evil or pathological individuals, Them, who are less human than Us. Police are the thin blue line between Them and Us. *Cops* accomplishes identification and distancing through five mechanisms. Some are intended by the producers as story-telling devices; others are more subterranean results of the program's content and form.

CONTEXT

The various categories of people shown on *Cops* are contextualized very differently. The first time the audience sees the host officer, his or her name, rank, and department are flashed on the screen as an introduction. Other officers are often identified by name in subtitles. Non-cops remain nameless. The host officer also often provides autobiographical information in the introductory phase of a vignette. Thus, the viewer gets to know the host cop personally. The officer will talk about why he – or, occasionally, she – joined the force, how long he or she has been a cop, and so on. One officer talked about how joining the military had helped him 'get some discipline and maturity.' Another said he became a cop because 'I suddenly realized I couldn't sit behind a desk ... I wanted to get out and make a difference.'

Another contextual device that promotes identification with the host cop in some episodes is that the viewer accompanies the host through various aspects of the latter's daily routine. For example, one officer was shown making tea in his kitchen with his wife, who was also a cop. The viewer even accompanied the officer to the pub after work, joining in the police camaraderie there. The viewer also spent off-duty time with the cop as he enjoyed his vintage Daimler automobile.

Responding to a suicide attempt allowed one host cop to express a human side of policing: 'The public does think that police officers have this thick skin and a lot of that is the appearance we have to present when we're trying to control a situation ... cops feel shock and anger and sadness and everything else that regular civilians feel.'

While police officers on *Cops* are humanized through such portrayals, the civilians shown are dehumanized in the way they are portrayed. The television spotlight focuses on the brief moment of police intervention, and does not provide any social context for the civilians portrayed or the alleged crimes committed. Police exist on the surface of social life (Ericson, Haggerty, and Carriere 1993); this applies especially to *Cops*, which offers only a superficial engagement with the world beyond the police cruiser. When any context is given, it is often the criminal record of the suspect as recounted by the officer. In one episode, for example, after a young African American man was arrested an officer stated, 'We've been chasing this guy around for years. He's got a drug problem. He was ... arrested last week. He ... got out of jail today. It just worked out pretty good. We just happened to be right there.' When civilians have their faces blurred or concealed by the editors to hide their identities, this further depersonalizes them.

POINT OF VIEW
Cops also encourages identification with police through its use of point of view. The lone camera in *Cops* simulates a single viewpoint – that of the police officer. This is analogous to the point-of-view shot used in film fiction to simulate the view of a particular character. Thus, viewers are not only placed in a personal relationship with the host cop, but are also positioned on-scene as if they themselves were cop's. For example, the viewer gets a cop's-eye-view through the cruiser window of the hunt for fleeing suspects. In this case, the attempt to get the viewer to identify through point of view is explicitly acknowledged by the producers. As executive producer John Langley states, 'The goal is to put [the viewer] in the passenger seat with them *so you can experience what it's like to be a cop*' (italics added). Langley also states that the program allows the viewer '*to share a cop's point of view*.' Thus, the 'raw reality' the producers talk about elsewhere is discussed here as 'reality' from a particular point of view.

IDENTIFYING WITH JOB SATISFACTION
Identifying with police may mean identifying with authorized power and its pleasures. In this vein, *Cops* also promotes audience identification – as the officers shown describe the sensations and satisfactions of their work. One officer described his job as 'like Disneyland.' Another's closing comment after an arrest was, 'I enjoyed that. It's a nice way to end the night.' A third said, 'I suppose the best thing is you never know what's going to happen next. Occasionally you get something exciting

happening and it makes all the boring bits worthwhile.' One host cop said, 'I don't like thieves ... I've had two cars stolen over the last ten years. When I pop a car thief and get to chase him and catch him, that's a good high there.' Thus the viewer is encouraged to share the satisfactions of policing.

IDENTIFYING WITH SUCCESSFUL VIOLENCE

Other research has indicated that *Cops* shows more violence by police officers than by suspects (Oliver 1994; Andersen 1996). Police officers on *Cops* are consistently successful in their use of violence, overpowering suspects. This is analogous to a recurring feature of television fiction, which is the successful use of violence by 'heroes' of dominant social groups rather than villains from subordinate social groups. Such violence becomes a metaphor for power relationships in society (Fiske and Hartley 1978; Fiske 1987: 9). Audiences are encouraged to identify with the power of heroes who use violence successfully.

IDENTIFICATION AND VOYEURISM

Identification is also bound up with the program's voyeuristic aspects. The supervising producer of *Cops*,' Murray Jordan, suggests that the program is successful in large part because of the 'inherent voyeuristic interest that most human beings have.' Scholarly analysts have also pointed out a voyeuristic quality in reality crime programs in general (Nichol 1994; Bondebjerg 1996; Andersen 1996).

Voyeurism is taking pleasure from viewing the private or forbidden. The viewer overrules the wishes of others that the object of viewing remain secret. Viewing may thus be experienced as an act of domination. The voyeurism of *Cops* is intertwined with its authoritarian pleasures. The seductions or pleasures of one type of power – voyeuristically intruding into the private or forbidden – are meshed with the seductions of another type of power – identifying with the sanctioned authority and sanctioned violence of the police.

A warning at the beginning of the show – that 'viewer discretion is advised' because of the 'graphic nature' of the program – may contribute to this sense of voyeurism. While there are legal reasons for concealing subjects' faces, this also adds a *frisson* of voyeurism through the suggestion that the viewer is being allowed to see 'private' incidents.

Survey research shows that the viewers who report the greatest enjoyment of *Cops* and other reality programs tend to be young males (Oliver and Armstrong 1995). A small portion of the material on *Cops* is explicitly sexual. For example, the opening montage of one episode began with a close-up of the bikini-clad torso of a woman – from which the camera pulled back to establish that the location was a Miami beach. The *Too Hot for TV* video marketed by *Cops* producers contains more explicit sexually voyeuristic material that seems to address a heterosexual male viewer. This includes footage of a sting operation in which the viewer is positioned with cops hiding behind a one-way mirror; the cops press against the glass to get a good view as they watch semi-naked female prostitutes with their male customers.

Another *Cops* vignette – one that did air on television – featured the arrest of a teenaged girl. This vignette most explicitly demonstrates the intertwining of the seductions of authorized power and of voyeurism. It may well have been included in the program for its sexually suggestive content, especially an extended sequence following the teenager's arrest. Police said the girl had led them on a drunken car chase. Once arrested, she was taken inside the police station. Tearful and not apparently resisting the police, the girl – clad in shorts and a revealing halter top – was kept in handcuffs. The cuffs were then chained to a bench as the camera lingered on her body. ('We have to keep the handcuffs on for your own safety.') Very drunk and continuing to cry, she expressed in a repeated, disjointed way the fear that people were going to hurt her. Her face was blurred by the producers to conceal her identity, but this also served to decontextualize and further objectify her body. She began to pull and fight against the chain, and then two cops seized her and bound her legs. Then the vignette jumped ahead in time. Her legs now cuffed together and her hands cuffed underneath her thighs, she was lifted into the back of a squad car by a team of cops – all the while fixed in the light of a Cops camera crew (the camera crew, while of course never acknowledged in the edited version, likely added to her terror). In sum, the young girl's body was the object of a display of converging practices of domination by both the police and the camera.

Just why exactly did the producers opt to show all this? The voyeuristic qualities of *Cops* are of course part of its commercial logic, rather than something introduced by the police. These seductive qualities help sell the program. Yet they may also contribute to viewer identification with the authoritarian pleasures of policing.

Closure

Promoting identification with protagonists is one key story-telling device. Another is closure. Because of the need for a relatively unambiguous storyline, the narrative structure of *Cops* imposes a closure on the events portrayed. Often the imposed structure encourages viewers to interpret events in ways consistent with law-and-order ideology.

One important way closure is accomplished is that the commentary of the host and other officers is used to impose an informal narrative framework on the televised events. This commentary often makes sense of a jumble of imagery that would be either meaningless or ambiguous without some imposed structure of meaning. There is no formal narration, but the material is edited so that the officers serve as informal narrators; the careful viewer can discern that their narration is edited over various visual sequences. Accounts of other officers, dialogue between officers, recordings from briefings and from police radio are also stitched together in the soundtrack to structure these storylines. Thus, viewers must rely heavily on officers' oral interpretation of events rather than the visual record. Because the role of police as narrators is informal and naturalized, the police definition of the situation, the 'authorized definition,' simply becomes the 'reality' of reality TV.

For example, one episode featured a raid on an alleged drug dealer's home in Riverside County, California. Without the host cop's narrative before and after the raid, all the viewer would have seen would be a short, confusing set of images featuring some figures in body armour running through the darkness, several explosions in the night, the sound of breaking glass, and then men in body armour standing in a hallway and a shot of a woman lying face down on the floor. However, on the way to the scene of the raid, an officer told the viewer that the man inside the house carried a shotgun at all times and had bragged that he had blown another man's head off. The cop described the villain as 'very paranoid, has a bulletproof vest, goes to the bathroom with a shotgun in his hand, has vowed to kill any law-enforcement officers that come on the property.' Then there was the short burst of images described above, lasting perhaps twenty seconds. Afterwards, as the camera showed the prone woman, an officer narrated, 'These doors were locked back here. We had to break them. We got one suspect on the ground right here. We got a shotgun [not shown]. He's the dude we were thinking about.' In this segment of reality TV, the reality was the narrative constructed by the officer. It was only through his account that the viewer knew police had succeeded in efficiently containing and controlling a 'dangerous criminal.'

One aspect of producing a coherent story from actuality footage, as mentioned above, involves removing potential ambiguity from events and introducing some form of closure. Police accounts – and the way in which they are edited by the *Cops* producers – may partially close off alternative readings of the televised events.

While the program announces at the outset that 'all suspects are innocent until proven guilty in a court of law,' most often all the evidence the viewer will ever get suggests they have been arrested because they are guilty. In one vignette *Cops* invoked its own closure, pronouncing on who the guilty party was in a highly ambiguous situation. A police cruiser pulled up on a suburban street to a scene where one man, armed with a metal baseball bat, raised it above his head and was threatening to strike another man sitting on the road. He had apparently already struck him. The beaten man staggered in front of the camera with one eye swollen shut, in tears and moaning, 'I'm hurt bad. I need help.' A third man stood by, a handgun protruding from the pocket of his sweat pants. Both he and the man with the bat were beefy individuals who seemed larger than the beaten man. 'I seen him come out of my backyard,' said the man with the bat. 'My gate has a lock and he ripped the gate open.' The beaten man said, 'I was walking down the street ... He said I was burglarizing his fucking house and he hit me with a bat.' The bat-wielding man said, 'He was banging on my door. He ripped the gate open. I stood there. We were scared to death. I had no weapon. I had my bat. That's all I sleep with. We ran across the street because we thought he was in the backyard. Then he comes walking around the corner. We approach him; we ask who are you, what's going on. He comes at us with his fists and I hit him.' A foiled burglary or a brutal assault on a passerby? The police officers made a decision. An officer said to the man with the bat, 'You want to press charges for prowler, right?' and directed him to place the injured man under 'citizen's arrest,' even though the latter was lying on a stretcher in an ambulance by this time. One officer commented that the beaten man 'lives in [another suburb]. That's kind of a bad area,' and asked, 'Why is he coming down to this area? It makes no sense.' Another cop, given the last word of the vignette by the editors, said the beaten man was 'a prowler and a thief who got caught. A prowler with a broken jaw.'

From the producers' point of view, this closure of meaning – by editing the vignette to make that the last word – provides a neat wrap-up and avoids any ambiguity that might leave the audience more troubled than entertained. Closure of meaning is negotiated between television editors and the front-line police who function as informal narrators. Police produce the authorized definition of an unclear situation, not only for the legal system, but also for the TV camera and its audiences. The result in this case was that producers and police constructed this highly ambiguous incident in terms of social class – as though it was clear that the 'bad guy' was the one who came from a 'bad area.'

The officers sometimes even seem to act deliberately to provide closure for the camera to record. For example, in another vignette, an ambiguous situation arose where a mother had apparently abandoned her baby: did she flee because of the threat of violence from the baby's father, or for some other, less excusable reason that would leave her open to criminal charges for neglecting the infant? In this situation, the moral ambiguity was resolved when the host cop took the camera right into the woman's jail cell and elicited from her the admission that she had not left the child because of the threat of violence, thus resolving the moral ambiguity and providing closure.

Not only do events have only one storyline, but it is one that can be swiftly diagnosed and dealt with by police. Police are the ones who know the reality of events. This creates an 'illusion of certainty,' as Haney and Manzolati argue concerning fictional police dramas: 'Police work ... is fraught with uncertainty ... this image of sureness and certainty may actually create in the minds of most viewers a presumption of guilt (1988: 127).' Haney and Manzolati surveyed television viewers and found that heavy viewers were significantly more likely than light viewers to be believe that defendants 'must be guilty of something, otherwise they wouldn't be brought to trial.'

There is usually a closing comment or 'last word' from a cop, voiced over a black screen featuring only the *Cops* logo. Some last words simply sum up the outcome of the vignette to offer closure. A number of others, however, provide a moral for the narrative that has just unfolded. These morals – interpretations from the viewpoints of front-line cops – often reinforce various aspects of the ideology of law and order. For example, in one episode, after a camera crew arrived to find a bloodied suspect subdued on the ground, the vignette closed with an officer's comment that 'the really important fact in this whole deal is that [the arresting officer] is tough as nails.' In another vignette, after two suspected burglars would not admit their guilt, the officer's last word was that this was 'just a sign of the times.' Other morals perpetuated this theme of the comfort of police protection in an uncertain world. These included, for example: 'That's it for today. Who knows what might happen tomorrow?' and 'We'll be sleeping safely in the knowledge that the night shift are on.' Frequently, the last word emphasizes that 'lives have been saved' or 'someone could have been killed.'

A vignette where an officer decided not to arrest a suspected drunk driver concluded with a moral about the 'technicalities' of due process interfering with crime control: 'It's a pity ... I couldn't get him off the street. He's probably going to kill someone.' Similarly, another episode incorporated a 'moral' about the need to get tough with teenage offenders. After some juveniles were arrested, a cop noted in a final monologue: 'They'll go ahead and say "release them to their parents"' ... They may not spend the night in jail. That's kind of frustrating ... It's a little bit of a letdown because they may walk ... they may be kiddie crooks but they grow up to be adult crooks.'

The content of these morals is not the result of some conspiracy between police management and media. It is simply that front-line officers, who provide these interpretations, are immersed in a 'cop culture' (Reiner 2000) that meshes well with law and order ideology.

Selection of Events and Situations

Cops is ideological not only in the ways it tells its stories, but also through the selection of events and situations it portrays. Other reality-TV programs such as *America's Most Wanted* and *Unsolved Mysteries* feature a high proportion of serious crimes – notably homicides – that are relatively rare in official and other statistics (Cavender and Bond-Maupin 1993). *Cops* tends to feature statistically more common or routine crimes, although it has aired multiple murders. In fact, *Cops* crews deliberately searched for murder footage to air in the November 1992 ratings sweeps week (Bernstein 1992). *Cops* shows many incidents involving crimes such as burglaries, robberies, less serious assaults, street-level drug busts, and incidents involving intoxication. Drunks are sometimes presented as clown characters in a kind of low comedy, falling down, embarrassing themselves with foolish statements, or failing simple practical tests of roadside sobriety. *Cops* also shows a large number of police chases, both auto and on foot, and has shown a number of drug raids. Domestic disturbances and domestic violence are a frequent focus, as well as a mixed assortment of other items deemed of viewer interest, such as a case where a man attempted suicide by shooting himself in the head, skydiving injuries, a car fire, and a single mother calling police to help try to discipline her teenaged son.

Nevertheless, in some respects *Cops* offers a highly selective vision of criminal justice. As Oliver's (1994) quantitative content analysis notes, reality crime shows, including *Cops*, tend to overrepresent both the amount of violent crime and the amount of crime that is solved by police. Oliver found that 69 per cent of the criminal suspects on *Cops* and four other reality-based crime shows were arrested, a dramatic improvement on the arrest rate in official and other statistics. In these respects, *Cops* resembles most fictional portrayals of crime, as a number of items of research demonstrate (Reiner 2000: chap. 5). More generally, *Cops* tends to show cases where police apparently deal effectively with situations, swiftly diagnosing trouble and resolving it.

Cops is also ideological in not airing material that will cast police in a bad light. Several factors explain the tendencies of *Cops* to portray police in a uniformly positive way: the producers are very dependent on ongoing co-operation from police; *Cops* producers themselves internalize pro-police attitudes; the producers also aim to give the audience what they apparently want.

The fact that many police forces are keen to cooperate with *Cops* is part of a broader trend towards proactive police self-promotion through the mass media (Ericson, Baranek, and Chan 1989; Schlesinger and Tumber 1994: chap. 4). However, while police forces are often active in promoting particular views of criminal justice, one must be careful not to ascribe a one-dimensional top-down instrumentality to police involvement in *Cops*. *Cops* is shaped as much by front-line police officers as by police management, although one may infer that the particular officers who receive management permission to appear on the program are carefully vetted. Instead, these officers' interpretations may be moulded more directly by front-line cop culture (Reiner 2000) than by the management line.

The relationship between police and television personnel in the production of *Cops* can be compared to police–news media relations. Police have often dominated such relations. The producers of *Cops* are like inner circle reporters who have close ties with police (Ericson, Baranek, and Chan 1989), yet their dependence on police is even greater. Unlike with news, there is no subcultural valorization of at least some degree of critical journalistic autonomy. Nor does the *Cops* format feature any perceived requirement for balance.

The producers of *Cops* acknowledge that, like inner circle police reporters, they have internalized pro-police attitudes. *Cops* creator and executive producer John Langley pondered whether his feelings about police had shifted:

To say 'yes' is to declare the understatement of the year. I'm a kid of the 60s. If you had asked me this in the 60s, I would have laughed and said I would never do a show called 'Cops.' Maybe 'Pigs' but not 'Cops.' Of course I was brash and immature back then ... I have developed a profound respect for police officers, firemen, paramedics, and everyone else involved in public service ... They put their lives at risk for others, and I think that's both admirable and inspirational.

Another *Cops* producer said she had been approached by several police forces about signing up as a cop herself once she left the program (Bernstein 1992). Debra Seagal, a former member of the production staff at a similar reality-based show, *American Detective*, noted that the camera crews for the program 'even wear blue jackets with POLICE in yellow letters on the back ... The executive producer ... frequently wears a badge on his belt loop' (Seagal 1993).

A Kansas City police officer who let a *Cops* crew accompany him on his midnight shift for two weeks told *Time* magazine it was an enjoyable experience. 'Most officers would be apprehensive to have the media ride with them ... But these guys proved themselves to us. They said that they wouldn't do anything to undermine us, and that we'd have final discretion about what ran' (Zoglin 1992). *Time* reported, 'each episode of "Cops" is reviewed by the police before airing, in part to make sure no investigations are compromised.' Hallett and Powell (1995) recount how *Cops* producers offered full editorial control of footage filmed in Nashville to the Chief of Police and to the Public Relations Officer of the Nashville Metro PD; after preliminary editing in Los Angeles, *Cops* personnel returned to Nashville so that those officials could approve the rough cuts. As one Nashville officer recorded for the program told Hallett and Powell: 'Most importantly, anything we didn't want kept on tape had to be erased – that was the deal – and each officer could have erased whatever he wanted to have erased' (1995: 115).

For these reasons, *Cops* does not air incidents that would cast police in a bad light. As Katz argued:

The cameras recording 'Cops' would probably not catch a Rodney King–style beating. The officers would know better than to behave like that; even if they didn't, it's unclear whether the broadcast's producers would show it, since the program depends on the voluntary co-operation of the police. (1993: 27)

For example, as reported in the *Seattle Times* (Scattarella 1992: A1) and elsewhere, in one notorious case in May 1992 a *Cops* camera crew recorded police on a drug raid bursting into a suburban Washington state home. They rousted a couple and their children from sleep and handcuffed the half-naked woman – before finally realizing they were in the wrong house. The woman complained, 'They pulled me out of bed and put a gun on me. Here I am with my butt showing, and I see the camera.' Police apparently had the address wrong on the crack-bust warrant. *Cops* decided not to broadcast any of the raid.

Seagal has described a similar incident she reviewed on *American Detective* videotape:

> Our cameramen, wearing police jackets, are in one of the [Santa Cruz police] undercover vans during the pursuit [of two Hispanic suspects] ... One of [the camera men] has his camera in one hand and a pistol held high in the other. The police don't seem to care about his blurred role ... the suspects are pinned to the ground and held immobile while cops kick them in the stomach and the face ... Our secondary cameraman holds a long, extreme closeup of a suspect while his mouth bleeds into the dirt. One producer shakes his head at the violence. 'Too bad,' he says. 'Too bad we can't use that footage.' This was clearly a case of too much reality for reality-based TV.' (1993: 55).

Another reality-TV show, *Real Stories of the Highway Patrol*, recorded a West Virginia state trooper pursuing a drunk driver until the drunk crashed his car into another vehicle and killed an innocent twenty-one-year-old woman. The camera crew then captured the trooper's reaction at the scene: 'I killed that girl, man ... I killed her, goddamn it.' However, the footage was never aired, as the police exercised a contractual option with the production company to suppress it (Vick 1997).

Cops is also selective in its portrayal of race. This reinforces ties between law-and-order ideology and racism. According to a content analysis by Oliver (1994) of five reality crime programs, including *Cops*, these programs tend to underrepresent African Americans and Hispanics and overrepresent whites as police officers, while overrepresenting minorities and underrepresenting whites as criminals. *Cops* also omits any portrayals of overtly racist police behaviour. Management would be unlikely to choose overtly racist officers to be filmed for the program; officers who were filmed would likely censor their own behaviour somewhat; and even if such material were recorded, producers would probably opt not to air it. According to survey research (of white viewers only), viewers who report greater enjoyment of reality-based programs, including *Cops*, also tend to show higher levels of racial prejudice (Oliver and Armstrong 1995).

The many episodes of *Cops* reviewed for this research focused exclusively on 'street crime.' *Cops* is also selective in focusing on crime in poorer neighbourhoods. This is apparent from watching the program, but was also revealed in a *Los Angeles Times* profile of a *Cops* co-producer: 'Most often, it's poor neighborhoods where "Cops" goes for its stories. Wealthy areas, while often host to the same domestic abuse and robbery problems that make up the program's stable of policing situations, are disdained as not crime ridden enough. "Traditionally, we don't go and ride in those areas," [the *Cops* co-producer] said. Things that happen in places like Beverly Hills, she said, "aren't the kind of things that are stories for us on the show."' (Bernstein 1992: F1). Thus, law-and-order ideology is intertwined with wider issues of class.

'Cops' and Other Cultural Products

Cops resonates with understandings of criminal justice that pervade the broader culture. One way in which this is most immediately apparent is in how the program fits together with other media products concerned with crime and policing. *Cops* does not operate in isolation of other media portrayals of criminal justice. Media products influence each other's meanings, for people do not consume them in isolation, but together. An evening's television may feature news, fiction, advertising, and reality TV, and viewers may often make sense of them through their interplay or intertextuality as a package (Barthes 1975; Fiske 1987). If we see the O.J. Simpson trial on the news, it will probably affect how we interpret a similar fictionalized trial later that night on *Law and Order*. The meanings of the particular visions of policing on *Cops* will be shaped in part by this interaction with the broader culture.

This notion of interplay or intertextuality is well established (Barthes 1975; Fiske 1987). However, it has not been considered much in social scientific work on crime in the media. Most analyses consider crime news, crime fiction, or reality-based TV in isolation, or treat them as discrete components of media content that may be considered in additive fashion. This approach ignores the extent to which these media products are intertwined and mutually constitutive. Together they make a whole that is more than the sum of its parts.

For example, a striking facet of the Fox TV network's Saturday night line-up is the interplay between different elements. *Cops* has repeatedly been situated as part of a broader package of television entertainment related to fear and loathing of street crime. During *Cops*, there are ads for *America's Most Wanted*, the other popular reality crime program that followed. After watching *Cops*, viewers can 'help the cops catch a killer on America's Most Wanted' because 'it's a night of non-stop action on Q13.' One segment of *Cops* immediately cut from the closing credits to a slogan saying: 'Real Cops,' an ad for another reality-based program, *Top Cops*, which features re-enacted scenarios of heroic police moments. Once, back-to-back episodes of *Cops* were followed immediately by *Front Page*, a Fox TV 'news magazine' that featured segments on the kidnapping and strangling of a young girl, on 'gangsta' rap music, and on 'locking up drug dealers ... how one state sends first-time drug dealers to prison – for the rest of their lives.'

Cops viewers were also repeatedly exhorted by advertisements to participate in hunting down wanted criminals. In the Pacific North-west, Saturday nights featured ads for Greater Vancouver Crimestoppers and Western Washington's Most Wanted, interspersed with episodes of *Cops*. Also featured repeatedly on *Cops*, in an apparent attempt at niche marketing, were ads for Pepper Mace spray. Airing shortly before Christmas, these ads concluded with the suggestion that Pepper Mace 'makes a great stocking stuffer.'

Cops and *America's Most Wanted* are sometimes even tied together thematically: on one occasion they featured back-to-back episodes set in New Orleans to mark Mardi Gras celebrations. *America's Most Wanted* is much more overtly ideological, and *Cops* will be read by audiences in the context of this. For example, one November 1996 episode of *Cops* featured video vignettes of a suspected assault/child neglect case, a drug raid, and a car chase. The closing credits for *Cops* were aired on one-half of a split screen. Aired on the other half of the screen, with a backdrop of dramatic fictional crime footage using actors, was a monologue by *America's Most Wanted* host John Walsh that encapsulated law-and-order ideology. Walsh said:

> You know what I'm sick of. Criminals who serve only a fraction of their sentences. Sexual predators who are released to live next door to you and your children and you don't even know it. Drug dealers who think they run these streets. This is a society where criminals have all the rights and victims don't have any. Well, it's going to change. You're going to make

that happen. The new *America's Most Wanted*. America fights back. Premieres next Saturday after *Cops* on non-stop Fox.

More broadly, viewers often consume crime news, reality crime programming, and crime drama in juxtaposition.[2] If one's daily rhythms include an hour of news at six o'clock, so that mealtime includes generous helpings of crime and punishment, topped off by a couple of hours of prime-time police dramas, one does not absorb these independently of each other. Being viewed in the context of news may add immediacy to crime fiction; being viewed in the context of fiction may add dramatic impact to crime news. Media consumers make sense of crime by juxtaposing countless crime stories from different sources in the mass media and elsewhere.

Cops is not simply more of the same. Through its claims to be 'reality TV' and its power to invoke the notion that 'seeing is believing,' *Cops* occupies a distinctive and crucial place in the wider media package. More generally, the more that 'real' footage of crime and policing appears on television – both on reality programs like *Cops* and in the news – it adds extra force to law-and-order ideology. This is because the footage offers visual 'proof' that powerfully reinforces the law-and-order messages in other programming. This is one key influence of TV as it comes to broadcast new situations in the realm of criminal justice.

Weekday episodes of *Cops* have often been broadcast immediately after the 6 o'clock news, bridging the gap between the news and prime-time crime. This bridging is both literal and figurative. As one television executive noted, the interplay between *Cops* and local television news may be an important part of its success in this time slot. Twentieth Television syndication president Greg Meidel told *Broadcasting and Cable* magazine, 'All our research indicates that viewers closely identify "Cops" content with that of similar sorts of law enforcement coverage on newscasts locally. That's why "Cops" has been so compatible as a lead-in or lead-out from local news programming. It looks, feels and tastes like a first-run news program' (M. Freeman 1993).

The story telling of *Cops* also resonates extremely well with fictional crime programming. *Cops* has the simple, unambiguous narrative structure, pumped-up action, heroic police protagonists, high arrest rate, and illusion of police certainty characteristic of much fictional crime drama. Like many such fictional dramas, the action on *Cops* ends with closure or summary justice at the arrest stage of the criminal process. *Cops* takes place in linear 'real time' in a fictional present rather than being recounted in summary form in the past tense like news. The presence of the camera is not acknowledged on *Cops*, which is also characteristic of fictional or dramatic realism (although it is an approach also adopted by some *vérité* documentarists).

Many viewers will likely draw on the experience of one form to interpret the other. For example, if people see that *Cops* is a lot like crime fiction, crime fiction may be seen as more realistic; conversely, the fact that *Cops* itself is structured like crime fiction may simply seem natural. More generally, the influences of *Cops* must be understood by situating it among a broader range of sources of crime stories. Combined, these sources form a package that is more than the sum of its parts. Thus, the broader cultural context in which *Cops* exists will reinforce its tendencies towards law and ideology.

'Cops' and Audiences

Clearly not all audiences will simply accept that *Cops* is reality. Yet audience research suggests that many viewers largely do see it this way. A survey of 358 television viewers in Wisconsin and Virginia (Oliver and Armstrong 1995) showed that audiences perceive *Cops* and four similar programs as significantly more realistic than crime fiction. Andersen (1996) notes that, according to a 1993 Times-Mirror survey, viewers tend to think of reality crime shows as informational programming rather than entertainment. Industry research also suggests that many viewers see *Cops* as very similar to local news (M. Freeman 1993).

Of course, audiences give their own interpretations to any media product. Not all viewers will take *Cops* the same way; some audience members will subvert the police definitions of the televised situations and make their own meanings (Fiske 1987). Yet many viewers are already inclined towards law-and-order ideology, and these are the people for whom *Cops* will most likely have the greatest appeal. This is confirmed by Oliver and Armstrong, who found that reality programs like *Cops* 'were most enjoyed by viewers who evidenced higher levels of authoritarianism, reported greater punitiveness about crime and reported higher levels of racial prejudice' (1995: 565). Other research showed that regular viewers of *Cops* and three other reality programs were significantly more fearful than infrequent viewers of being sexually assaulted, beaten up, knifed, shot, or killed (Haghighi and Sorensen 1996: 23).

The influence on audiences of crime in the media has been very extensively investigated (Gunter 1987; Sparks 1992). Research has repeatedly found that viewers who watch large amounts of crime on television strongly tend to be more afraid of crime and more inclined towards law-and-order ideology. However, the extent to which each circumstance causes the other has proved difficult to ascertain. Do people want more law and order because they watch crime on TV, or vice versa? The relationship is most likely one of mutual reinforcement. Like many media products, *Cops* is not exactly preaching to the converted, but is more preaching to those who lean that way – reinforcing fear of crime and law-and-order views among people already predisposed to them.

It is particularly hard to demonstrate empirically how media reinforce existing viewpoints (Livingstone 1996). Nevertheless, mainstream and critical communications literatures converge on one point – the strongest socializing influence of media may be precisely that: to reinforce existing views (Curran 1990, 1996; Surette 1997). There are strong indications, then, that *Cops* does not simply allow viewers to see unproblematically into a previously hidden situation, as Meyrowitz would argue. Instead, *Cops* offers an ideological vision of criminal justice that will more likely tend to reproduce hierarchy and inequality than eliminate it.

'Cops' Feeds Back into the Criminal Justice System

The question of how *Cops* portrays crime and policing is bound up with how it feeds back into criminal justice situations themselves. *Cops* helps constitute events in the justice system, so that criminal justice events also become television events. It does not simply offer a distorted representation of some 'real world' of policing; it helps shape that world. *Cops* illustrates the more general point that 'the mass media do not merely report on events but rather participate directly in processes by which events are constituted and exist in the world' (Ericson 1991: 219; see also Altheide and Snow 1979, 1991).

There are numerous indications that police tailor their behaviour to the program. For example, outtakes from *Cops* reveal both police and camera crew members giving stage directions during 'real' incidents. The most controversial such incident, involving stage directions given to police by a reality-TV crew, occurred with another program, *Real Stories of the Highway Patrol*. As described above, in November 1996 the crew of that program recorded a police pursuit gone awry. The crew were riding with a West Virginia State Trooper as he chased a drunk driver until the impaired driver collided with another vehicle, killing an innocent twenty-one–year-old woman. The woman's parents launched a wrongful death suit, charging that

> the presence of the camera crew further excited a perilous situation. The allegation is supported by a vivid moment picked up on the videotape: the sound of one of the TV crew members apparently urging [the trooper] on ... 'That has to affect him,' says [the dead woman's] mother ... 'They are hyping the situation ... Had they not been there, would my daughter be sitting here?' (Vick 1997)

Many on-the-spot interrogations of suspects and conferences between officers during *Cops* seem staged for the camera's benefit. *Cops* has also displayed small-scale sting operations that illustrate a convergence of police and media needs. One episode featured a sting conducted by police in which a Mack truck was intentionally abandoned outside a housing project and in other impoverished urban areas. Police and cameras were concealed in the truck, and within a short time males in the area, usually young and African American or Hispanic, would break into the truck's container to see what kind of valuables were inside. This yielded not only ready-made arrests and charges, but also ready-made footage for *Cops*. As one of the officers noted, it was 'Christmas in August' for all concerned – except, of course, the African American and Hispanic youths breaking into the truck, who simply wound up 'gift-wrapped' for police and media consumption.

Another way in which television coverage reshapes criminal justice practice is through the emergence of informal rituals of punishment for the camera. The result is the spectacularization of arbitrarily selected day-to-day instances of crime and punishment. For example, police sometimes parade arrested suspects in handcuffs in strategic locations so they can be visually recorded by the media – a ritual known colloquially as the 'perp walk' (Doyle and Ericson 1996). Similar practices are evident on *Cops*. As well, the narrative structure of *Cops* works to provide closure for each vignette, and police often seem to deliberately shape their actions to produce such closure.

One occasional way of giving the stories closure is to show suspects on *Cops* being subjected to informal shaming rituals by police. These offer a kind of summary justice that provides closure and a moral to the particular vignette. Police often may offer some form of lecture or shaming to suspects regardless of whether or not television cameras are present, but of course their presence redefines the situation dramatically for the participants. For example, in one vignette a man was pulled over by police while he was driving to a funeral with his female partner and small children. The man was found to be in possession of a small amount of marijuana. He was not charged, but was instead subjected to a roadside lecture by police, as he pleaded by way of mitigation that he was unemployed. The humiliating effect of the lecture was likely magnified powerfully because he was in front of a camera and would later appear on national television.

This example raises the more general point that *Cops* also alters the experience of criminal justice for particular civilians who are recorded. Media attention may cause police to alter their behaviour, but also redefines the situation for other participants. For example, media coverage of the criminal process may make the experience of that process more punitive for suspects. Being recorded for *Cops* becomes itself an informal shaming ritual. Certain suspects may be excited by the attention, and a surprising number do sign the releases. However, being taped for *Cops* may often be painful and humiliating for many other civilians, as television cameras intrude on some of the unhappier moments of their lives. This is evident from outtakes of the program, although footage of viewers reacting to the camera is edited out when the program airs. Even if suspects do not consent to the footage being aired, being filmed may be highly unpleasant for them.

Nor does the blurring of faces always conceal the identities of civilians. Producer John Langley told one newspaper, 'We don't disclose someone's identity without their permission,' but this was not the situation in at least one controversial incident in Los Angeles. The identity of a fourteen-year-old alleged statutory rape victim was revealed on *Cops* without either her or her family's permission (*Los Angeles Times*, April 20, 1991, p. B3). During televised footage of a police interview, a nineteen–year-old suspect mentioned the girl's unusual first name and admitted having sex with her. The footage made it clear in which locality the events were taking place. The result was that the fourteen-year-old girl was verbally harassed and 'pushed around' by schoolmates and temporarily removed from her school by her parents. The teenager said, 'I was very embarrassed to find out that many students in my school were talking about me and it upset me to hear the things they were saying ... If I had known my name would be given out, I never would have spoken to police ... Now when I go out, if I mention my name, it's "Oh, you were the girl on *Cops.*" I just don't want to be known as the girl on *Cops.*'

While police may tailor their behaviour for the program, a key point is that they do not feel compelled to constrain their actions very much because of their possible visibility on TV. As Debra Seagal, former production staffer of a very similar reality-TV program, *American Detective*, noted in a letter to the *Columbia Journalism Review* (March/April 1993: p. 4):

> This footage, before it's transformed into an acceptable episode, features cops and detectives at their uncensored 'best,' which invariably includes slander against every minority under the sun, as well as numerous acts of excessive physical and verbal harassment. The cops are well aware of the fact the viewer will never see any of this, since they have a tacit agreement with the producers that they will be shown in a positive light.

Cops also feeds back into policing more broadly by influencing police and would-be police who are viewers. There has been massive study of the influence of crime in the media on individual audience members, but little research on how crime in the media influences the particular audience of criminal justice personnel. According to Mary Beth Oliver, who has researched *Cops* extensively, instructors from police academies around the U.S. have indicated that such shows inspired many of their students to pursue law enforcement careers. The students' 'whole idea of what it means to be a police officer is based on these very shows,' Oliver said (Perigard 1995). Similarly, one would-be police officer interviewed for this chapter said that he watched *Cops* often and saw it as part of his training: each episode taught him how to deal with particular situations.

As *Cops* feeds back into policing, it begins to blur the worlds of television and 'real life.' For example, the possibility that police officers may one day appear on *Cops* suggests a continuity between their working worlds and the world of crime on TV. One California police officer, who was being recorded in action for *Cops*, told the *Los Angeles Times* that he and his wife were also regular viewers and big fans of the show: 'I watch it all the time ... I like the action ... which is also what I like about being out here [on the beat]. It's an adrenalin rush. It's what a lot of us like about police work – the excitement' (Bernstein 1992). How did viewing many previous episodes of *Cops* shape his behaviour when *Cops* began recording him on the job? For police officers being recorded, *Cops* may represent a fantasy come true in that they were raised on the fictional heroics of police crime dramas: now they have their chance to be a 'television hero.'

These diverse examples demonstrate that *Cops* influences policing and the criminal justice system in ways that are much more varied and pervasive than is first apparent. *Cops* has now televised over 1500 vignettes of police activity. This means the program has videotaped something like ten thousand hours of policing since 1989. It has thus affected numerous instances of police activity and touched the lives of many individuals in this way. However, *Cops* has further effects on the criminal justice system that range far beyond the particular incidents it has recorded. It has spawned many imitators, such as *American Detective, LAPD: Life on the Beat*, and *To Serve and Protect*. In fact, in St. Petersburg, Florida, the increasing media consciousness of police has pushed this influence to the next step: St. Petersburg police are now bypassing the media and producing their own *Cops*-style reality-based program on local cable television. These police sometimes take video cameras along as they work, and film their own activities for the show. The program, *Police Report*, combines footage of their real-life operations, in *Cops* fashion, with interviews with police. They have also created their own media shaming ritual in the form of televised naming of prostitutes' johns (Getz 1995).

Video cameras are becoming omnipresent in criminal justice, and *Cops* has attempted to expand its reach to obtain footage from all of them. In the spring of 1996, the official *Cops* website on the Internet was advertising an appeal to 'officers, deputies, corrections officers, troopers,' and others. The advertisement stated, 'The producers of *Cops* are looking for amazing, unusual, exciting or weird videotape: crazy arrests, angry suspects, hot pursuits, bloopers from in car cameras, cam corders, surveillance cameras.' The footage was sought for a new home video that would be entitled *Caught on Camera*. First prize for the best footage was a trip for two to Hawaii.

Thus, the influence of *Cops* has penetrated ever deeper into the criminal justice system. Word would have spread among criminal justice personnel so that, conceivably, any footage from any video camera in the system anywhere at any time might appear on *Cops*. Increasingly, any criminal justice moment might become a media event.

Conclusion

There has been copious research on how individual media products affect the views of audiences. Unfortunately, such research employs a conception that is too narrow to capture fully the force of media influence. Certainly, *Cops* may influence many viewers' attitudes. *Cops* demonstrates profoundly how the story telling of reality TV can be ideological, as its narrative techniques – such as naturalization, positioning of viewer identification, closure, and selectiveness – shape 'raw reality' into made-for-TV stories. Thus, *Cops* does *not* simply include viewers in a new 'information system' (Meyrowitz 1985) or make visible the back regions of policing, leading to pressure for social change, as Meyrowitz claimed. *Cops* offers a particular portrayal of criminal justice, one that works not to reduce but to perpetuate hierarchy and social inequality. The definitions of the criminal justice situations recorded for *Cops* are negotiated in unequal power relations among police, television personnel, 'suspects,' and audiences. This occurs in ways more consistent with the account of Ericson, Baranek, and Chan (1989) and with other research on the sociology of news production that has demonstrated extensive police control over the media (Chibnall 1977; Hall et al. 1978; Fishman 1978, 1980, 1981; Schlesinger and Tumber 1994; Sacco 1995). Ironically, compared to relations with journalists, police seem even less vulnerable in *Cops*, even though their activities are recorded directly for television. For television broadcasters who are allowed to record policing for *Cops* do so on terms dictated by police. Power relations affect which situations of crime and policing are selected for broadcast, how these situations are packaged; the resulting portrayal of policing is an artifact of police power. Power relations also influence the ways of understanding criminal justice in the broader culture that are drawn on when these images are interpreted by audiences.

The key to understanding the various influences of *Cops* is the role of the police as authoritative definers of the events that are recorded. Police are both informal narrators of the footage and those who largely define the criminal justice situation for the various front-line players, including defining particular behaviour as criminal. Clearly not all audience members will simply accept the police definition of what they see (Fiske 1987), but audience research suggests those viewers who are drawn to watch *Cops* are also more likely to accept its purported 'reality.' Audiences tend to see *Cops* as informational programming, like news, and in any case the particular audience segment that favours *Cops* tends to have authoritarian tendencies that make them likely to identify with police and accept their accounts (Oliver and Armstrong 1995).

Power is in large part the ability to define a situation so that others act on that definition (Altheide and Snow 1991: 4). In the case of *Cops*, the ability to present the authorized definition of the situation before the cameras, an ability held mostly by police, is the key to controlling television's influence not only on audiences, but also on the situation in front of the camera and the institutions beyond it. *Cops* not only portrays events and practices in the criminal justice system, it actually helps reshape them. For example, *Cops* functions as informal promotional and teaching footage for would-be police officers, influencing their behaviour in future situations. As well, it alters practices by, for example, prompting informal rituals of summary justice by police or reshaping the experience of criminal justice as more punitive for suspects. Day-to-day policing activities are imbued with a spectacular, ritualized shaming quality, consistent with a media tendency to foster spectacular behaviour in the institutions it records. Through an infusion of media logic (Altheide and Snow 1979, 1991), the routine crimes and arrests captured by *Cops* are reshaped into media spectacles.

CHAPTER FOUR

Surveillance Cameras, Amateur Video, and 'Real' Crime on Television

The medium of TV is not static; it cannot be analysed as though it never changes. The influence of television on other institutions cannot be understood as if TV itself exists in a single, unchanging, final form. TV and related technologies perpetually evolve, continually altering the social relations that surround them. For example, as I have noted, the advent of smaller, more portable video cameras for television crews was one factor that led to the emergence of *Cops*. In this chapter I discuss two similar examples of advances in TV technology, and their influences.

The previous chapter began to show ways in which TV does not simply record criminal justice, but reshapes it. In this chapter I discuss the similar effects of other types of 'real' footage of crime and policing, broadcast not only by reality programs, but also in TV news and advertising. I look at the impact of two new kinds of media technology: the surveillance camera and the home video camcorder. During the 1980s and 1990s, both of these new technologies increasingly provided footage for TV to broadcast of 'real' crime and policing. How might these new video technologies have altered the situations they record? What wider impacts might this have on the world of crime and control? These two sources of footage – the surveillance camera and the camcorder wielded by the amateur videographer – provide an interesting contrast. How might the impact differ when the footage comes from an unofficial source, an ordinary citizen with a home video camera, as opposed to a more authoritative source, a surveillance camera operated by public or private police?

There has been very little previous social science work dealing with the use of either kind of video on the news. Surveillance camera footage is mentioned in some of the literature on reality TV (e.g., Schlesinger and Tumber 1993). Two authors – Young (1996) and Fiske (1996) – have analysed prominent incidents in which a crime was recorded by surveillance cameras and then displayed on television news (the James Bulger killing in Britain and the Latasha Harlins shooting in the U.S., respectively). Some works on trends in TV news comment briefly on the increasing use of amateur video in the 1990s (e.g., Lichty and Gomery 1992; Bird 1997). There have been several scholarly analyses of the politics of interpretation of the notorious Rodney King video (Gooding-Williams 1993; Goodwin 1994; Fiske 1996). Yet there has been no investigation of the more general trend towards the use of these kinds of footage.

In this chapter I use various data to generate an exploratory typology of the uses of surveillance camera footage and amateur video of criminal justice incidents on broadcast television, and to examine the implications in light of my research questions. From the Nexis database, I collected transcripts of dozens of television items featuring either surveillance camera video or amateur video of crime and policing. I collected further examples as I came across them in my own viewing, and from a variety of secondary sources.

Surveillance Camera Footage on TV News

During the mid-1970s, a crude but dramatic piece of surveillance camera footage captured the U.S. TV news spotlight. The footage, from a California bank surveillance camera, featured kidnapped heiress Patty Hearst brandishing a gun as she accompanied her captors during a hold-up. Such cameras were relatively rare then, but the televising of this flickering piece of black-and-white footage taken at multi-second intervals marked the beginning of a trend. As surveillance cameras have spread, authorities have also taken the initiative more in providing the news media with surveillance footage of many crimes.

Closed-circuit television (CCTV) surveillance of public spaces is increasingly pervasive in Britain (Norris and Armstrong 1999). Publicly owned and operated surveillance cameras are also spreading in North America, having arrived by the late 1990s in cities such as Tacoma, Newark, and Baltimore (Surette 1997: 175). In Vancouver, a proposal was under consideration to mount twenty-three surveillance cameras to monitor fifty-nine blocks in the downtown area (*Vancouver Sun*, 13 March 2000, p. B1). Cameras now frequently mounted in police cruisers have become another source of TV footage. Of course, surveillance cameras also now blanket commercial spaces such as shops and malls, one part of a major expansion of private policing (Shearing 1992; Law Commission of Canada 2002).

Surveillance footage on TV news not only spotlights high-profile crimes like the Hearst kidnapping, but also more routine and prosaic incidents. These are crimes that make the news simply because they happen to be caught on camera. Such footage is also picked up in various other TV formats. Surveillance footage has been regularly used in British *Crimestoppers* television ads since 1988 (Moran 1998: 280) as well as on the popular television program *Crimewatch UK* (Schlesinger and Tumber 1993). In the U.S., the Fox network's weekly hour-long program *World's Wildest Police Videos* has been a key outlet for police surveillance cameras. The British Carlton Television program *Police! Camera! Action!* features surveillance footage of dangerous and disturbing driving incidents (Moran 1998: 283). So do commercially released videos, for example, *Police Stop!* and *Police Stop! America*. Another commercial video, *Caught In the Act!*, marketed a montage of events captured by surveillance cameras monitored by local authorities and by the police (Moran 1998: 285).

Video Wanted Posters

Surveillance capability of the cameras is enhanced by working with TV news and programs like *Crimestoppers* and *Crimewatch UK*. This is because police can call on the TV audience to identify suspects recorded on camera but not known to authorities. (I will call this tactic the 'video wanted poster.') Television not only reshapes the social situation by including the audience in a new 'information system' (although in a situation quite different from that envisioned by Meyrowitz's [1985] medium theory analysis), but creates a new institutional role for the audience as a participant in surveillance.

The video wanted poster has enjoyed a number of success stories. A man who held up a Louisiana convenience store was caught on surveillance camera pounding the clerk's head against the cash register. His father saw the footage on local news and turned him in (*The Rivera Show*, 30 May 1998). Proponents claim broadcast of surveillance footage also led to two other, high-profile captures: of the young killers of James Bulger in Britain, and of a suspect in the bombing of an American federal government building in Oklahoma (Graham 1998: 90). A British subway bomber was reportedly captured through the use of this tactic (A. Freeman 1999). And enterprising police are using video wanted posters to identify suspects in the aftermath of riots, as I discuss in the next chapter.

While they help in the hunt for suspects, video wanted posters simultaneously dramatize and sensationalize particular crimes. Perhaps the most prominent example was the Bulger case in Britain. Sixteen cameras captured a two-year-old being led away from a shopping mall by two ten-year-old boys. The older children would later murder the youngster. The public furore over the Bulger case was magnified by the repeated airing on TV news of footage from the sixteen security cameras that recorded the two-year-old's abduction.

Video from public and private surveillance cameras is sometimes given to the news media even when there is no obvious investigative purpose. For example, in the Latasha Harlins case in the U.S., TV news repeatedly aired surveillance footage of a Korean shop owner shooting a young black woman in the back of the head and killing her (Fiske 1996).

Some surveillance footage seems to make the news purely because it is dramatic, even in the absence of any other obvious news value. For example, on 25 May 1999 a Seattle television station aired surveillance footage of an unidentifiable thief removing a painting from the wall of a Salt Lake City art gallery. There was only a very brief verbal description accompanying the image. A painting being stolen in far-away Utah was certainly not local news, and airing the footage apparently did nothing to further the investigation.

These examples suggest that a secondary function of surveillance cameras has developed: to produce for public broadcast what I will call 'promotional footage.' These video clips of crime promote a particular image of criminal justice, one that may serve the purposes of police and other authorities. John Daly is host of the American reality program *Real-TV*, which offers dramatic video clips of actual events – including a number of criminal justice incidents – purely for entertainment. Daly said a key source of video footage for *Real-TV* is government agencies – local, state, and federal – along with private surveillance cameras in businesses (*The Rivera Show*, 30 June 1998). *Real-TV* has even featured footage from hidden cameras used in FBI undercover operations. Other televised criminal justice footage comes from camcorders mounted in police cruisers. For example, another reality program, *I Witness Video*, featured footage from a Texas constable's police car of suspects gunning down the officer, followed by footage from a second police car of one of the suspects in turn being killed in a shoot-out with police (*LA Times*, 22 February 1992). Footage from in-car cameras is also central to *World's Wildest Police Videos*. In Britain, controversy developed after police released footage from their own surveillance cameras to the producers of *Police Stop!* which features video footage of high-speed pursuits:

> The Association of Chief Police Officers [ACPO] is in two minds about Police Stop! It didn't like the emphasis on white-knuckle pursuits, but it welcomed, with qualifications, the road safety messages. Nevertheless, it is now rethinking its guidelines to forces on the future provision of reality footage. This follows the case of the Birmingham father whose two-year-old daughter was in a car that was rammed by a suspected armed robber in a police chase crash. Repeated requests by the father for police footage to support his claim for compensation – he felt the police had needlessly endangered his daughter's life – got nowhere. But the footage was made available to Labyrinth Video, maker of Police Stop! (*Daily Telegraph*, 2 July, 1994)

There was confusion, too, on the question of payment. An ACPO spokesman said, 'We are not in a position to sell our footage.' Yet Labyrinth confirmed that it had made 'donations' to some of the police forces. 'In some cases, we've given [video-making] equipment or cash for them to buy equipment,' a spokesman said (*Daily Telegraph*, 2 July 1994).

I call this type of video 'promotional footage' because it often promotes the problem of crime and the solution of 'law and order' in general, or in particular the use of surveillance cameras themselves as a solution to crime. It has long been observed that police news often promotes a law-and-order approach to crime (e.g., Hall et al. 1978; Sacco 1995; Potter and Kappeler 1998); surveillance cameras are used to supplement the package with dramatic visuals.

One widely reported example of use of surveillance cameras for such promotional footage occurred when a video camera captured a forty-year-old man trying to commit suicide outside an apartment building in Brentwood, England. Police rescued him after a camera operator noticed what was going on; however, the surveillance tape was then released to TV news without the man's permission, in order to publicize the effectiveness of the town's security system (*Globe and Mail*, 5 April 1996, p. A20).

Surveillance footage of crime is often used in news stories publicizing the effectiveness of the technology itself. This is one partial explanation for the rapid spread of public surveillance cameras (CCTV) after its initial introduction in Britain: once it is introduced, CCTV very effectively provides its own dramatic visuals for media promotional material. As McCahill points out, 'there has been widespread media coverage of several tragic cases, including, of course, the abduction and murder of James Bulger ... As Beck and Willis (1995: 166) argue, the media coverage of such cases has given an almost irresistible impetus to the introduction of CCTV in Britain. For example, in July 1994, less than a year after the James Bulger case, a large scale CCTV system "went live" in the centre of Liverpool' (1998: 59).

What I will call 'found television crimes' are otherwise undistinguished crimes that are elevated to media fame simply because they happen to be captured by a surveillance camera or a home video operator and they offer dramatic footage. Such crimes become 'bigger than life' (Altheide and Snow 1979) due to the influence of media. In 1989 a secret camera captured a nanny in Tennessee slapping the infant she cared for. After the nanny had already pleaded guilty in court, the footage was released to TV news and broadcast widely. Normally, this type of crime, while repugnant, would receive little media attention. Thanks to the shocking imagery and resulting public outcry, however, the ex-nanny will probably never outlive the incident, said her lawyer: 'It was like taking a sledgehammer to an ant' (*Newsweek*, 22 July 1991: 45).

Trial by Media / Intensification of the Formal Process of Punishment

While the media attention given such cases can be quite punitive in itself, it may also influence the formal justice process. Television broadcast of video may pre-empt the accused's right to a fair trial, resulting instead in 'trial by media' (Altheide 1993). The heavy publicity surrounding such crimes may also result in an intensification of formal punishment.

The television culture of criminal justice is not something that exists separate and apart from the justice system itself. Instead, TV culture feeds back into the justice system itself, shaping both particular day-to-day practices and broader policies. For example, crimes that receive media attention may be less likely to be plea-bargained, and more likely to be pursued vigorously by media-conscious prosecutors and judges and to be punished to the full extent of the law. Pritchard (1986) studied 90 Milwaukee homicide cases and found that the amount of news coverage given to the cases was the strongest predictor of whether or not prosecutors would plea-bargain. This confirmed findings of earlier research (Utz 1976; Jones 1978): the more news coverage, the less likely prosecutors would be to negotiate a bargain for a lesser penalty. While, as Pritchard admits, one must be cautious about inferring a causal relationship here, previous research also suggests prosecutors pay close attention to news coverage (Dreschel 1983), particularly in the United States, where district attorneys are elected officials.

Altheide (1995) describes other ways in which media culture feeds back into the day-to-day practices of criminal justice. He offers examples of what he calls 'gonzo justice,' where judges pass spectacular individualized sentences apparently designed to achieve media attention. Sometimes gonzo justice even directly involves media in the execution of the sentence, for example, by forcing convicts to buy advertising shaming themselves. Even if such sentences do not directly involve media in this way, they often receive massive media attention, adding to their punitive shaming effect. In June 1999 the Associated Press reported a media shaming ritual that exemplified gonzo justice. Ironically, the criminal receiving the sentence was a TV executive:

> A former TV station executive who rigged a contest last year so that his mother-in-law would win a pick-up truck was given 60 days in jail, fined $10,000 U.S. and ordered to attend a Sept. 25 college football game wearing a sign declaring: 'I am a liar, a coward and a thief. I rigged the Channel 51 contest so my mother-in-law would win the pick-up truck and give it to me.' (*Vancouver Sun*, 5 June 1999, p. A14)

Publicity-loving sheriff Joe Arpaio of Phoenix, Arizona, personifies this trend towards media considerations influencing the day-to-day practices of criminal justice. Arpaio has employed numerous spectacular media-friendly measures, such as scouring the streets with volunteer posses, putting up a two-metre-long neon 'Vacancy' sign outside his tent city prison, and forcing his inmates to wear humiliating pink boxer shorts (Appleby 1996). The sheriff is

> savouring every moment of a publicity extravaganza that (by his count) has encompassed 111 radio shows, 38 national TV shows, 27 national print stories, 24 foreign radio shows, 15 foreign print articles and 14 foreign TV

stories. 'It keeps building,' he said excitedly. 'It's a runaway train.' (Appleby 1996: A1)

The influence of television in particular may reshape even the smallest details of police practice:

> The standard issue shoulder stars on the sheriff's uniform, for instance, were a tad small for the TV cameras. So he had larger ones sewn on. (Appleby 1996: A1)

While an orientation to TV and other media may simply lead criminal justice to be more visual and colourful, it may also lead to a push for intensified formal punishment. For example, media attention given to the Bulger case in Britain – partly via the frequent broadcast of surveillance footage – led to a massive public appeal for harsher sentences. The Home Secretary eventually intervened in the Bulger case, raising the sentences of the ten-year-old perpetrators to nearly double their original length (Young 1996: 126).

Biases in Surveillance Camera Footage

Thus, certain crimes may be spectacularized by television simply because they happen to be captured by surveillance cameras, with various consequences for the players. The selection of such crimes may result from somewhat arbitrary factors, but they are certainly not a completely random sample of all crime. The surveillance produced by the interaction of cameras, authorities, and broadcast television will be a selective one that will tend to work to the advantage of police and other dominant institutions and groups, and to work against the less powerful. To go back to our broader theoretical concerns, this would mean that how television brings audiences into these particular situations would tend simply to reproduce social inequality, instead of resulting in social levelling as Meyrowitz's (1985) medium theory predicts.

Why is this kind of surveillance likely to be an unequal one? Firstly, public surveillance cameras are more likely to be present in poorer areas. For example, Davies notes, 'Rather than focusing on town centres (arguably democratic) particular residential trouble spots are being singled out for special attention: the Meadowell Estate in North Shields and Chapeltown in Leeds to name two examples. Rather than equalizing the rates of detection of middle class and working class delinquency, the effect is to intensify an already unequal pattern of policing' (1998: 270). Similarly, the twenty-three surveillance cameras proposed for Vancouver would all be located in poorer parts of that city: the Downtown Eastside, Chinatown, Gastown, and Strathcona areas (*Vancouver Sun*, 13 March 2000, p. B1).

Camera operators cannot monitor every camera all the time. A second kind of bias occurs in whom the camera operators choose to monitor. Norris and Armstrong (1999) found, in a study of British surveillance camera operators in three areas covered by 148 cameras, that the young, the male, and the black were systematically and disproportionately targeted. As they wrote: 'It will come as no surprise to anyone who is aware of the literature on police suspicion that CCTV operators adopt similar criteria to construct the target population: focusing on the young rather than the old, disproportionately targeting blacks rather than whites, men as opposed to women, and the working rather than the middle classes' (1999: 119; see McConville, Sanders, and Leng 1991 and Norris et al. 1992 on police suspicion in general; see McCahill 1998: 51–3 and Fiske 1998 on targeted surveillance in particular).

The knowledge produced by surveillance cameras always involves interpretation. Surveillance cameras do not simply 'make visible' what they record; instead, those who have the power to interpret the images – who produce the authorized definition of the situation – are the ones who hold the upper hand. Police also dictate which footage from public surveillance cameras is available to the news. Not surprisingly, the broadcast of footage from police surveillance cameras showing police in a bad light is apparently rare.

In sum, as with *Cops*, surveillance footage on the news probably features a structured bias towards reporting certain types of crimes. In particular, it may tend towards street crimes committed in poorer urban areas and by nonwhite populations.

The Convergence of Police Surveillance and Television News Surveillance

The above examples feature the televising of surveillance footage that was recorded for other purposes. One police operation, however, actually produced its own surveillance footage designed first and foremost specifically for TV news. This extreme example indicates the extent to which broadcast TV can ultimately transform policing. Altheide (1993) conducted a case study of an Arizona police sting operation in 1990 and

1991 known as Azscam. In this ground-breaking initiative, the police used hidden cameras to record an undercover operative offering bribes to numerous state politicians. The politicians were not under any previous suspicion of wrongdoing. Nevertheless, some politicians accepted the bribes and were videotaped in the act by hidden cameras. Instead of presenting this video material in the courts, Arizona police turned it into prepackaged news releases and went directly to TV news with the footage, well before any trials. In the words of one reporter, 'evidence in the case was literally pushed on us ... evidence was made available to the media in wholesale lots, with the video provided by direct uplink from police headquarters.' This led seven members of the state legislature to resign. Most accepted plea bargains and went to prison. In sum, it was a situation of trial by media for nearly all of the accused. This preempted troublesome questions about entrapment that may have arisen in court. Public opinion was very much in favour of the police. Altheide (1993) suggests Azscam was 'a turning point in mass mediated justice and social control' (1993: 66) and that it represented a 'major refolding of social control and mass communication.' Azscam presents an extreme case of how, in the interaction of surveillance cameras and broadcast television, policing and criminal justice may be transformed. It remains to be seen to what extent other police operations might adopt this approach, not striving simply for criminalization but primarily for publicity and public shaming of suspects.

A Parallel Trend: Amateur Video on the News

In addition to the increasing use of surveillance footage on TV, a parallel trend since the late 1980s has been the increasing use of home video footage. Like surveillance cameras, home video camcorders have spread rapidly. In 1987 only 3 per cent of American homes had camcorders (*Nightline*, 14 May 1992). By May 1998 this figure had increased more than tenfold: about one in three American households owned a camcorder, according to ABC's *20/20* (11 May, 1998). As of 1995 about 1.5 million Canadian families owned a video camera (*Toronto Star*, 25 February 1995).

The boom in home camcorders, combined with the tightening budgets of TV news organizations (Kimball 1994; Baker and Dessart 1998), led to rising use of amateur video footage on television news in the late 1980s and early 1990s. This trend was noted by numerous industry observers (e.g., Robins 1989; Luft 1991; Lichty and Gomery 1992: 14;

Bird 1997) and encouraged by influential consultants, such as the firm Frank N. Magid Associates. These consultants urged local news producers to institute procedures to collect amateur footage (Lichty and Gomery 1992: 15). 'Using home video is especially important for small stations with limited budgets, because people who live where news happens can cover it quicker and cheaper,' said Jeff Bartlett of the news consulting firm Audience Research and Development (Luft 1991: 35). In January 1987 CNN inaugurated its *News Hound* program, in which viewers who had amateur footage for CNN could call a 1-800 number. As of January 1989 CNN was airing three or four such *News Hound* stories a month. Philadelphia's WCAU *Newswatchers* program generated five to eight stories a month (Robins 1989: 30). By 1991 KSNW in Kansas had aired about 100 stories using amateur video. In Canada, Edmonton's A-Channel began a 'Street Shooter' promotion to collect home video.

The world-wide attention given the notorious Rodney King video in 1991 was a massive further stimulus to amateur videographers. 'The King tape made more people think how to put their cameras to use and how to make money from them,' said the news director of KTLA television (*Electronic Media*, 23 September 1991). A 1993 survey of 100 television news directors found that 77 per cent now used camcorder video from amateur sources (*Electronic Media*, 27 September 1993).

Much amateur news video focuses on incidents like tornadoes, fires, and car accidents, but home cameras also capture a range of criminal justice events. Home video (like surveillance footage) became a staple of reality-TV shows, both for programs focused on criminal justice and for those with a more general focus, such as *Real TV*, *Amazing Videos*, and *I Witness Video*. (Even the latter programs offer a good deal of criminal justice footage.)

Certainly the camcorder can sometimes protect citizens in their dealings with police. The Rodney King case is the most notorious example of a series of incidents where civilians recorded police brutality. The politics of interpretation concerning the King video have been analysed in some depth (e.g., Gooding-Williams 1993; Goodwin, 1994; Fiske 1996). I will not revisit these issues here other than to point out that, despite the conflicting interpretations given it, the King video was indisputably a source of massive trouble for L.A. police and a highly effective means of resistance against police brutality. There have been a number of less well-known examples. In Fort Worth, Texas, in 1991 a tourist videotaped a patrolman clubbing a handcuffed man twenty-four times. The officer was suspended after the incident played repeatedly on local TV news (*Newsweek*, 22 July 1991). Another home camcorder captured the controversial shooting of twenty-year-old James Quarles by a police officer in Baltimore in 1997. In Brazil, the popular TV-news program *Jornal Nacional* broadcast an amateur video showing military police beating and even killing civilians (*Human Rights Watch* 1998). Indeed, whether or not their video footage is submitted to the news, some members of the public have taken to videotaping police interactions they witness as a check on such brutality (Fiske 1998; Haggerty and Ericson 2002). Others use camcorders for vigilante crime-fighting themselves, for example, neighbourhood 'video vigilantes' who tape suspected drug dealers or prostitutes either to intimidate them or to turn the footage over to police. This footage often winds up on TV. For example, the 11 May 1998 episode of the ABC newsmagazine *20/20*, used extensive amounts of such footage in chronicling the video vigilante phenomenon.

The King video triggered a chain of events that led to the bloody Los Angeles riot of May 1992, but had further ripple effects on criminal justice. When the King beating received such wide publicity, it prompted other members of the public to step forward with complaints of police brutality. 'After seeing the King tape, people who have been mistreated are finding the courage to come forward,' said John Crew, an attorney for the American Civil Liberties Union. Police brutality complaints 'increased markedly' nationwide following the airing of the King video, and the Department of Justice considered hiring extra lawyers, said Assistant Attorney General John Dunne (*San Francisco Chronicle*, 2 April 1991).

There was also speculation that with the emergence of the camcorder, police behaviour would be constrained. Doug Elder, the President of the Houston Police Officers Association, said, 'These cameras are so popular I'm worried that we're going to have a case where because of intimidation, an officer didn't use a necessary level of force and we'll get somebody hurt or killed because of it' (*Newsweek*, 22 July 1991).

Amateur video of policing of demonstrations and riots, such as that in New York's Tompkins Square in 1988, and various demonstrations by the AIDS activist group ACT-UP, also finds its way onto TV news, and supports accusations of excessive police violence. However, such video is subject to a complex politics of interpretation that may constrain its effectiveness as a tool of resistance. In the next chapter I talk about these constraints, using the example of the recording of a particular riot.

Many other civilian videographers are just after the token amounts of money that local stations will pay for amateur footage, or the symbolic recognition they will receive. In this way, media logic (Altheide and Snow 1979) has spread not only through contemporary institutions, but through much of the general public as well. As one American TV news director said, 'In many cases people are just interested in getting their footage, and their name, on TV ... People are even starting to ape TV reporters and do their own on-the-scene interviews' (*Electronic Media*, 23 September 1991). Some amateur videographers listen to police scanners at home and race to potential news events to record them for possible sale to TV news. News director Bob Yuna, formerly of KSNW-TV in Kansas, said, 'Many people feel as though it's almost their duty to go out and get those pictures. It becomes a symbiotic relationship – the people actually feel bonding between themselves and the TV station' (Luft 1991: 35).

Arrests initiated by civilians may be prompted by the possibility of recording them for television. For example, one anonymous tipster who turned in a fugitive to the FBI also arranged for a friend to be on hand to record the arrest with a camcorder for Seattle television news (Lichty and Gomery 1992: 14).

Criminals Who Record Their Own Crimes

As with surveillance cameras, home video can thrust relatively mundane crimes into the spotlight. Criminals sometimes even videotape their own crimes for personal gratification, which may result in the spectacularization of otherwise more routine crimes. For example, a group of criminals who carried out a series of robberies in Washington, D.C., videotaped their efforts, producing footage which aired repeatedly not only on local and national news but also at their trials (Robins 1989; Lichty and Gomery 1992: 15). On 11 March 1999 the tabloid-TV program *Fox Files* featured an item on such 'video crimes' recorded by criminals, calling these the 'crime of the 90s.' ABC's *Prime Time Live* (15 July 1998) featured blurred home video footage a rapist took of himself with his drugged victims.

A group of American teenagers videotaped themselves driving around shooting at passersby with a paintball gun. When this video was televised, it captured the spotlight because the dramatic footage mirrored 'real' drive-by shootings. Even though the paintball spree was relatively harmless, the paintball gunmen subsequently received prison sentences; media coverage evidently made their crimes 'bigger than life' (Altheide and Snow 1979). Similarly, a Michigan couple became the subject of a nationwide outcry after the parents videotaped two of their children fighting each other. The parents were heard on tape egging on their children to fight for the camera. After the tape was broadcast on national news and shown as evidence in court, the couple had their four children taken away by the government, were charged with first-degree child abuse, and faced a possible twenty-year-sentence (*NBC News*, 7 March 1997). A sixteen-year-old Nebraska high-school student videotaped a friend beating up one of his peers at school. After the footage was broadcast, the teenaged cameraman was himself arrested for assault for his role in wielding the camera. A reporter with the local NBC affiliate noted the impact the television images had on this situation of schoolyard bullying, again making it 'bigger than life': 'The community in general seems to be pretty shocked about it ... the police don't want to minimize it ...because most people don't know what a fistfight looks like, and they have to see it firsthand... that is shocking. It's as shocking as the Rodney King beating' (*Rivera Live*, 5 June 1996).

The Surveillance Camera Versus the Camcorder

There are a number of similarities between amateur video and surveillance camera footage that is broadcast, and between these and the reality-TV footage of *Cops*. Like the video shot for *Cops*, amateur video and surveillance footage both have a strengthened claim to authenticity because of their crude, underproduced quality. This property works to deny the existence of artifice, suggesting the tapes have come, undoctored, from a 'real' source. Their crudeness or starkness, and the graininess of surveillance video in particular, suggest a grim, harsh, street-level 'reality,' evoking for the audience a gritty realism that the audience may, ironically, have learned from viewing fictional crime programming (Cavender and Bond-Maupin 1993). The grey-and-black palette of surveillance footage has the same kind of *film noir* quality as *Cops*, which seems most often to be recorded at night with limited lighting. These visual properties fit with a 'common-sense' view of crime – committed on dark, 'mean' (i.e., poor) streets at night by strangers – a vision of crime that is so naturalized it may take the critical observer a while to realize that this is a particular, ideological way of understanding crime.

As discussed in the previous chapter, *Cops* attempts to naturalize the verbal narration that accompanies the footage, stitching together an unofficial narrative through the soundtrack of police officers' verbal accounts. In contrast, both surveillance camera footage and home video are often accompanied by more explicit narrative dissection, as well as overt manipulation of the footage to assist the narrative, for example, the use of slow motion, repetition of key sequences, and on-screen arrows or diagramming to clarify the imagery. It is easier to see in this case that much depends on verbal interpretation of the video footage. Here the interpretive activity is much more explicit.

These similarities aside, there are also key differences when considering the impacts of surveillance footage versus home video on TV. Civilian sources will face more difficulty than police in publicizing their preferred video imagery of criminal justice. The Rodney King video showed some of the potential of the new camcorder technology in resisting the power of police. Yet episodes such as Rodney King's will necessarily be much scarcer than the use of surveillance footage on TV. Official sources have a huge sweep of available surveillance footage to draw from, as opposed to the haphazard availability to private citizens of small amounts of camcorder footage.

Although there has been no social scientific research on the trend towards amateur video on the news, the issue has prompted much discussion and debate in both broadcasting and journalism industry publications and in the popular media itself. Both have raised extensive concerns about the increasing use of amateur video on the news. Yet the parallel rise in the use of surveillance camera footage on the news has received little critical comment. In contrast to home video, surveillance camera footage apparently comes from an unquestionable source.

Criticisms of the use of amateur video reveal an interesting tendency towards what I will call 'selective epistemology,' or the questioning of the truth-value of video evidence in certain situations but not others. The kinds of questions raised about amateur video present an interesting contrast with normal attitudes toward visual material on TV news. Similar questions do not seem to be raised about other forms of video evidence on the news, such as that from surveillance cameras. Apparently, critics doubt the validity of video evidence only when it suits them.

The more optimistic observers heralded the tendencies toward use of amateur video on TV as resulting in 'video democracy' (Ted Koppel, *Nightline*, 14 May 1992) or adding a 'democratic dimension to television journalism worldwide' (Luft 1991: 35). 'Now anyone can be Dan Rather,' *Newsweek* enthused (22 July 1991). Of course, these are arguments similar to the medium theory analysis of Meyrowitz: increased visibility due to exposure on television leads to social levelling.

However, many critics and media personnel argue that, with amateur video, seeing is not believing. Not surprisingly, the trend towards amateur video has provoked a fair amount of unease among TV news professionals, who saw themselves as potentially displaced from their jobs. Journalism professor Roger Bird saw the use of home video as a 'threat to the authenticity of news,' and questioned the 'motives, skill and honesty of the amateur sources. Their choice of what to record and sell is constrained by no journalistic tradition, ethics, or training' (1997: 127). He charged that amateur video would make the news vulnerable to new technologies that would allow altering or morphing of footage.

David Bartlett, president of the U.S. Radio-Television News Directors Association, said, 'Seeing is not always believing in the world of video, so television stations have to apply rigorous standards to this material and not just stick it on the air' (*Toronto Star*, 25 February 1995).

Media writer Howard Rosenberg of the *Los Angeles Times* (3 April 1992, p. F28) was highly critical of local television stations for airing footage in early 1992 of an event that echoed the Rodney King incident. In this case the footage was of a police officer kicking a Santa Cruz man and striking him with a baton as he sat on the ground. The target was a suspect in a child molestation case who was later found to be wrongfully accused. The man was being beaten, it was argued, as he was still moving around against the officer's orders. The suspect's wife recorded camcorder footage of the police beating.

Firstly, Rosenberg criticized the verbal interpretation by television reporters that accompanied the footage, and specifically the statement that the officer was 'beating' the 'wrong man.' He Rosenberg did admit, however, that the man – who was undoubtedly being kicked and clubbed over and over again – had been wrongfully arrested and wrongfully accused of child molestation, so he was indeed the 'wrong man.' Nevertheless the TV critic concluded that it was inappropriate for television news to air the footage because the police officer 'appeared to be acting properly in using the level of force that he did.'

Rosenberg further charged that the officer was a victim of 'guilt by association' because the footage was aired alongside another item updating the King case. He stated, 'There was no word on why the ... footage was released to TV at this time. Some observers feel that the move may have been instigated by proponents of review boards for both the Santa Cruz police and sheriff's departments.'

Regardless of the authenticity of the home video footage, then, it was impugned because of (1) the context in which it was shown, and (2) the possible motives of those who may have supported its release to TV. Clearly, much other TV news footage is open to such criticisms, yet does not seem to undergo similar scrutiny.

A former TV journalist who moved on to public relations work for a non-profit organization described the problems he faced in his new job in getting amateur video footage shot by volunteers onto the news: 'Response from the media has been cautious because there is still some doubt that ordinary people can produce this stuff. There are ethical concerns and concerns about quality.' (*Toronto Star*, 2 February 1995).

Again ABC-TV journalist David Marash commented (*Nightline*, 14 May 1992) about the use of amateur video that, 'One scene on videotape can yield many interpretations. The physical position of the camera can define how it captures an event, and so can the camera-person's point of view.'

When pushed, these critics might admit this was true of *all* video used on television. However, the point is they are not pushed. Their silence accedes to the common sense that, in other situations, video seeing is believing – yet here it is questioned.

Although the Rodney King footage is the most prominent example of amateur video as resistance to police power, its aftermath was beset with legal complications for the man who recorded it. George Holliday, the plumber and amateur cameraman who taped the King beating, received only a token amount of money for the footage. Holliday launched multi-million-dollar lawsuits against various television outlets after the footage was aired massively worldwide without his consent. He lost. Numerous stations now ask amateur videographers to sign waivers absolving the station of any liabilities incurred during the taping of the story (Luft 1991: 35).

One key difference between surveillance and amateur video footage is that the former is more likely to come to television news in a package with an authorized definition from police; amateur video footage must speak much more for itself. Home video footage may carry less weight independent of an official definition that says what it is, that imbues it with significance. Hence, the media's different treatment of the two types of footage simply extends a trend documented in much previous media research: journalists rely heavily on official sources as 'primary definers' (Hall et al. 1978) or 'authorized knowers' (Ericson, Baranek, and Chan 1989). Similarly, research on which letters to the editor are published by newspapers reveals that those from official or institutional sources are significantly more likely to get published (Ericson, Baranek, and Chan 1989: 338–76). In the same way, even when there is video footage of actual events, it is more likely to make it onto the news if it is officially approved footage accompanied by an authorized definition from police, as opposed to the work of an ordinary person's video camera.

Conclusions

To sum up, TV's broadcasting of surveillance camera footage and home video reshapes selected social situations in the world of criminal justice. However, to suggest that these technologies simply include viewers in new 'information systems,' as Meyrowitz's medium theory account might argue, ignores the ideological tendencies that mark the resulting visions of criminal justice. I have indicated apparent potential biases in the availability of footage from both surveillance cameras and home video that tend to reproduce an ideological vision of crime and policing. For example, surveillance footage from public cameras will tend to be of lower class neighbourhoods. Surveillance cameras produce 'promotional footage' that dramatizes a particular vision of the crime problem. Similarly to *Cops*, this particular vision will tend to resonate with law-and-order ideology and thus work to reinforce the status quo rather than undermine it.

While it offers some new potential for resistance to police power, amateur video faces more challenges in making it onto the TV airwaves than does surveillance footage from police cameras. Some hopeful observers believed that the rise of amateur video on the news would result in 'video democracy.' This would fit well with Meyrowitz's arguments, if it were in fact the case. However, the various power imbalances discussed in this chapter make it more appropriate to speak of 'video inequality.' Powerful institutional players encounter much less difficulty in getting their preferred video on to the news, fitting more with the institutional perspective of Ericson, Baranek, and Chan (1989).

The examples in this chapter again reveal how the introduction of television not only records but reshapes front-line criminal justice situations themselves. For instance, I have shown how surveillance and camcorder footage can lead to the somewhat arbitrary spectacularization of particular crimes. When particular crimes are recorded and broadcast, this may in turn lead to intensification of the criminal process itself, to harsher punishment in those cases, as media logic makes them bigger than life. In the extreme case analysed by Altheide (1993), the introduction of television prompted a whole new form of control: police recorded surveillance footage apparently with the primary goal of releasing it to TV news as a kind of 'trial by media.'

One key way television reshapes the police institution is shown in the advent of the 'video wanted poster.' Not only is police surveillance capability expanded considerably, but a new institutional role is created for the audience. Those in front of the TV are not only viewers but also watchers, engaged in surveillance of each other. Viewers are indeed placed in a new information system, as Meyrowitz (1985) suggested; however, what they do with that new information largely serves dominant institutions, especially the police.

More generally, these two new media technologies, working with broadcast TV, do influence criminal justice. However, these influences do not flow simply from the formal properties of the technologies in question. Changes do not occur just because new technologies have the potential to make things 'visible.' Instead, the particular forms these media influences take are most often shaped by the most powerful players in each situation.

CHAPTER FIVE

Television and the Policing of Vancouver's Stanley Cup Riot

The previous two chapters have looked at situations in which TV footage of policing is recorded quite selectively. The choices about what is televised – and what is ignored – mostly favour police. In this chapter I look at a contrasting situation in which police might have less control.

Another key way police will be recorded for TV is at a public event where they must manage a crowd. Police are more potentially vulnerable when they must deal with a mass of rioters or demonstrators with cameras present. In contrast to the making of *Cops*, the media are not there by invitation. There may be conflict between police and news media interests. Reporters want a story; police might not want visibility if the situation becomes violent. How much does the balance of power shift in this less controlled context? How might this affect how TV reshapes the criminal justice situation itself? This chapter considers ways in which the rise of TV may affect the policing of 'public-order events' like riots or demonstrations. Other researchers have identified a trend towards a less coercive approach to policing mass protests. Since the 1960s, they say, police have adopted a gentler approach with disorderly crowds, at least sometimes. Has TV contributed to this shift? What other influences might television have in such situations?

I explore these questions through a study of TV's various influences in one controversial crowd-policing situation, the Stanley Cup riot in Vancouver, British Columbia, on the night of 14 June 1994. Police and rioters clashed that night in a maelstrom of tear gas, thrown bottles, and billyclubs. TV news footage of Vancouver police violently attempting to subdue the rioting crowd aired often in the days, weeks, and months following the riot. I focus on the role that TV played in how the various players made sense afterward of the riot, and of the police role in it.

Riots are highly complex events; how the 'authorized definition' of the televised riot emerged was much more complicated than with an episode of *Cops*. Ultimately, police had the power to say what the footage meant. This definitional power of police proved crucial in shaping the various influences that TV had in the riot aftermath.

Previous Research

What does previous research tell us about such situations? Police, the crowd, and the media all work together in shaping public-order events such as riots or demonstrations. All three groups interact to shape how the event will be understood after the fact. Yet the three-way dynamic[1] here has not been considered much by social scientists, apart from an isolated handful of works. Social scientists need to broaden our analyses to consider all three players in this triangle.

This chapter looks at a sports riot and generalizes to other kinds of public-order situations[2] (e.g., disorderly demonstrations or political protests) that feature the same combination of high visibility and violent chaos. This combination of chaos and TV cameras rolling makes it difficult for police to maintain control over their public image. 'The whole world's watching,' demonstrators chanted at the 1968 Chicago Democratic national convention, as Mayor Daley's police billyclubbed them in front of network news crews. Chicago 1968 was perhaps the most controversial episode of televised protest policing. Powerful images of police brutality on TV news fed a crisis of institutional legitimacy. The 'police riot' (Stark 1972) of Chicago 1968 is seen by previous researchers as a watershed in two ways. After Chicago, media accounts became generally more sympathetic towards protesters (Gans 1979: 54). And police began to adopt softer styles of protest policing in response to the dangers of increased media visibility (Fillieule 1998). British police faced a similar crisis of legitimacy over their role in the riots at Brixton and elsewhere in 1981, partly due to TV coverage (Reiner 2000: 146). The resulting criticism, notably in Lord Scarman's report on the riots, led to significant police reforms.[3] Similarly, network footage of police pepper-spraying student protesters at the APEC 1997 summit in Vancouver led to massive controversy. This focused especially on one widely aired TV news clip of Staff Sergeant Hugh Stewart spraying not only the demonstrators, but also a news cameraman. The aftermath was a great deal of trouble for police and the Canadian Prime Minister's Office, leading to the lengthy APEC enquiry (Ericson and Doyle 1999; Pue 2000).

To sum up, a number of accounts suggest that the introduction of TV into these crowd situations has led to changes in policing. Certainly, since the 1960s police in Western Europe and North America have widely adopted less coercive styles of protest or crowd policing (Waddington 1994; Della Porta and Reiter 1998b; McPhail, Schweingruber and McCarthy 1998). One gentler strategy now often used by police is 'negotiated management' of protest (Della Porta and Reiter 1998b). A departure from the more heavy-handed protest policing styles of the 1960s and 1970s, negotiated management works to avoid violence by emphasizing peacekeeping rather than strict law enforcement, and through the increasing formalization of negotiation between police and protest organizers.

As Gary Marx suggests:

> Police may conclude that rigidly enforcing the law through use of overwhelming force will be counterproductive, whether in the short or the long run. The presence of the mass media is an important factor here serving to moderate police behaviour. The symbolic importance of always being in control is given lesser importance than the harm that might befall police, demonstrators, and third parties and the longer negative consequences that might flow from media accounts of police violence. (1998: 257)

Some call police adoption of these gentler tactics 'the mediatization of protest policing' (Fillieule 1998: 14; see also Geary 1985; Della Porta 1998). The term 'mediatization' locates this shift as one part of the much broader trend of increasing news media awareness in contemporary institutions, and in particular in recent years by police (Ericson, Baranek, and Chan 1989; Schlesinger and Tumber 1994).

This argument is subject to two qualifications. Firstly, some key researchers of protest policing, such as Peter Waddington (1994) and Olivier Fillieule (1998), argue that the shift to gentler crowd policing has been quite selective (see also Wisler and Giugni 1999); that police still adopt more repressive tactics in some situations, particularly when dealing with crowds or protest groups who are more socially marginalized. Secondly, another body of social scientific research takes quite a contrary position. This work – mostly emanating from British critical sociologists and criminologists – suggests that news coverage of riots tends simply to legitimate police violence. These researchers argue that such news coverage often demonizes rioters or demonstrators (e.g., Murdock 1984; Young 1986). David Waddington (1992) summa-

rizes extensive literature in this vein arguing that media provide insuf-
ficiently critical reporting of violent police suppression of riots or protests. Justin Wren-Lewis (1981) argues that television's tendency to
select visuals of the most violent sequences as legitimating a law-and-
order approach to riot policing, by exaggerating the threat of violence
by crowds (as also argued by Halloran, Elliott, and Murdock 1970). This
literature is, of course, consistent with the large body of research cited
in earlier chapters that suggests that police and other official sources
tend to dominate the news.

Fillieule (1998) suggests that – just as there is substantial variation in
how heavy-handed police are, depending on just who is protesting –
there is also significant variation in how the media cover such events.
In his ethnographic research on French protest policing and the news
media, Fillieule found that 'the sensitivity of the police forces to media
surveillance is highly variable depending on the nature of the demonstrators' (14). Thus, the news media sometimes, but not always, give
critical coverage of police brutality during suppression of crowds,
depending on just whom the brutality is directed against: 'The less
social power the demonstrating group enjoys on the local level, the
better the chances that the police will manage to impose its vision on
the event' (18).

Even though my research looks at a sports riot, not a political demonstration, it is still useful for testing a key premise of this literature. This
premise is that harsh police suppression of crowds in front of cameras
will lead to negative TV coverage that is damaging for police. A key
question I will ask is: How vulnerable were police because TV recorded
them violently controlling the Stanley Cup crowd?

This leads us to the question of how the meaning of a riot is negotiated after the fact. Most of the literature on the policing of demonstrations or riots focuses on the events of the day as being simply fixed in
definition, as static, stable entities (but see Tumber, 1982, and P.
Waddington, 1998, for two key exceptions). In contrast, this chapter
explores how the meaning of clashes between police and rioters or
protesters may undergo a lengthy process of re-negotiation after the
fact. This process involves reconstructing not only the events themselves, but also their causes (P. Waddington 1998). I contend that even
when such events are televised widely, their meanings are not fixed.
Fillieule (1998) quotes a French police official who said, 'I never know if
the demonstration has been a success until after the press reports come
out.' Media accounts are the first draft of history, only part of a wider

process of retrospective reconstruction. Riots are highly complex and chaotic, and necessarily feature a swirl of many different perspectives and narratives, even if such events are recorded by television. The televised accounts interact with and are reconstructed and rewoven into subsequent accounts in various ways. Criminalization of rioters (and very occasionally police) involves building criminal justice system accounts of the events. There may be formal inquiries. All these varying accounts of the riot then re-enter and re-shape ongoing media coverage and public debate.

It is apparent from my data that footage of policing the Stanley Cup riot – and, by extension, all television footage of policing crowd disturbances – is open to a great deal of retrospective reinterpretation shaped by political considerations. In other words, television does not simply 'make visible' riot policing; seeing is not simply believing in this case. This is the key point to keep in mind when we consider how television has influenced the policing of public-order events.

Finally, I should point out here that there seems to be an unspoken or implicit premise in much previous research on media coverage of riots: that the words, not the images, count the most in television coverage. I should be clear that none of the authors in question state this point explicitly; I have inferred it from how they target their analyses. For example, Justin Wren-Lewis (1981) in his piece 'The Story of a Riot: The Television Coverage of Civil Unrest in 1981' focuses almost entirely on television's verbal portrayal of events rather than on visual imagery. He provides over forty examples of what presenters and interviewees *said* on television. In contrast he refers to television imagery of the riot only twice: once talking briefly about television riot imagery in general, and again when discussing a particular image of policing the riot – but only in the context of discussing the oral interpretation of the presenter of that image. This example might simply reflect the bias of Wren-Lewis in particular, were the same tendency not evident in nearly all of the social scientific literature on media coverage of riots reviewed by D. Waddington (1992)[4] – there is a heavy emphasis on TV's words, not its visuals. As we will discover, verbal accounts also seemed to dominate in media coverage of the Stanley Cup riot.

I will now move on to the specifics of TV's role in the Stanley Cup riot. I rely on numerous sources of ethnographic data collected through participant observation, informal interviews, and qualitative analysis of media texts and official documents.[5]

Unlike print media coverage, TV footage airs and then is gone. Recordings can be recovered only with considerable difficulty, if at all. In the politics of events such as the riot, this privileges institutions able to access such recordings – broadcasters themselves and, in this case, the police who confiscated copies of the television tapes – as opposed to members of the public, who have no access to the footage. This situation also makes life difficult for those researching television. Only with some difficulty was I able to obtain videotapes of a number of television newscasts about the riot and its aftermath.[6]

The Evening of the Riot, and After

On the evening of 14 June 1994, many thousands of people gathered in front of TV screens at various venues in downtown Vancouver to watch the concluding game of the Stanley Cup hockey final, being played in New York, and potentially to celebrate the city's first Cup win. Following the Vancouver Canucks' defeat by the New York Rangers, a crowd estimated at 40,000 to 70,000, a large number of whom had been drinking for several hours, choked downtown Vancouver streets. Over 500 police attempted to maintain order. Shortly after 10 p.m., Vancouver police's recently created Crowd Control Unit advanced in paramilitary formation, clad in armour and wielding batons. They moved on a rowdy throng at the intersection of Robson and Thurlow.

There has been considerable dispute about whether the so-called flashpoint of the riot occurred before or after the Crowd Control Unit moved on the crowd. All sides agree, however, that there was an explosive mêlée following the unit's advance. Police maced people in the face and clubbed their heads, and fired tear-gas canisters into the crowd until they exhausted their supply. Rioters taunted police and hurled bottles and bricks, overturned a squad car, shattered retail display windows, and made off with piles of stolen goods. Assorted residents trapped at the scene stumbled about vainly trying to escape the bitter pinch of tear-gassed eyes. The chaos lasted for hours. In the most controversial single incident, one officer shot nineteen-year-old rioter Ryan Michael Berntt in the side of the skull with an Arwen riot gun, leaving the teenager in a coma for nine days. He was not initially expected to survive. Berntt was left with a cavity in his skull, his intellectual functioning, speech and walking permanently impaired. Another man shot by the Arwen gun needed thirty-two stitches to close the hole in his chin. Over one hundred others were injured, and ultimately over one hundred people faced criminal charges. The riot cost an estimated $1.1 million as a result of property damage and theft.

Competing stories soon emerged about how and why the riot occurred, and who was to blame for the destruction. One story, told by a sizable group of those present and in some media accounts, was that a full-scale riot did not erupt until the Crowd Control Unit marched, unleashing tear gas, pepper spray, and batons. The concept of police iatrogenesis in crowd situations – simply put, police making things worse rather than better – is well known in the literature on public-order policing (e.g., Stark 1972; Marx 1981; Waddington, Jones, and Critcher 1989; D. Waddington 1992), in connection with both political demonstrations and sports crowds (Marx 1981). The Vancouver police Crowd Control Unit was created in 1993 for the Clinton–Yeltsin summit meeting in Vancouver, but its first real action did not come until the 1994 hockey riot. Relative inexperience in public-order situations is one factor that might have meant the police response that night could possibly have featured an element of panic and overreaction. For example, one police officer gave the following account of his experience of the riot:

> In a matter of seconds I saw a diverse collection of individuals transform into one snarling salivating monster. I looked into the crowd, and the thousands of faces disappeared to be replaced by one. The face of evil was staring back, grinning in anticipation ... with shaking knees, we watched its appetite for violence grow ... Those who claim we joined the fray too eagerly will realize the folly of their statements if they ever look into the eyes of the Beast. For five hours, or lifetimes, we did battle with an enemy unlike anything I've faced before.' (*Vancouver Sun*, 23 June 1994: p. A3)

It is clear that police did adopt a highly coercive approach to subduing the crowd. In what follows I show that the narrative of police escalating the situation was widely circulated immediately following the riot. However, it is not my aim to make a definitive assessment of how much police might have actually triggered or worsened the Stanley Cup riot or simply responded in necessary fashion to a crowd that was already running amok. This is not the question I am trying to answer. Instead, my focus is on the role television and police played in the politics of how the story of the riot came to be told.

From all the evidence, it seems clear that the presence of television cameras had little restraining effect on police behaviour during the riot. Vancouver's Crowd Control Unit seemed to have enough difficulty staying in touch with its own command that night, and dealing with the immediate crisis, let alone worrying about media considerations.

Given this, the key question then becomes: What are the consequences for police of neglecting the problem of media visibility? Was ignoring the presence of cameras during the riot a blunder for which police would pay dearly in terms of damaging media coverage? If so, then policing the Stanley Cup riot would be a kind of exception that proves the rule. If crowd policing were not conducted with a gentler touch, this would be how police paid the price. On the other hand, if police were able to engage in coercive policing in front of the cameras that night with relatively little consequence, this would call for some qualification or modification to the 'mediatization of protest policing' argument.

Unlike riots with a clear political grievance – such as the much bloodier 1992 Rodney King trial riot in Los Angeles, or various riots in Thatcherite Britain – there was no apparent complaint that enraged the Vancouver crowd. Nevertheless, the Vancouver riot, with its televised images of armoured police raising clubs and transgressive youth looting stores, represented a dramatic yet ambiguous symbol that could be tailored to competing ideologies. Many different explanations of the riot soon appeared in the media, each with its own political bent.[7]

One factor in making sense of the Stanley Cup riot after the fact was that it was recorded extensively on video. This was facilitated in part because television cameras were already in place on a rooftop at the intersection of Robson and Thurlow to record the post-game celebration.[8] Some initial coverage by television news and other media outlets raised questions concerning the police's role. As Margo Harper of the CBC evening news reported the following day: 'Today there was criticism that police didn't act soon enough ... and that when they did it was without warning and with excessive force.' In the days following the riot, however, accounts critical of police actually appeared more often in the print media than on TV. The critical newspaper accounts depended largely on recounting of events by participants rather than on a visual record. Local CBC-TV news seemed to encounter difficulty in finding eyewitness sources for such retrospective accounts, apart from one young man recorded on the night of the riot chanting that 'police are idiots.' While television had recorded the whole riot, the most critical coverage by CBC-TV concerned two police shootings of members of the crowd with the Arwen riot gun.[9] In the more serious shooting, there was footage from immediately before and after the shooting, showing the fallen victim. In the other shooting, there was no such footage; a critical CBC television news story depended simply on after-the-fact recounting of the shooting by the man who was shot and by witnesses.

BCTV produced a lengthy chronological account of the riot for its news the following day. This also relied heavily on after-the-fact interpretation. While CBC reporting suggested that its journalists were trying to sort among competing accounts of causes of the riot, the BCTV version had a much more unitary narrative: it blamed 'thugs' and 'punks.' In dealing with the question of possible police mismanagement, BCTV chose to air a 'talking head' interview conducted with one of its own cameramen (who thus underwent a strange shifting of roles, becoming a witness in front of the camera). 'Did police over-react?' the cameraman was asked. He held up a brick and responded: 'I don't see how you can over-react to a crowd that's carrying bricks like this.' BCTV opted to rely on the cameraman's verbal recollections rather than his extensive video record of the riot.

Both CBC and BCTV aired snippets of graphic footage of police beating individual crowd members with batons, but in the absence of any verbal interpretation of this police behaviour, the footage proved not particularly damning.

In short, although television cameras had taken massive footage of the Stanley Cup riot, critical (and supportive) reporting of policing the riot relied more on after-the-fact verbal interpretations from witnesses, experts, or those who had seen the footage rather than on the footage itself as a visual record of the events. The visuals of the riot were not self-explanatory. This is consistent with what I identified earlier as an unspoken theme evident in previous research: that even in TV accounts, the words are more important than the pictures in fixing the meaning of a riot. TV footage of a riot is too complex and chaotic to simply 'speak for itself.'

Print media coverage of the Stanley Cup riot is interesting to consider in contrast to the television reporting. Print news outlets offered more critical coverage than television, even though they lacked the same body of extensive visual evidence to rely on. For example, a front-page headline above the fold in the *Globe and Mail*, on 16 June 1994, two days after the riot, read, 'Probe ordered into hockey riot – Vancouver residents at the scene say police provoked melee.'

Other quotes from the print media:

'I personally think it is the cops' fault,' said Jeff Murphy, manager of the Cows clothing store at the corner of Jervis and Robson. 'They started shooting tear gas when it wasn't needed. They provoked it.' (*Vancouver Sun*, 15 June 1994, front page)

'I do not blame the crowd,' said Thane McLennan, a 47-year-old bookstore manager who mingled with the revelers until police moved in. 'The police turned it into a situation.' (*Maclean's*, 27 June 1994, p. 13)

Simon Ng, a systems manager at an investment company, said, 'he witnessed a savage beating. Near midnight, he saw a small group of men heckling a riot squad on Burrard St. When the officers suddenly lunged at the group, the name-callers turned to flee. But a thin man in his 20s tripped and fell. "They gathered around him and began to beat him with nightsticks," said Ng. "Later he was so badly beaten up he got up to run away, but collapsed in pain."' (*Vancouver Sun*, 18 July 1994, p. A4)

Clearly, one factor here may have been that television cameras simply did not capture incidents such as this one that might have provided more unambiguously telling visuals. A 'smoking gun' piece of TV footage never emerged from the Stanley Cup riot.

'I'm going to file a complaint with police,' said Shawn Sheehan, 18. 'Police should have given a warning, saying we're going to fire tear gas, rather than going in and bashing people.' He said he was in the centre of the action at Robson and Thurlow when the riot squad showed up, blocking his exit to his apartment a block away. He politely asked police if he could cross through the police line. 'I got maced.' (*Vancouver Sun*, 16 June 1994, p. A3)

David Neylan, 17 ... said he was taken by surprise when a tear gas canister exploded in front of him. He pulled off his No. 10 Canucks shirt and bunched it over his face to protect himself from the fumes. He said that by the time he lowered it to see what was going on, police were upon him. 'They billyclubbed me to the ground and kicked me when I was down,' he said. His shirt had been wrenched from his hands in the scuffle ... 'As I reached for my shirt they stomped on my wrist, breaking my wrist,' he said. (*Vancouver Sun*, 18 June 1994, p. A4)

In a column headlined 'The violence escalated when police moved in,' the Sun's 'Town Talk' columnist, Malcolm Parry, wrote:

I was there – mingling with prudence but little fear at the centre of the crowd until an unannounced tear gas barrage drove us, blinded and retching, along Robson Street. Most present likely will agree that crowd violence suddenly escalated after the police squad's unannounced and disorienting action. We had seen a shirt-sleeved fellow walk in front of the armored officers, casually spraying them with beer from a shaken can. Then we were all being counter-attacked with major force. (*Vancouver Sun*, 18 June 1994, p. A6)

Police Reaction to the Riot

Several days after the riot, police executed search warrants at the three local television stations for videotapes of the riot. Police also attempted to seize still photos from local newspapers. BCTV and UTV co-operated with police immediately; CBC-TV joined two local newspapers in a brief court battle resisting the warrants, but soon succumbed.

Police used the seized videotapes for a variety of purposes. These included some innovative police tactics that called on members of the public to identify anonymous rioters recorded by television, so these rioters could face criminal charges. To this end police used the riot footage to produce television news spots and advertising. Police also arranged an 'interactive video kiosk' in shopping malls in which members of the public could view segments of the footage to identify rioters. As well, the footage was used to produce a television special about the riot as part of the subsequent enquiries. Frames of the video were frozen to help create a public display on the riot at the Vancouver Public Library; the frozen video images were accompanied by captions giving the official interpretation of the images. Finally, the television tapes were viewed as part of the B.C. Police Commission's review of police behaviour.

In the face of considerable criticism, the Vancouver police soon displayed 'account ability' (Ericson 1995) in responding publicly to the riot. Police focused on arguing that the public supported their actions, rather than justifying those actions per se.

Constable Anne Drennan, well known to local television audiences, was the public relations officer who handled most media contact for Vancouver police in that era. In the aftermath of the riot, she was quick to construct a vivid image of a public that was supportive of police action:

Drennan said police appreciate the support they have been receiving from the public in the aftermath of the Tuesday night riot ... 'I'm told it's 99 in favor, one against,' she said. Supportive calls are flooding in from the Lower Mainland and from viewers in other parts of Canada and the United States who saw scenes of the riot on television. 'Our switchboard is jammed. People are calling in on 911 in huge numbers to thank us.' Drennan said members of the public have sent police gifts of flowers and chocolates to show their support for officers who battled rioters and looters. (*Vancouver Sun*, 17 June 1994, p. B1)

However, accounts from the tear-gassed crowd were not all flowers and chocolates. Controversy arose both through media coverage and through direct complaints to authorities from many members of the public who were present during the events. Within twenty-four hours a review process was announced.

Controlling the Retrospective Account: The Riot Reviews

Politicians announced a review to post-mortem the riot, or rather three separate reviews. At this point, it I should lay out the political context of these three reviews.

As I have suggested in the introductory chapter, it would be naïve to take the conspiratorial view that the police are simply some omnipotent arm of the state and that, for this reason, any official review would automatically legitimate them. Instead, police are a semi-autonomous institution, which negotiates with political constraints and is sometimes highly vulnerable to a critical public airing of dirty laundry (Reiner 2000). As the context of the Stanley Cup riot reveals, however, police often wield very significant political influence.

The three-part structure of the riot review process reflected the complex political status of the Vancouver police. The City of Vancouver conducted its own review, but the city review deliberately avoided any consideration of the police role in the riot. The B.C. Police Commission conducted a second, separate review looking at the police role. Vancouver police themselves conducted a third process, their own internal review of policing the riot.

Ultimately, this three-part structure precluded much public criticism of police behaviour during the reviews. The city's review made the strongest effort to get public input, but as I will show, any input that questioned the police role was deflected as not relevant. The other reviews did look at police behaviour, but solicited only very limited public input. In short, one review invited public input on all aspects of the riot except the role of the police. The others did look at the police role, but allowed very little input from the public. These two components of the review were isolated from one another, which meant there was almost no opportunity for citizens to question the police role.

Another key factor limiting criticism of the police was the way in which the confiscated videotapes of the riot were used. In the public forum, the City of Vancouver review, the videotapes collected by police were not used at all. Thus, no unfavourable interpretations of their contents by members of the public could enter into the review process. In the closed-door review conducted by the B.C. Police Commission, on the other hand, the tapes were actually reviewed and used as evidence. Thus only interpretations of the TV tapes by the Police Commission – which, as I will discuss, is notoriously pro-police – would enter into the process. In short, police maintained control of the TV tapes, and the Police Commission were the only ones allowed to say what the images on those tapes meant.

A key political factor shaping the enquiries was that the two levels of government involved, the provincial New Democratic Party (NDP) government and Vancouver City council, seemed to lack the will to question the police role in the riot. The provincial government, nominally a social democratic one, was evidently keen to adopt a centrist tack, given its low standing in the polls at that time and the fact that an election was forecast for 1995. Pundits said that the NDP, traditionally seen as soft on crime, wanted to be seen instead as provincial advocates of law and order. For example, legislative reporter Keith Baldrey of the *Vancouver Sun* stated in his year-end political analysis and predictions (6 January 1995, p. B2): 'Law and order will also dominate the political agenda as each of the three parties tries to capture that issue as its own. ... In a move consistent with the government's strategy for the past year, [the NDP premier] will try to become personally identified with the government's law and order initiatives.'[10]

Meanwhile, at the city level, Vancouver council was dominated by a right-of-centre political organization, the Non-Partisan Association (NPA). The NPA have always been strongly supportive of police.[11]

Another key political factor was the relative powerlessness of the rioters as a group. They tended to be young, diffuse, and anonymous, although with a number of exceptions. Unlike, for example, the protesters at APEC 1997, the Stanley Cup rioters did not have a political organization in place to advocate for them, nor the legitimacy of a recognized cause that was supported by significant segments of the community.

Within such a political context, then, it seemed unlikely the reviews would turn out badly for police. I will now analyse the three reviews, beginning with that conducted by the City of Vancouver.

The City's Review

Although the city's riot review was supposed to steer clear of police matters, paradoxically the police nevertheless seemed very actively involved in it. Then-Vancouver mayor Philip Owen said at the time that the police were 'observing' the city process, and that there was a 'very close liaison' between the city's review and the police reviews. Although it was not supposed to be about policing, close ties with police were evident throughout the city's review: I saw several high-ranking Vancouver police officials in extensive discussion with city officials at each of the four city review meetings I attended. In fact, a police officer was one of the four-member team who wrote a key document on the riot, the city's 'Background Paper.' As I will show, this document tended to shape the course of the whole process. It appeared prior to the review's public meetings, but very much telegraphed the final results of the review.

Given these factors, and the apparent co-operation of city staff, the city's review was an interesting study in the social organization of knowledge: it functioned as a 'procedure not to know' (Smith 1984) about police misbehaviour. It was instead structured in a way that led it toward blaming the riot on several other factors, notably the media, and in particular television.

The city's review proceeded as follows: first, a team of four researchers, including a police officer, developed the lengthy document *Riots: A Background Paper*. Once this was completed, the city set up a large display in the Vancouver Public Library concerning the riot and review, and began gathering public input. They widely distributed a public questionnaire called a 'feedback form' and gathered the results. Four meetings with the public and community representatives were held in October 1994. City staff then produced a final report that was formally presented to city council at a last public meeting on 23 November 1994.

The question of possible police wrongdoing was a spectre that hovered over the city's review process, leading to some interesting silences.

For example, the key document *Riots: A Background Paper* included a four-page section on crowd behaviour. This offered a variety of reasons why some crowds 'turn ugly,' drawn from an article in *Police Journal*. Yet the section contained no reference to the possibility that police behaviour itself could cause or worsen riots, even though this factor is well documented in the literature on riots (e.g., Stark, 1972; Marx, 1981; D. Waddington 1992).

Similarly, the city collected several hundred letters and comments from individuals concerned about the riot, numerous quotations from which appeared in *Riots: A Background Paper*. Yet none of the published quotations involved any questioning of police behaviour, even though, as city staff admitted to me at the time, concerned individuals had actually frequently commented on police behaviour. One city staff member told me privately after one of the public meetings, 'Frankly, [the role of the police] is top of most people's list. People have very strong feelings about it.' One would never know this from reading any of the quotations from the public in *Riots: A Background Paper*.

The city's review instead pushed individual public input in other directions, or preformatted other public concerns. For example, at the display on the riot in the Vancouver Public Library, passersby were asked to fill out feedback forms that included the question 'What do you think are the causes of the riot?' Yet the same display itself featured a detailed account of the riot already indicating what the causes were. The public display featured selected frames frozen from the television footage with captions interpreting the television images in a way favourable to police. One read: 'The fact that looting started after the Crowd Control Unit was used to regain control of street space can be understood to be part criminal behaviour and part psychological. Confronted with an unbeatable enemy, the bystander leashes [*sic*] out at the nearest undefended target.' Thus, those at the library display who offered public input about the causes of the riot did so while standing next to an official account that already spelled out the causes.

Ironically, the city's final administrative report on the riot and review, produced *after* the public input sessions in October, was much shorter and less comprehensive than the background paper, which was distributed *before* public input from the meetings. The latter – 'intended to provide background information for the information center, the public forum, and the working sessions' – seemed to preordain the final results of the review.

According to the background paper, one key cause of the riot was the television cameras themselves. The background paper contained an extensive section titled 'Role of the Media,' which suggested, for example, that 'the presence of TV cameras in a volatile situation can cause violence to escalate ... Media forecasting of an event has been blamed for the event occurring ... Researchers have stated that the media's use of violent, adversarial language can influence the mood of the crowd' (p. 6), and so on. This section did not, however, cite research evidence that is more dubious about the media's role in fueling riots. It is difficult to see how the authors of the background paper could simply have overlooked or not come across the only published book specifically on this topic, Howard Tumber's *Television and the Riots* (1982: see especially pp. 45–6).

Below I will discuss these criticisms of the media's role in the riot. Regardless, for the city, the media was apparently a more acceptable target than the police.

The whole situation was encapsulated by the two-page feedback forms widely distributed by the city to solicit public input. More people filled out these feedback forms – about 285 according to one consultant – than were involved in any other aspect of the public process. The feedback forms began with the open-ended question: 'What do you think were the causes of the June 14 riot and how can we prevent it from happening again?' The space allotted to answer this question was quite limited compared to that allotted to questions about more favoured causes. Thus, most of the form contained a number of questions designed to elicit responses about the role of the media, particularly television, in causing the riot, as well as two other factors, the spatial arrangements on Robson Street and the role of alcohol.

In fact, approximately 20 per cent of the space on the feedback forms was devoted to eliciting concerns about the media. For example, the forms asked: 'What influence did the media have in creating this gathering?' and 'What role should the media have during a disturbance?' and 'How can the media assist in preventing another riot?' Furthermore – and this is perhaps the most striking demonstration of how 'public opinion' was pre-formatted – the feedback forms were actually sometimes distributed stapled to a four-page summary of the background paper!

To put this whole situation in a nutshell, the city review asked the public respondents: 'What influence did the media have in creating this gathering?' on one form that was often distributed stapled to another document that, on the next page, contained a summary of assertions criticizing the media, including, for example, criticisms of 'violence on TV' and the media's 'use of inflammatory language.' This second document – actually stapled to the very survey people were answering – suggested further that 'some people say the media's intense and immediate coverage actually incites violence.' The summary did also contain some arguments in defence of the media, though these were lower down in the document and given considerably less space. Even so, the exercise was methodologically as faulty as a social scientist circulating a survey to which she had stapled another sheet of paper with suggested answers.

Given all this, it is not surprising to read in the city's final report that the public had expressed a number of concerns about the media's role in the riot! For example, 'many suggested pre-game media stories created an environment which made a riot more likely ... they suggested that cameras filming the looting and rioting actually encouraged such behaviour,' and so on. I should make it clear here that I believe the media may well bear some responsibility for the riot, so such concerns may be legitimate. I am merely suggesting that, either way, the review pushed public input in this direction.

In vivid contrast, there was only one question on the feedback forms that mentioned the police at all: 'What advance measures should the city and Police take to prevent major disturbances in the future?' One should note the focus on 'advance measures' as opposed to police behaviour on the evening itself. Encapsulating the broader situation, the forms did not ask specifically about the police response to the riot.

As I observed first hand, the public meetings during the review were also conducted in a way that shifted blame from police to television and the other media. When we split into small discussion groups at the first city public meeting on 1 October 1994, a Vancouver police inspector joined our group. The police inspector sat in, even though, as I pointed out earlier, the review had already formally excluded discussion of the police role. As the discussion proceeded, the moderators deflected questions and comments by people in our group that challenged police behaviour; for example, one moderator redirected the discussion away from police issues by saying, 'We want to keep this focused on the future.' Other questions by people in the group looking at the role of television (and other possible factors) in causing the riot were drawn out; for example, a moderator said to one group member, 'You started out saying you thought the media played a big role ... could you expand on that?'

On the other hand, when participants in our group began to praise rather than criticize the police, the police inspector joined in the discussion, even though the review was not supposed to examine police behaviour. At this point the inspector offered his account of why police did what they had done. A businessperson asked for more time at this point for the group to talk with the inspector. In contrast, this part of the discussion – focused on a more positive account of police behaviour at the riot – was not curtailed by the moderators, even though it was off the ostensible topic.

Following the meetings, unsurprisingly, the city's final report offered a narrative of events on 14 June that did not implicate the police in any way: 'A crowd, estimated between 40,000 and 70,000, gathered ... in the course of a few hours, looting, vandalism and open violence developed. Store windows were smashed, bottles and rocks thrown, and cars trashed. Many people were injured, some seriously. The police crowd control unit eventually dispersed the crowd' (p. 2).

Instead, the final report blamed the same factors that had been presented throughout the review: the media, event planning and security, and alcohol. In contrast, 'the subject of violence (especially youth violence and its causes) is beyond the scope of this review, but many individuals expressed their concerns about what happened on 14 June and how our values are changing. The ideas expressed varied significantly – from changing the Young Offenders Act and our educational system, to developing more activities for youth.' In other words, the proposed solutions ran the gamut from *A* to *B*. While denying ownership of the problem of 'violence,' the city's report simultaneously constructed it as a problem of 'youth violence' rather than as at all stemming from police crowd management.

The city's review process was supposed to culminate in a public meeting at City Hall on 23 November where this final report was to be presented to council. However, advertising for this meeting was quite limited. I searched in vain in local newspapers like the *Kitsilano News*, *Vancouver Courier*, and *Vancouver Sun* for display ads similar to those by which the city had advertised other recent public meetings.

As it turned out, there were only a handful of people at the final meeting in the review process who did not have some institutional affiliation. Only four of these people spoke. Then, a final incident occurred that showed once more how the politics of the review precluded criticism of the police: Dr. Stuart Rulka, a Burnaby dentist who had been in the riot crowd, spoke up. Dr. Rulka seemed to me a dramatic symbol of the missing public in the review process. He certainly presented a visual contrast with the image that had been constructed of crowd members as 'young punks': the balding dentist appeared to be in his mid-forties, wore a muted sports jacket and tie. He was accompanied at the meeting by his wife and school-aged daughter. Dr. Rulka said he had not attended any of the previous meetings because, as he lived in suburban Burnaby, outside the City of Vancouver, he had not seen any advertising or otherwise heard about the review.

Standing at the microphone, the dentist narrated – with considerable length and clarity – his experiences in the crowd that night. Dr. Rulka told the meeting that, based on his first-hand knowledge, both the city's report and the B.C. Police Commission report gave a false accounting of the events leading up to the riot. He suggested instead that the advance by the Crowd Control Unit at Robson and Thurlow was the flashpoint of the riot – in short, that police had triggered the worst of the mayhem. 'I state categorically that the first window on Robson was not broken until after the tear gas ... I just don't buy that section of the report,' he said. His statement was a jarring moment. A police inspector seated next to me in the audience covered his face with his hand.

After Dr. Rulka spoke, one councillor said he appreciated the 'lucid account' but raised no additional questions. Then two other members of council launched verbal attacks on the dentist. Councillor Craig Hemer noted that Dr. Rulka and his daughter had wandered away from Robson and Thurlow earlier in the evening and then returned. Councillor Hemer said, 'I don't have a great deal of sympathy for individuals who return to a riot site.' Dr. Rulka was clearly one member of the public that this public review did not want to hear from.[12] With no further discussion of the concerns he had raised, Council voted to accept the city review's final report and follow its recommendations.

In sum, the city review was set up in such a way that it could not address any concerns about police behaviour on the evening of the riot. The 'public process' instead seemed structured in a way that pushed the review to produce other findings, notably that there was 'public' concern about the role of television and other media in the riot.

The Police Reviews

While some effort was made to involve the citizenry in the city's review, public involvement was minimal in the other two reviews, conducted respectively by the B.C. Police Commission and by the Vancouver police themselves. In contrast to the city's review, these two – the reviews that *were* actually mandated to examine the police role – offered no feedback forms or any equivalent method for soliciting public input. One review only offered a brief series of newspaper ads asking people to write letters commenting on the riot; the other made no attempt to invite public input.

The B.C. Police Commission, like similar bodies in Canada (see, e.g., McMahon and Ericson 1987; McMahon 1988), had been under fire for being too cozy with the police. In fact, just three months after the riot review was announced, a different public enquiry recommended that the Police Commission itself be abolished because it was not suffi-ciently impartial.[13] Certainly, in the case of the Stanley Cup riot, it turned out that the recommendations of the Police Commission would be very similar to those of Vancouver police themselves (*Vancouver Sun*, 4 February 1995, p. A5).

In any case, public involvement in the Police Commission's review of the riot was quite limited (B.C. Police Commission, 1994b: 5–6). The commission's research included 'interviews with people who were downtown that night, including people working downtown' (with whom, how many, and how they were contacted were never stated). Research also included 'a review of written comments about the riot from members of the public. Some of these were unsolicited and others came about as a result of newspaper advertisements published by the Commission asking for such comments' (p. 6). This methodology re-stricted the type of individuals who would respond. For example, teenaged street people would be unlikely to see a newspaper ad and then sit down and write a letter to the commission.

Nonetheless, critical public viewpoints do occasionally appear in the Police Commission's report, such as this one: 'One member of the public who was at the corner of Robson and Thurlow on June 14 following the hockey game states that "There were a few rowdies and a lot of commotion, but otherwise the crowd was extremely well behaved and very civil"' (p. 12). The Police Commission, however, immediately undercuts this statement by constructing its own version of public opinion: 'This opinion appears to be the minority view of what was taking place downtown that evening and is not borne out by a review of the video tapes. Our examination shows that some of the crowd that gathered downtown after the game were looking for trouble, whereas others were there just waiting for something to happen' (p. 12).

This demonstrates how the Police Commission used the confiscated TV footage. As the only parties authorized to interpret the TV footage, they could baldly state what the footage meant without having to provide much of a justification. There was, for example, no need to explain how the Police Commission was able to discern the state of mind of all these crowd members – that they were 'looking for trouble' or 'waiting for something to happen' – simply by reviewing the tapes.

The report also says 'a review of the video footage reveals a crowd composed almost entirely of teenagers and young adults' (p. 11). In contrast, this chapter offers comments from members of the public present that night who were in their thirties, forties, and fifties.

The Police Commission report absolved police from triggering the chaos, stating that the atmosphere 'seemed to reach a "flashpoint" of sorts' around 10 p.m. – that is, just *before* the Crowd Control Unit advanced at 10:09 p.m. (p. 13). Like the city's review, the B.C. Police Commission review instead found that the media, and particularly television, were partly to blame for the riot (pp. 40–5). Why? Firstly, for playing up the rivalry between the Canucks and Rangers: 'for the type of broadcasting that heightens the rivalry and aggressiveness of a sporting event' (p. 41); secondly, for advertising a 'party atmosphere' downtown (p. 41); and thirdly, for placing cameras in a fixed location that encouraged crowd members to gather and perform for the cameras.[14]

Given the cozy relationship (Oppal Commission 1994) between police and the commission, and the limited attempt to solicit input from members of the riot crowd, one can hardly be surprised by the commission's conclusion that 'the police did a commendable job considering their lack of experience in dealing with a hostile, unruly crowd' (p. 71). Apparently referring to Ryan Michael Berntt, the nineteen-year-old who was shot in the side of the head, the commission noted that 'the importance of respecting agitators as "skilled alchemists" is emphasized by riot study literature; there must be a means to remove those alchemists from a crowd in some circumstances' (pp. 66–7). However, they recommended that the Arwen gun not be used in future because it might hit somebody who was not an 'agitator.'

The commission further pointed out that 'there were *only* five complaints of misconduct filed against Vancouver police department officers; four of these were informally resolved (italics added).' The fifth

complaint was 'considered withdrawn' because 'the complainant refused to cooperate with the investigation (p. 71).

The B.C. Police Commission report, then, offered very little possibility for input from concerned individuals, constructing its own version
of public opinion, one highly supportive of police.

The third and final review was an internal one conducted by
Vancouver police. While these various reviews were announced as a
response to public concerns, the ongoing reviews were cited several
times as a reason why Vancouver police could not comment to the
media on aspects of the riot. Thus, ironically, professing to address
public concerns about policing was used as a justification to keep the
review process secret from the public.

As part of this third and final review, Vancouver police arranged a
public meeting to talk about police behaviour, held 11 October 1994.
Vancouver police chief Ray Canuel said that night, 'The Vancouver
Police Department is committed to open public communication. That's
why we're here this evening.'

Despite the police chief's claim, one senior city staff member told me
privately at the time that, in fact, initially no public meeting at all was
scheduled by the police. Indeed, I was told, the Vancouver police only
made a last-minute decision to hold any kind of public meeting at all to
look at police behaviour – deciding this just days before the meeting
was actually held – because of criticisms of a lack of public input into
the police review process.

As it turned out, the meeting to examine police behaviour was scheduled for a weekday evening, little advertised, and even by official
estimates drew only twenty to twenty-five people. Only two of those
present at the meeting had actually been at the riot. A consultant hired
to assist with the review process blamed the low attendance on lack of
advertising due to financial constraints. He said the police did not have
much of a budget for publicizing this type of event. This explanation
seemed highly unlikely given the large amount of resources police
normally commit to public relations (Ericson, Baranek and Chan, 1989,
chap. 2; Schlesinger and Tumber 1994).

Nevertheless, Vancouver police chief Canuel commented at the meeting, 'We hoped there would have been a lot more people than we have
here now.' This meeting was the only public meeting held for either of
the police reviews.

Vancouver police at first said they would not release their internal
report to the public at all. This secrecy met with substantial criticism

from the news media. The Vancouver police review was finally released in early 1995 and, of the three reviews, was actually the most critical of police operations on the night of the riot. Its criticism was, however, limited to police training, operational procedures, and equipment: no individual officer was found blameworthy, and the key question of whether police had used excessive force was not addressed. Much of the criticism in this third report was focused on the limitations of the communications technology police used during the riot. This criticism would be used to justify a call for funding a new $12 million regional communications centre. The report was also used to warrant a request to council (quickly approved) for $238,700 worth of new riot equipment for police (*Vancouver Sun*, 17 May 1995, p. B3).

Media Coverage of the Reviews

Media coverage of the riot story – from both television and newspapers – tailed off as the reviews progressed. Ultimately, news coverage of the reviews was much less intense and critical than initial coverage of the riot itself. The way the reviews were set up seemed to defuse media interest over time. A number of journalists attended only portions of the evening review meetings, leaving long before they finished. After the early meetings, some journalists produced stories commenting on the low turnout. The media began to read the absence of the public at these meetings as a message, and began describing the public as either apathetic or simply satisfied and secure with current arrangements. 'June outrage turns into October indifference,' ran a headline in the *Province* newspaper. With some notable exceptions, media accounts did not suggest the low public turnout might instead be a result of the way the reviews were being conducted.

By November, there was very limited media coverage. Most media outlets mentioned the final public meeting in the review process – if at all – lower down in stories focusing instead on security preparations for the upcoming Grey Cup football championship festivities in Vancouver. Dr. Rulka's account of police escalation of the riot was not mentioned in any of the five newspaper and television stories that referred to that last public meeting. Dr. Rulka was one of the few members of the public who actually attended the meeting. Yet his 'lucid' account of the riot – contrary as it was to the official reports – seemed to sink without trace. Why?

One journalist with a television news organization spoke to me privately for a long time after the last public meeting. He said the tale of the riot and its aftermath was 'the most frustrating story' he'd ever worked on. In his view, questions about police behaviour had simply not been addressed in the reviews. However, in stark contrast to his comments to me, when his story on the meeting appeared the next day, it made little mention of any of these concerns. Despite what he told me, his TV news story focused instead on security for the upcoming Grey Cup festivities. The television journalist told me those in his newsroom were 'gun shy' about pursuing the riot story, partly because of what they perceived as strong public support for the police. Perhaps this is why he produced a story so at odds with his comments of the night before.

More generally, why was media criticism of the police curtailed during the review process? Obviously, the review process lacked the drama and spectacle of the riot itself, though television stations sometimes used the review as a reason to recycle footage from the riot. More speculatively, the media may have grown cautious after coming under fire themselves for their role in the riot. They may have been intimidated by the riot review's criticisms of the media.

There was, at any rate, not much to report: few sources critical of the police emerged from the review process. In ways I have outlined, the review itself did not allow much criticism of the police.

Another factor was that journalists apparently perceived that public interest in the riot had diminished because few people were showing up for the meetings. Thus the review was seen as less newsworthy.[15]

Nevertheless, some harsh media criticism of police persisted throughout the review process and afterward. For example, in late December local CBC television news did a story with a critical tone reporting police's decision not to charge anyone over the Berntt shooting. The *Globe and Mail* ran a lengthy column on the review process on 12 November (p. D2). The headline summed it up: 'Vancouver turns blind eye to the police role on the Night of Shame.'

The *Vancouver Sun* newspaper also continued to run some critical comments. For example, the *Sun* encapsulated the riot in its year-end review (31 December 1994: p. B1): 'A B.C. Police Commission report found that police performed well. But some observers felt that the police panicked and provoked much of the looting with their aggressive tactics.' On 14 June 1999, on the five-year anniversary of the riot, CBC-TV ran a long news story suggesting that the reviews never got to the bottom of what happened that night. The story said that later controversial problems with crowd policing in Vancouver, for example at APEC 1997, might have been avoided had the reviews looked at policing of the Stanley Cup riot more critically.

Television's Other Roles in the Riot

We have thus far discussed the role television played in interpreting what happened the night of the riot. I now move on to focus on other roles that television played in the riot and its policing.

Did the Media Cause or Exacerbate the Stanley Cup Riot?

The central premise of this book is that television may shape what is in front of the camera. As noted above, the riot reviews suggested the media – mostly referring to television – were partly to blame for the riot. It is difficult to address the truth of this claim with the available evidence. Similarly, for example, there has been widespread criticism of the media's role in possibly fuelling the Los Angeles riot of 1992 (O'Heffernan 1992). Not surprisingly, the media have been considerably less critical of their own role in the Stanley Cup riot than they have of the police.

There have been a handful of earlier pieces of research on the media's possible role in causing riots (Tumber, 1982; D. Waddington, 1992), but these have not uncovered much evidence that media played a key role in causing the riots studied.

The Stanley Cup riot reviews cited both immediate factors and broader cultural concerns in examining the media's role in the riot. At the most immediate level, it was suggested that placing TV cameras in fixed locations on Robson Street rooftops encouraged crowds to gather and 'perform' for the cameras. The media were also accused of inviting audiences to come downtown and join the celebration. (This ignored the role that police played in extending this invitation through the media.)[16] Broader cultural concerns suggested by various sources included the media's involvement in perpetuating the spectacle of sports violence.

By arguing that the reviews helped shift the blame to television, I am not implying that TV was blameless. On the face of it, there seems some plausibility to arguments suggesting television contributed in some ways to causing the riot, but I do not have enough evidence from the night in question to give a very definitive evaluation of them. I have focused instead on the post-riot politics. Whether or not TV actually helped cause the riot, various factors worked to blame things on television.

Television and Police Surveillance

Television also dramatically enhances police surveillance capability through the use of 'video wanted posters.' The Stanley Cup riot is a cogent example of this. Police used a massive collection of media video-tapes, photographs, and negatives to enlist public help in identifying members of the crowd. This led to over one hundred rioters facing three hundred charges. A high-technology video kiosk was set up in local shopping malls and other public locations, moving around the Greater Vancouver area for many weeks (*Vancouver Sun*, 7 October 1994, p. A1). In the kiosk, passersby could use interactive computer technology to call up on a screen segments of video footage from the riots. They could then type in information identifying individuals featured in the footage, as well as details such as those individuals' school or place of work. The information went by cellular phone directly into the Crimestoppers computer. Those who could identify suspects were given a tip number. They could check in later with this number, and if their tip led to charges they could claim a reward.

A similar approach was used after the Tiananmen Square uprising in Beijing in 1989, employing video footage from what was nominally an 'advanced traffic control system.' The system was used to record the protests at Tiananmen, and the images were repeatedly broadcast over Chinese television along with an offer of a reward for information. Numerous Tiananmen participants were captured and punished (*Vancouver Sun*, 1 June 1999, p. B1). Police used television footage in the same way after the Los Angeles riot of 1992 and after riots in Toronto and Carbondale, Illinois.[17]

The Stanley Cup riot demonstrated a point familiar from the previous chapter: how this kind of surveillance is selectively deployed. In this case, surveillance was used against members of the crowd but not against police themselves. Reviewing the tapes resulted in over one hundred rioters being charged, but the process led to no charges or complaints against police. Rick Brooks, the lawyer for Berntt, criticized the kiosk for precisely this reason: 'It's very one-sided, isn't it. I don't see any police officer in here misconducting himself or herself.'

Local media outlets showed varying degrees of resistance to involvement in the post-riot surveillance program. Some were quite co-operative. For example, television stations BCTV and UTV initially offered special video segments enlisting help in identifying rioters. In any case, the video kiosk effectively bypassed the news media – essentially giving police their own media outlets.

Indeed, one may argue that the video kiosks were useful not only for enlisting help in surveillance. These visuals of the riot, produced by police, served a second function: to publicize the police version of events. They were a highly visible outlet for police-controlled 'news,' repeatedly displaying the police's own edited version of the riot, from which any footage casting police in a bad light was cut out.

Conclusions

How does the addition of TV into the situation influence a riot? There is some evidence that TV can contribute to the complex chain of events leading to a riot. Furthermore, television has changed riot policing in various ways. Some researchers have optimistically argued that, by making visible violent police tactics, TV has led to gentler police behaviour in controlling crowds. While there is evidence to support this (e.g., Fillieule 1998), the Stanley Cup riot shows the situation is a little more complicated.

It is clear from my data that footage of policing a crowd or riot is open to a great deal of retrospective reinterpretation shaped by political considerations. Such footage seems to rely heavily on verbal explanation of its meaning. While this is the case with many kinds of TV footage, it applies particularly in the complex and highly ambiguous realm of public-order events such as riots or demonstrations, which may unfold in a wild, rapid blur. The Stanley Cup riot footage was too chaotic simply to 'speak for itself.'

Many people said, immediately after the riot, that police caused or escalated it. However, this narrative from the public was largely silenced in the subsequent review process. The fact that a television record existed of virtually the entire riot did very little to halt this silencing, given the political context. Police became the players in a position to authoritatively define this TV footage in the various reviews. Even when police do adopt more violent tactics in public-order policing, my research shows how they can retrospectively achieve control over televised accounts.

This is not to say that police are always able to achieve such control.

Certainly, the fallout from television coverage of police suppression of protest at APEC 1997 in Vancouver was damaging to police and government officials (Ericson and Doyle 1999; Pue 2000), as was the case with Chicago 1968. Yet whether or not TV coverage is damaging seems to depend a great deal on the political context, not simply on the availability of the television images themselves. This point fits with previous research (Fillieule 1998; P. Waddington 1994) indicating that the trend towards gentler public-order policing has been a selective one, depending on just how socially marginal the protesters or rioters are.

The case of the Stanley Cup riot shows again how the most powerful players, in this case police, tend to produce what I am calling the 'authorized definitions' of televised situations, and thus control their consequences. Invoking the notion that 'seeing is believing,' TV is uniquely effective at warranting these authorized definitions. TV did reshape the situation in various ways, and take on a number of other roles – TV as facilitator of public surveillance, TV as scapegoat – but because police had the power to define the footage, these influences mostly served police.

It may seem strange, and perhaps a little frightening, that, even when such a hugely public and visible event as the Stanley Cup riot was witnessed directly by hundreds of people and recorded and broadcast massively by TV, it ultimately was the words of police that mattered. This begins to suggest a broader point about television: that many understandings of TV might overemphasize its visual aspect. In the examples we have looked at so far, verbal interpretations of televised events by the most powerful players seem more important than TV images. A theory that suggests TV simply makes things 'visible' ignores this point, as it ignores the power relations involved in how TV reshapes social situations.

CHAPTER SIX

The Media Logic of Greenpeace

My final case study turns the tables. In this fourth study it is the criminal, rather than police or journalists, who initiates televising of the situation. This chapter asks: How has the presence of television affected law-breaking political protest, and the activists that use it?

This case study focuses on the premier creators of television activism, Greenpeace. Born as a tiny band of protesters in Vancouver in 1971, Greenpeace is now the world's largest and best-known environmental organization. While it has achieved a great deal in protecting the environment, Greenpeace has also swollen into a wealthy and powerful international institution[1].

After reviewing previous research, I will offer some history, showing how Greenpeace has from its birth been a creature of the media, particularly television. Carefully choreographed made-for-TV stunts are Greenpeace's signature tactic. I examine how activists, journalists, and police treat these media stunts. Mostly, they simply go along with them. However, Greenpeace imposes significant constraints on itself in designing its actions for the media. As TV influences what happens in front of the camera, TV also has had broader effects on Greenpeace. It has fed back on and shaped the style and direction of the whole Greenpeace organization, including its structure, its goals and philosophies, and its relationship with its members. This case study is based on varied sources of ethnographic data. Key data come from numerous Greenpeace documents and texts I have obtained, and from hundreds of newspaper clippings and television news items about the organization. I also draw on interviews with Greenpeace staff, with other environmental activists, and with journalists covering environmental issues.[2]

Previous Research

Previous Research on Greenpeace

Greenpeace and its media tactics have been discussed by a number of academic sources pursuing different theoretical interests[3] (e.g., Eyerman and Jamison 1989; Cassidy 1992; Hansen 1993; Shaiko 1993; Rucht 1995; Anderson 1997; Carroll and Ratner 1999). A discussion of this previous research is woven throughout the chapter. Journalist Stephen Dale (1996) has written an excellent history of the organization, focusing on its media tactics. None of these previous works have, however, explored the broader implications for theorizing television's influences of how Greenpeace's approach to media has fed back on and shaped the whole organization.[4]

Previous Research on the Media and Social Movements

Greenpeace is the example *par excellence* of how social movements have increasingly become media movements. More generally, the news media and particularly television are increasingly the crucial playing field for contemporary politics (Ericson, Baranek, and Chan 1989; Jamieson 1992; Blumler and Gurevitch 1995). Like many other institutions, social movement organizations and interest groups that used to work behind the scenes are adopting a higher media profile, becoming increasingly professionalized in media relations or 'mediatized' (Grant, 1989: 80; Ericson, Baranek, and Chan 1989; Doyle and Ericson 1996; Anderson 1997; Carroll and Ratner 1999).

Ideally, at least, media coverage can give social movement organizations a kind of standing in public debates. The news media allow movements to advance their preferred messages or frames of meaning concerning issues, in order to gain public support, pressure governments and corporations, and boost the morale of existing supporters (Gamson and Wolfsfeld 1993). The increasingly central place of television in society is implicated in the 'mediatization' of social movements from the 1960s onward (Tarrow 1994). Television, for many years now the source of news most relied on by audiences (Baker and Dessart 1998: 127), has offered tantalizing new opportunities for social movements to capture attention with a striking image or sound-bite.

Much previous research has examined how social movements receive favourable or unfavourable news media attention (e.g., Gitlin

1980; Gamson and Modigliani 1989; Entman and Rojecki 1993; McCarthy, McPhail, and Smith 1996; Couldry 1999). Such research has explored in detail how activists may (or may not) shape news content. However, there has been little empirical exploration of the alternative question I raise here: How do media feed back on protests and on social movement organizations? Theoretical discussions have raised the point that media coverage can help to reshape movements themselves (Kielbowicz and Scherer 1986, Gamson and Wolfsfeld 1993), but the nature of this impact has not been examined much empirically. Todd Gitlin's (1980) classic analysis of media coverage of student protest against the Vietnam War in the mid-1960s did touch on this question. Gitlin argued that the student anti-war activists were unprepared for media attention. Thus, media attention had a divisive influence, helping to fracture the activist organization Students For A Democratic Society (SDS). I focus instead on what happens when social movement organizations are less naïve, and show more sophistication in dealing with the news media. What happens when movement organizations shape their actions more professionally and proactively to gain media coverage?

Previous Research on Media and Political Demonstrations

Inquiries about the media and activism quickly lead one to consider the political demonstration and how it plays in the news, particularly on television. A central way social movement organizations obtain media attention is through such demonstrations. As Ericson, Baranek and Chan (1989: 299) note, 'the contemporary political demonstration owes just about everything to news media coverage, especially to television. It is the marginal organization's press conference.' This was epitomized in the violent confrontations between police and demonstrators at the Chicago 1968 Democratic convention, with protesters' repeated chants that 'The whole world's watching! The whole world's watching!' Political demonstrations have become increasingly commonplace and institutionalized in Western nations since the 1960s (Etzioni 1970; Meyer and Tarrow 1998; Della Porta and Reiter 1998a; McCarthy and McPhail 1998; Cleveland 1999); a great many do not receive any media attention at all. For example, McCarthy, McPhail, and Smith (1996) found that only a small fraction of political demonstrations in Washington, D.C., that received official permits in 1982 and 1991 were even mentioned in the *Washington Post*, in the *New York Times*, or on national television news.

Furthermore, simply getting media attention may not be enough for social movements. Outsider or challenger organizations may be constrained from effectively communicating their messages by having to use demonstrations and stunts to get into the media. A well-known case study by Halloran et al. (1970) examined one day's television coverage and two weeks' newspaper coverage of a British anti-Vietnam war demonstration. The researchers found that nearly all news outlets they studied focused on violence in the demonstration as the defining element of the story. Other research has confirmed this tendency, suggesting that media accounts of demonstrations or political riots tend to portray the demonstrators as deviant rather than conveying their grievances (D. Waddington 1992; McLeod and Hertog 1992), although the spotlight sometimes shifts to portraying police as deviant when crowds are violently repressed in some political contexts. According to Gitlin (1980), the media covering anti-war demonstrations in the U.S. in the 1960s zeroed in on violence, on the presence of communists, and on the carrying of Viet Cong flags. McCarthy, McPhail, Smith, and Crishock (1998) analysed 766 newspaper and television reports of political demonstrations in Washington, D.C., in 1982 and 1991. They found that 42.7 per cent of the newspaper stories and 61.9 per cent of the television stories did not even mention the policy goals of the protesters. Hackett (1991: 214) studied coverage by three Toronto daily newspapers of mass protests against the 1986 American bombing of Libya. He also found that the arguments of the peace protesters received little attention. A content analysis of newspaper coverage of British Columbia environmental protests (Tindall and Doyle 1999) showed a similar pattern. When environmentalists were quoted in news coverage of protests, most of the time they were talking about the protest itself; only 33 per cent of their quoted statements actually touched on any aspect of the environmental questions that had triggered the protest. When they were quoted in non-protest stories, in contrast, environmentalists were able to focus much more on the environmental issues themselves – 77 per cent of the time. These numbers pose a dilemma for activists: they can get more media attention by staging protests, but this coverage may come at the cost of deflecting media focus away from the underlying issues, towards the protest action itself.

TV news provides even less of a window to get the activists' messages out. McCarthy et al. (1999) compared television news coverage of protests to newspaper coverage and found that television focused on the underlying issues even less. This previous research thus points to a key question: How much can Greenpeace overcome the news media's general tendency to focus on the spectacle of the demonstration rather than on its message?

Previous Research on Social Movements and the Rise of Television

A small number of works by historians and theorists of social movements come at these problems differently. They take a longer term historical view of the influence on social movements of shifts in the predominant media of communication. Interestingly, these analyses are considerably more optimistic about the relationship between media and movements. In his book *Power in Movement*, Sidney Tarrow (1994) describes what he sees as the liberating potential of the advent of new communication media, first print and then TV. Tarrow argues at length (1994: chap. 3) that social movements developed in their modern form over the past two centuries partly due to the rise of the commercial print media. He goes on to argue that the advent in the last several decades of the 'new social movements,' such as environmentalism and feminism, is linked in part with the rise of television.[5]

Certainly, the civil rights movement in the southern U.S. in the early 1960s gained massive momentum through network television footage, particularly that of Southern police brutalizing civil rights crusaders (Kielbowicz and Scherer 1986: 83; McAdam 1996). Some analysts have linked the development of 1960s counterculture resistance in the U.S. in part to the coming together of the Vietnam War and the rise of television, such that Vietnam became the first 'living-room war,' because of the emotionally charged impact of these television images (Rutherford 1989). Thus Tarrow writes:

A tidal wave of movements ... arose [in this era] amid technological and social changes that gave them a new set of resources and connections with which movement organizers could work ... The expansion of mass media from print to electronics – and especially the advent of television – was the most important of these developments. (1994: 143)

In a later piece, Meyer and Tarrow develop these arguments:

The growth of the mass media, along with citizens' capacity to both consume and participate in it, has also increased the velocity of diffusion of contentious politics, for at least three reasons. First, when ordinary citizens see others like themselves demonstrating on television, they learn how protests can be mounted and occasionally how they can succeed – demonstrations have a demonstration effect. Second, television focuses attention not on discrete issues that can divide viewers from those they see protesting on screen but on visual images that diffuse information about the routines of contentious politics, which can be used regardless of the content of demands. Third, because television broadcasters attract viewers through visual images, social actors with claims to make may learn to mount them through dramatic public performances that are more likely to attract the attention of the media than through less public forms of collective action ... Contemporary activists, recognizing the critical role of the media in projecting their activities and claims, have developed more sophisticated ways of influencing how their activities are covered ... And an organization like Greenpeace maintains a skilled staff that instantly diffuses images of its activists' dramatic activities to news sources around the world. (1998: 13–14)

On the one hand, we have more tightly focused empirical research on what the news media actually report concerning protests and demonstrations, and on the other hand, we have broader, more speculative historical analyses of the role of television in the evolution of activism. Putting these two sets of literature side by side raises important questions. Does the experience of Greenpeace fit with the generally negative prognoses of researchers who studied news media coverage of protest? Or does it fit with the more optimistic account of Tarrow, who suggests liberating potential in the television form? Note that these alternatives repeat a pattern in literature: focusing on the formal properties of a medium leads one to be optimistic about its liberating potential; empirical research into the actual circumstances of media production and content often leads to more pessimistic conclusions.[6]

Greenpeace and the Media

Early History

Many social movement groups and other non-governmental organizations experience a lot of difficulty in gaining access to media. Greenpeace, however, has repeatedly been successful in mobilizing the media to its own ends. Greenpeace has been very geared to the news media since its birth. The group was created by a small group of anti-nuclear activists in Vancouver in 1971. Its initial target of protest was a scheduled American atomic bomb test on Amchitka in the Aleutian Islands. A demonstration by seven thousand protesters at the Canada–U.S. border failed to attract much media attention. After this, as one Greenpeace founder, Jim Bohlen, said, 'We decided to start an organization, informing the public in a way the media cannot ignore' (Cassidy 1992: 168). The new group conceived a media stunt: sailing a boat close to the test area, putting the crew in danger and thus preventing the detonation. They recalled that Quakers had some years earlier tried a similar tactic to protest testing in the South Pacific. Marie Bohlen, Jim's wife and another founding member, said, '[The Quakers] were arrested in Hawaii before they got to the site, and that made all kinds of national news ... [We thought] why don't we get a ship and take it up there?' Jim Bohlen recounted, 'I liked the idea. Then the phone rang. Some reporter wanted to know what was going on in the environmental movement ... The next day, there it was in the newspaper' (Brown and May 1989: 8).

Even in its embryonic stage, Greenpeace was proficient at dealing with the media – because some of the key players who started the organization were themselves journalists. Three journalist/activists were among the twelve-person crew on the initial Greenpeace protest voyage towards the Aleutians.[7]

Greenpeace's early media tactics had some interesting theoretical underpinnings. They were rooted somewhat in a kind of theory of the media that Robert Hunter had developed in two philosophical books, *Enemies of Anarchy* and *The Storming of the Mind* (1971). These books discussed ecology, media, and changing public consciousness, among many other things. Hunter wrote:

> As we have seen, even operating mindlessly and at random, mass media have helped to reshape human consciousness. That initial period of 'accidental effects' is passing. We see the media are now deliberately being brought to bear in an effort to stimulate further changes in consciousness ... If the pen was a hundred or thousand times mightier than the sword, we can only estimate that television is at least a million times more powerful ... Marshall McLuhan has been our greatest prophet. (1971: 217–21)

Hunter suggested that the new technology of television allowed a 'revolutionary strategy that was not possible in any previous historical context' (1971: 221) and that 'the new consciousness revolutionaries are now hurling mind-bombs through the delivery systems of the mass media' (1971: 223). He argued that revolutionaries could help bring about a major shift in public consciousness through the media.

Until the mid-1970s, Greenpeace focused its actions on nuclear issues. Then it began to diversify its focus, first extending it to whaling. For their next campaign, the activists 'took musical instruments with which to serenade the whales, and most important, film cameras to document their work' (Yearley 1991: 69). From this point on, Greenpeace became ever more oriented towards television in particular.

Difficulties in Presenting Environmental Issues on TV

Environmental organizations like Greenpeace face specific problems in trying to present their concerns in the media, most notably on television. Environmental problems are difficult to communicate in the media because they are often geographically distant or dispersed, multinational or international, have a slow onset, are invisible, and are technically complex (Yearley 1991: 44–5; Beck 1992; Medler and Medler 1993; Hannigan 1995). Some environmental concerns do become highly tangible and visible in the most horrific way, as with the holocausts in Bhopal and Chernobyl. Others remain intangible and are difficult to make visible.

A second problem concerns the key task of portraying governments or corporations as deviant. These may be faceless villains. Unlike the criminal justice system, the enforcement regime that deals with environmental concerns, based on an administrative compliance model, tends to operate with minimal publicity (Hawkins 1984). Some environmental problems may be easy to represent visually, for example, the devastation of a clear-cut forest or the clubbing of baby seal pups. Other problems, like the ozone hole, are more difficult to make visible for the media: both the 'crime' and the corporate or government 'villain' may be abstractions.

Environmental problems may also be situated in isolated locations in the wilderness or on the high seas, far from major news outlets. A further difficulty is the 'event orientation' of the news media (Ericson, Baranek, and Chan 1987; Hannigan 1995). An environmental problem most often involves a long-term situation rather than the distinct dramatic event that fits news media formats (Ericson, Baranek, and Chan 1987). As Hansen notes, 'the environment and "environmental issues" do not ordinarily – other than in the form of major disasters and accidents – draw attention to themselves' (1993: 158). The need to overcome these problems helps explain Greenpeace's particular approach to media.

Greenpeace's Media Stunts

Greenpeace's central tactic for much of its history has been the creation for media consumption of brief vignettes – micro-dramas, often in the form of daring direct action – that dramatically encapsulate an environmental problem. By using these stunts, Greenpeace tries to overcome the difficulties outsider organizations face in getting news media attention in general, and media attention for environmental problems in particular.

Greenpeace's stunts are well planned and organized and are announced to the media in advance. They are timed to suit media deadlines and executed with precision by a small number of professional activists, rather than involving a large crowd of demonstrators. The stunts always involve visually striking, made-for-TV elements such as acts of physical daring, wearing of costumes, or unveiling of a banner with a very brief message. They often involve calculated nonviolent law breaking, such as a sit-in or blockade, with the deliberate goal of prompting on-the-spot arrests to add television drama. As a former Greenpeace campaigner indicates in a media handbook he wrote to instruct other activists, an 'arrest scenario' might be negotiated in advance with police, timed for television deadlines. In addition to making the maximum effort to facilitate media coverage in any way possible, organizationally and technically, the organization has its own videographers record the stunts for release to television outlets that are unable to send cameras.

Greenpeace's media stunts have included 'hanging banners from smokestacks, plugging industrial sewage pipes, and buzzing around ships in inflatable dinghies' (Gorrie 1991: 50). In particularly spectacular stunts, Greenpeace climbers scaled Big Ben and the Statue of Liberty in the summer of 1984 and hung banners (Brown and May 1989: 99). The stunts sometimes involve placing trained activists in highly visible situations from which they cannot easily be whisked away by police. The stunts have temporal qualities crucial to the media, particularly television: they are brief dramatic events, which fit with the news media's event orientation, and they are prescheduled at convenient times to allow television news assignment editors to plan to record them in time for deadlines.

Greenpeace also provides various forms of expert technical assistance to the media to ensure the stunts are recorded optimally. In its B.C. forests campaign in the late 1990s, Greenpeace used a floatplane to fly out news footage from the remote forests and provided its own helicopter to ferry journalists in and out (*Province*, 15 June 1997, p. A11). Greenpeace will, if necessary, make sure the area is appropriately floodlit by arranging for a light truck to be present (*Vancouver Sun*, 10 November 1993, p. A3).

One frequent and key element of the stunts – of conducting direct action for media purposes – is that Greenpeace activists deliberately get arrested on camera.[8] Deviance is a defining characteristic of newsworthiness (Ericson, Baranek, and Chan, 1987). As a veteran Greenpeace campaigner explained in his media how-to book for activists:

> Arrests can make stunts by activists more newsworthy – perhaps elevating them out of the stunt category altogether. 'I wouldn't encourage people to get arrested,' says Greg Todd, a former editor for the Rocky Mountain News, 'but that definitely adds to the news value of the story.' (Salzman 1998: 19)[9]

Indeed, televised arrests were deemed to be such an effective communication tool that another environmental group working alongside Greenpeace, the Friends of Clayoquot Sound, supplemented news coverage by buying television ads repeatedly showing the same video footage of its members getting arrested. As televised images of the arrests played, a narrator stated:

> These are people you may know – accountants, teachers and carpenters. They are not against logging. They are against the continued clearcutting of Clayoquot Sound ... MacMillan Bloedel has been convicted 23 times for destroying fish habitat, negligent logging and other environmental offences. 50 more cases are pending. Who are the real criminals? For more information, call the Friends of Clayoquot Sound.

This ad displays a tension or paradox that is apparent in many of Greenpeace's media stunts (and indeed more generally in media culture): a surface fascination with deviance existing in tension with an underlying pervasive ideology of support for the status quo. The ads' imagery relies on the attention-grabbing value of showing the environmental group's supporters being arrested, yet it simultaneously argues that MacMillan Bloedel are the 'real criminals' and thus the environmentalists are actually the ones who are upholders of consensus values. This is very similar to how, to use another cliché, Greenpeace tries to have its cake and eat it too. Greenpeace grabs attention by using some of the symbolism of deviance – its members being taken away by police in handcuffs – but simultaneously aims for a broad general appeal, and so cannot push the deviance very far beyond this surface level. Clearly, a social 'movement' operating within these conditions can only 'move' so far.

Related to this strategy, another defining element of Greenpeace media stunts is that they are nonviolent, at least to the extent that the activists will not engage in any deliberately violent activity. Greenpeace does not adopt the active violence or property destruction practised by more radical environmental groups such as Earth First! and the Sea Shepherd Society. Ironically, violence perpetrated by others has often been a key media selling point for Greenpeace: the bloody, harpooned whale, the bludgeoned baby seal, and the apex of Greenpeace's notoriety, the single media episode that most propelled it to global prominence: the sabotage bombing by French spies of the Greenpeace vessel *Rainbow Warrior* and killing of a Greenpeace photographer in New Zealand in 1985. Media culture is enthralled by violence as long as it can be expressed in a context that simultaneously supports established norms. Indeed, if there is a suitable violent aspect to a Greenpeace action, such as the summer 1999 injury of a Greenpeace activist by the Norwegian coast guard, Greenpeace press releases will spotlight the violent component. Nevertheless, Greenpeace must never be seen to initiate this violence.

Obviously, civil disobedience, or nonviolent, calculated lawbreaking for protest, had a long and noble history before the advent of television, and activists engage in it for a number of strong reasons other than garnering media attention. In the original Greenpeace philosophy, getting media attention was one of two 'philosophical bases,' according to Greenpeace co-founder Robert Hunter. One was 'to try to focus the mass media on the issue, which is otherwise like a mugging going off in a back alley' (Dale 1996: 17). As well, Greenpeace's early direct actions were rooted in the Quaker idea of 'bearing witness,' which 'is supposed to change the observer and increase their level of activism, compassion, anger, whatever it is.'

Acts of daring by Greenpeace members, individually or in small groups, are another telegenic aspect of many of these micro-dramas. If the Greenpeace activists make themselves outlaws, they are heroic outlaws. Part of Greenpeace's appeal is the daring of its eco-cowboys, its rebels, its 'rainbow warriors.' The stunts are presented as David standing up to Goliath, as acts of desperate courage by small bands of individual underdogs and individual heroes, like Robert Hunter, against international corporate villains. This belies Greenpeace's latter-day status as a large multinational organization.

In tandem with the media stunts is the use of direct mail fundraising (Shaiko 1993) and door-to-door fundraising, to elicit financial support from the passive television constituency fostered by Greenpeace media actions. To coordinate its media tactics with its fundraising efforts, Greenpeace conducts audience surveys that gauge how successful its various media tactics are.[10]

Media stunts are only one of a range of Greenpeace approaches and tactics, but they are the central one, as repeatedly emphasized by the organization itself. They have remained the organization's trademark activity. 'Greenpeace is really re-emphasizing a return to its direct action roots now,' Gerry Leape, the group's legislative director for ocean ecology, said in 1995. 'It's what we do well' (Motavalli, 1995: 30). As the president of Greenpeace USA, Barbara Dudley, put it: 'People remember the actions. It's the same image that's been going for Greenpeace for 20 years, and it still works' (Dale, 1996: 27).

Responses to the Stunts

How do police respond to such tactics? Advice from a media handbook written by a former Greenpeace campaigner reveals how all parties may co-operate to execute the well-choreographed ritual of televised arrest: 'If possible, conclude your protest with the media in mind. Sometimes you will want to negotiate an arrest scenario with police. If so, settle on a time for your arrest to coincide with live TV or before deadlines' (Salzman 1998: 130). An extensive review of media reports of Greenpeace's law-breaking stunts suggests that in many or most cases police simply arrest the participants, as the activists intend.

How do journalists react to Greenpeace stunts? Whether or not they are sympathetic to Greenpeace, how much influence do these journalists have on television coverage of Greenpeace demonstrations? Greenpeace publicity director Nick Gallie describes Greenpeace stunts as 'totally pre-packaged ... packaged in such a way that the media – newspapers as well as TV – could swallow them without having to chew' (Porritt and Winner 1988: 94).

'A package the media could swallow without having to chew': Gallie's comment offers a neat metaphor for what Altheide and Snow (1991) call 'post-journalism.' Altheide and Snow make the provocative argument that contemporary journalists are increasingly redundant as they become mere conduits for stories that are essentially prepared by source organizations. Greenpeace could be a prime example of such an organization.[11]

Negative framing of Greenpeace stunts is very unusual on television news, although it does happen. Of the dozens of television items and transcripts I reviewed concerning Greenpeace law-breaking actions, only two were framed in a negative way. This is what one would expect: if Greenpeace stunts were more frequently depicted in a negative way, the organization might have second thoughts about using this approach so consistently.

Greenpeace cultivates friendly relationships with key sympathetic journalists. From the beginning, Greenpeacers have often enjoyed favourable relationships with journalists, unsurprisingly, as many of its activists have been former, and sometimes current, journalists themselves. As Hansen (1991: 451) notes, a number of researchers have suggested that reporters who cover environmental issues tend to be positive about environmental groups as news sources. One aspect of this is that these journalists have an ongoing interest in maintaining good relations with the groups; the groups are no longer marginal in this respect (Ericson 1994). Beyond this, however, numerous journalists have demonstrated sympathy with the environmental movement. Front-line journalists who are low in the editorial hierarchy may be seen as belonging to a particular class of young, university-educated people in the social and cultural fields (Doyle, Elliott, and Tindall 1997). Research (Kriesi 1989: 1083,1111) suggests this particular group is particularly inclined to 'post-materialist values' and to supporting new social movements such as environmentalism.

There continues to be some notable intertwining of Greenpeace and media organizations. For example, Robert Hunter, the *Vancouver Sun* columnist who became president of Greenpeace, later moved on to become environment reporter for CITY-TV in Toronto.[12]

Greenpeace-Produced News

Greenpeace has become more and more proactive in prepackaging the news it creates. This, as we have noted, fits with the broader trend towards what Altheide and Snow (1991) call 'post-journalism,' in which institutions that are frequent news sources have become so effective in packaging their activities for the news that journalists are becoming increasingly redundant. Greenpeace produces a great deal of photographic and video documentation of its own activities and makes this available to the media. It took advantage of economic pressure and cutbacks in the television news world (Kimball 1994; Baker and Dessart 1998) to get more of its own footage on the air (Anderson 1993). Press releases I found on Greenpeace websites now give information on how television news outlets can obtain Greenpeace-produced video footage directly via satellite link-up. The websites also give the media access to digital photographs taken by Greenpeace operatives of Greenpeace activists getting arrested.[13]

Greenpeace's television profile has risen dramatically since the late 1970s in part because of its close relationship with the international television newsbroker Viz News, which was co-owned by NBC, the BBC, and other broadcasters. It was at that time that Greenpeace began tailoring its direct actions to TV. 'Our idea was to reach a global audience through the agencies,' said Greenpeace communications expert Tony Mariner. 'And the direct action [law-breaking incidents] gave us a product to sell, if you like, in terms of a news event' (Dale 1996: 114).

How Television Has Helped Shape Greenpeace

If Greenpeace is seen as expert at manipulating the media, it may be argued that the media have conversely shaped the activities of Greenpeace.

Televised direct action may constrain the kind of messages Greenpeace can communicate. It may limit the ability to place particular environmental problems in the context of broader concerns about, for example, consumerism and capitalism, global social inequality, or unbridled technological advancement. Furthermore, particular environmental issues or campaigns – such as the baby harp seal hunt in Newfoundland – may be chosen for their mediagenic qualities, while others are ignored.

Because Greenpeace actions are designed for TV, the resulting form of protest has three elements: simple messages, media-friendly goals, and a passive public.

1. SIMPLE MESSAGES
Firstly, its media approach limits Greenpeace to simple messages. Eric Draper (1987: 8), a campaign co-coordinator for Clean Water Action in Washington, D.C., gives an example:

Four years ago, I stood with a group of citizens and environmental activists in front of a burned-out hazardous waste dump in Jacksonville ... We shouted to be heard ... but the camera-operators, already looking bored, were dismantling their recorders. Then two members of our group, campaigners from Greenpeace, vaulted the yellow cordon that surrounded the site and attempted to plant our banner in the toxic-saturated soil. Guards quickly dragged them off site, but the image of confrontation was permanently recorded ... The event, as retold by photo editors, took on a different cast ... Lost was the statement by neighbourhood residents that they, as injured persons, no longer trusted the health authorities' bland reassurances. Lost was the connection between their local struggle and the broader national movement against toxics. Instead our audience got videos of a barricade standoff.

Direct action stunts may be particularly effective at publicizing the organization itself and the fact that there is a confrontation over a single issue. A stunt such as floating a giant inflatable whale into Yokohama harbour with a banner saying 'Let the Whales Live – Greenpeace' (Brown and May 1989: 142) is superb for getting a bite-sized message across that includes promoting the organizational brand name. The banners that Greenpeace frequently uses in its stunts are a literal representation of the way in which those stunts limit the complexity of messages that can be communicated: they are simply too small to contain much information. In March 2000, twenty-five Greenpeace activists blockaded a Romanian goldmine and unfurled a huge banner saying, 'Stop Cyanide.' It might be argued that this is simply effectively communicating the nub of the issue, but it does represent a considerable constraint. The most extreme example of simplistic communication was a stunt in which Greenpeace hung banners on eight smokestacks spelling out 'Stop Stop' (Brown and May 1989).

Television tends to reduce politics to a spectacle, inhibiting more complex forms of political discourse that may lead to a deeper critique of contemporary social relations. The news media's orientation to distinct dramatic events in the immediate present (Ericson, Baranek, and Chan 1987) and focus on short-term monocausal explanations (Hannigan 1995) may displace a focus on broader social issues. By its very adeptness at utilizing media formats, Greenpeace buys into these limitations. As one local Greenpeace campaigner said in an interview:

It looks easy to just get on the camera and say what you think, but when you're under a tremendous amount of pressure and you have fifteen seconds to convey an idea ... Noam Chomsky talks about how it's very difficult to change the status quo in fifteen seconds but incredibly easy to reinforce it.

As a veteran Greenpeace campaigner advises activists:

> Your first task in creating a media event is ... to identify one simple message you want to communicate. Your message should be contained in one simple phrase; following are some examples of messages for the news media:
> The incinerator will cause cancer ...
> Stop hunting whales ...
> Vote yes on amendment one. (Salzman 1998: 9)

As the Greenpeace campaigner explains, this is imperative with television news, which is most often Greenpeace's primary target:

> Journalists – television journalists in particular – rarely confuse their audience with complex information, which might prompt some lazy people to change the channel. For this reason, the script of a newscast is generally written with the assumption that viewers comprehend at a sixth-grade level. To fit this format, your message needs to be simple, clear and easily understood.

This quotation dramatically illustrates just how much Greenpeace has taken on board the constraints of the television form. Clearly, this Greenpeace activist had internalized media constraints to a point that greatly limited the kinds of messages he would attempt to communicate, specifically to the sixth-grade level. And arguments have to be more than simple: they must also be middle-of-the-road, resonating with dominant cultural understandings.

2. MEDIA-FRIENDLY

Secondly, television has helped to reshape Greenpeace's organizational goals. Reliance on the televised stunt thus feeds back on Greenpeace more broadly as an institution. The story of Greenpeace is one of a shift from concern with the broader philosophical and political roots of environmental problems to a focus on more narrowly defined goals (Eyerman and Jamison 1989). The limitations of communicating through televisual media stunts can be linked to this shift.

Greenpeace also appears to target particular environmental issues precisely because of their capacity to provide strong images for television. Not only their tactics but the choice of whole campaigns may be driven to a considerable extent by media considerations. As Eyerman and Jamison note, (1989: 106), 'the selection of which environmental issue to tackle next [is] made by the board of Greenpeace International ... the criteria used in selecting a campaign are the following: its suitability to the Greenpeace profile and its 'visibility,' i.e. connection to marine life or to 'innocent nature'; and that a campaign must appear winnable' (1989: 106). Such 'visibility' involves, in part, the potential that a campaign offers for gripping TV images.

As Cracknell suggests, 'the issues on which groups choose to campaign are undoubtedly influenced by considerations of likely coverage. This is important as it can mean that "non-sexy" and unmediagenic subjects are targeted less than those with instant media appeal, regardless of the intrinsic importance of the issues in question' (1993: 5–6). This is not to say Greenpeace always relies simply on media campaigns; for example, its long-term, world-wide effort to eliminate hydrofluorocarbons focuses to a large degree on extensive negotiations with various governments and industrial boards. However, as British environmental journalist Chris Rose describes, media considerations often seem to have shaped the campaign choices of Greenpeace:

> You've got to have the pictures, it doesn't matter what they're talking about, you've got to have the pictures ... if you can't deal with it in those terms, and their formula, they can't really campaign on it. (Anderson 1997: 126)

For instance, the Greenpeace campaign focusing on the baby harp seal hunt in Newfoundland was made for television. The power of the TV imagery of the baby seals being clubbed to death overrode opposition arguments.[14] Environmentalists who have worked to save less telegenic creatures have had more difficulty. Not surprisingly, for example, there has been little success in generating public concern over the possible extinction of the 'giant earwig of St. Helena,' a nine-inch monster insect (Yearley 1991: 46).

3. GREENPEACE'S PASSIVE PUBLIC: 'COUCH POTATO ACTIVISM'

Thirdly, reliance on televised stunts also reshapes Greenpeace's relationship with its constituency, with its members or publics. Greenpeace's reliance on media stunts executed by a small number of professional activists contrasts with earlier demonstrations and protests, which historically have depended on mobilizing large crowds. Public-order events involving such crowds are much more difficult for both police and activists to control. As well, as Ryan (1991: 106–7) argues, it is difficult to give large crowds a sympathetic, personalized appearance for television, because of the distance the television camera must maintain. Finally, the advent of TV means it is no longer necessary to assemble a large crowd to provide the audience for one's message. These various factors underlie a shift to a more tightly controlled and choreographed, ritualistic form of protest, epitomized by the actions of Greenpeace.

This shift raises questions about the limited role of 'the public' in Greenpeace's kind of activism. As Tarrow (1994) suggests, the new, television-driven social movements require a form of organization that is quite different from mass mobilization:

> The implications for movement organization [of the arrival of television] were profound: If movements could transmit their messages to millions of people across the airwaves, encouraging some to follow their example and larger numbers to take sympathetic notice of their claims, it was possible to create a movement without incurring the cost of building a mass organization. This had been true in the past with the advent of cheap newspapers. But where the press only described what movements wanted, television showed graphically how they behaved, and how their opponents responded, in a form of public spectacle that required little in the way of formal mobilizing structures. (143)

On the one hand, this is enabling for social movements, which require fewer internal resources to seize the political spotlight. Meyer and Tarrow (1998: 13) argue that television thus facilitates social movements. Yet this situation arguably has a very significant downside for movements. Tarrow (1994: chap. 6) traces a long-term trend prior to the age of television from violent direct action to nonviolent mass mobilization. Now, in the TV age, Tarrow argues, such mass mobilization is no longer required. Television communicates to vast numbers of people, but it is also a unidirectional medium – its large audience is a silent, passive one. Greenpeace epitomizes this historical shift from active to passive engagement. In Greenpeace Germany, for example, 'the great majority of registered Greenpeace supporters – that is, about 99.7 per cent – are limited to the role of spectators or regular or occasional contributors' (Rucht 1995).

Tarrow argues that the advent of this kind of television politics interacts with the increasing affluence of movement supporters to encourage passive support rather than action:

> If the spread of affluence and mass communications has given organizers
> at the summit new resources, it has also deprived movements of the
> steady participation at the base that prewar movements could count on
> through party branches and union locals. People who watch television in
> the evening and go away for long weekends are less interested in attend-
> ing meetings and marching in Sunday demonstrations than their parents
> were in the 1930s and 1940s. (1994: 146)

Greenpeace supporters fit this description: the Greenpeace public is
constituted by the organization's tactics as a dispersed group whose
political role is simply to watch demonstrations on TV and then mail in
money. An activist for another B.C. environmental organization, speaking in an interview of this drawback of televised protest, captured how
Greenpeace's reliance on television has transformed its relationship
with its publics:

> I think to a certain extent what we've done with civil disobedience unfor-
> tunately is, we've created this sort of couch potato activism where people
> sit at home and they watch the news and they see people getting arrested
> and they go, 'Oh gee, isn't that horrible' and then they turn the TV off and
> they go to bed.

Greenpeace's physically heroic stunts may also help to position the
audience as bystanders to the spectacle. As one Greenpeace staffer
stated:

> I think that seeing someone as a hero is rather disempowering ... most
> people can't really see themselves driving a Zodiac, stopping a warship,
> or something like that ... I think the majority of people put us up on a
> pedestal and say 'You're Greenpeace; you're doing the work ... It's not me;
> I can't do that.' (Carroll and Ratner, 1999: 14)

A key point is that, whether or not activists are right in viewing
public attitudes as increasingly passive, the way Greenpeace and similar organizations treat their publics make such observations a self-
fulfilling prophecy. Greenpeace sets its publics up to be passive in
practice: it simply does not provide the mobilizing structures that would

give its publics a more active role. In conceiving of its publics as passive, Greenpeace creates them as passive.

Thus, the type of media politics Greenpeace practices may be seen as inherently disempowering. Like many contemporary institutions, Greenpeace deals very much in constructing 'phantom' images of the public (Lippmann 1925, Robbins 1993) shaped for institutional use, rather than actually mobilizing its diverse audiences.

Greenpeace relies on a top-down approach with power centralized in the hands of a small number of professional experts. 'Greenpeace International is organized like a multinational corporation, with a five-man board of directors answering to a general council made up of individuals representing the seventeen national corporations ... Greenpeace has a policy of not using too many volunteers in their office work and especially not in any key positions' (Eyerman and Jamison 1989).

Greenpeace's ability to mobilize miniature environmental dramas for the media does not necessarily have to speak to the public so much as merely make politicians think it is speaking to the public. Greenpeace claims millions of 'members' – yet in practical terms an elite professional hierarchy conducts the activities of the organization. Much sociological literature on social movements concerns itself with how movements gain and keep adherents, yet, as the case of Greenpeace indicates, this may not be crucial for the achievement of movement goals. As Eyerman and Jamison suggest, 'Success is not measured in how many new converts have been added to the cause, although membership rates are very important to Greenpeace both in its lobbying work ... and in its finances' (1989: 104). The membership rate – the constructed representation of the public – becomes more important than the members themselves.

Conclusions

Former president Robert Hunter's early philosophizing suggested that a change in 'public consciousness' would be wrought by Greenpeace's media campaigns. This now seems very secondary to achieving the organization's financial and political goals. One of Greenpeace's founders, journalist Ben Metcalfe, left the organization in the 1970s and now argues it has lost much of its effectiveness. Metcalfe suggested that Greenpeace opponents, governments, and corporations have learned to accommodate the protest. They'll do something and wait for the protest and just keep doing it. The protests are accommodated like Christmas or Easter ... they're just part of the agenda. Greenpeace is now institutionalized. (Dale 1996: 84)

It is in large part because the requirements of television have fed back on Greenpeace that it has been tamed, been institutionalized. In making its central *modus operandi* televised stunts, Greenpeace has allowed its protest activities and its broader organization to be largely shaped by the needs of television. Made for TV, such protests are carefully organized and planned in advance, nonviolent, middle of the road, conducted by a little group of professionals.

Previous research suggests the news media tend to focus on the deviant action or spectacle of the demonstration rather than on the message of the protest. Greenpeace is partly, but only partly, able to overcome this problem with its bite-sized messages. My data on Greenpeace fit with earlier research suggesting that because TV has a limited capacity for complex communication, this inhibits political discourse, and in particular, critique of the status quo (Postman 1985; Herman and Chomsky 1988; Gamson and Wolfsfeld 1993). My data are less supportive of accounts suggesting a liberating potential for television, by either movement historians and theorists (Tarrow 1994; Meyer and Tarrow 1998) or communications theorists (Meyrowitz 1985). Compared to print media, TV has a limited capacity for complex messages. This is a result of the limited space and time TV has to communicate. It is also a consequence of television's ephemerality (Ericson, Baranek, and Chan 1991). Most of the time what is shown once on TV is, unlike written text, simply gone and cannot be reviewed. A further constraint on the complexity of messages stems from the way TV is consumed: by an audience who may be attending selectively rather than fully. Attempting to hold the interest of a very diverse audience who often pay attention inconsistently, and mostly in their leisure hours, TV often features a strong entertainment imperative (Altheide and Snow 1979; Postman 1985). For these reasons, in communicating through TV, Greenpeace must restrict itself to simple messages. This constrains Greenpeace's ability to bring about any substantial transformation in political consciousness.

According to Altheide and Snow (1979, 1991), 'media logic' means in part that particular phenomena in other institutions which are mass mediated will have tendencies to be more dramatic, spectacular, enter-taining, simplified, presented in the form of a story, and shaped to fit more with conventional values. The pivotal point is that such phenom-ena are not simply *portrayed* that way by the media – they also *become* that way. Media logic has fed back on and shaped the contours of the whole Greenpeace organization. Centring the organization on televi-sion, Greenpeace also chooses particular telegenic campaigns, and has reoriented itself to short-term goals that fit better with TV communica-tion, rather than aiming to bring about a long-term shift in philosophy or consciousness, as it had originally intended. Finally, I have argued that the transformation of protest due to television is a key factor shaping Greenpeace's structure of a small elite leadership and a huge passive membership.[15] Greenpeace exemplifies Altheide and Snow's point that the more dependent an institution is on media, the more likely it is that media logic will dictate its operations (Altheide and Snow 1979: 238–9). This can occur even to the point where the organiza-tion is consumed by media considerations.

CHAPTER SEVEN

Conclusions

To capture more fully the range of TV's influences, we need a new critical model of how TV influences other institutions. At the close of this chapter, I will lay out some key propositions of such a model, from which we may generalize to various other situations of media influence.

One key point that I have been developing throughout this book is that too many of us, both social scientists and everyday people, too easily assume that TV is largely a visual medium. We need to think of TV somewhat less as visual and to focus somewhat more on its properties as an oral or verbal medium, on the interaction between the words and images, and on the defining force of the words. In my studies, the most powerful players have tended to assume the key role of providing the verbal scripting of TV's images.

Marshall McLuhan once drew attention to TV's neglected properties as an oral medium (although he saw their consequences very differently: see McLuhan 1964; Silverstone 1988). Medium theory, which Joshua Meyrowitz built on the work of McLuhan, Innis, and others, offers numerous other suggestive insights. It opens up new lines of investigation as it moves us beyond a narrow focus on media effects on individual audience members. However, medium theory needs to take more account of the social contexts in which media operate, and the power differentials in those contexts. It needs to be resituated in a more critical vein.[1] In the cases I have studied, rather than having a liberating effect (Meyrowitz 1985), TV most often has the opposite kinds of impacts. TV has a range of influences beyond simply helping to shape the beliefs and attitudes of individual audience members. Yet in my four studies, TV largely helped reproduce the established institutional order and often strengthened the position of those who already hold the upper hand.

My four studies have shown that these newly televised situations are altered in fundamental ways by 'media logic' (Altheide and Snow 1991), the conception that most fully captures the range and diversity of media influences. However, powerful source institutions, like the police, usually control the nature and form of such influences (Ericson, Baranek, and Chan 1989). TV does change things, but in ways tailored by police and similar dominant players. The medium is thus not simply the message.

What I found thus fits with some key aspects of both the media logic and the institutional perspectives. These two perspectives need to be synthesized. I will quickly summarize the answers to each of the research questions I posed in Chapter 2, and how they led me to these conclusions. I will finish by briefly outlining what I see as key points of a new, synthesized model that accounts for the influences of television I have found.

First I will talk about the factors that shape what is televised and how it is presented, or packaged interpretively. Discerning these factors is key to explaining how these situations are altered as they are televised. Whoever controls what TV shows largely controls TV's influences on other institutions.

To what extent does TV 'make visible' new social situations or reveal secret back region information from them?

Meyrowitz's medium theory (1985) suggested that television 'made visible,' 'exposed,' or 'revealed' social situations that it broadcast. TV let viewers into newly seen 'back regions' to view 'back stage behaviour.' However, the general tendency across my four studies was that police most often controlled which criminal justice situations were broadcast. This was not always the case: I have also explored the televising of a couple of potentially dangerous situations that police might well have preferred to keep shrouded in the back regions.

My studies show that, even when thinking about the changes introduced by TV, we need to return to Goffman's (1959) original use of the terms 'front regions' and 'back regions' to describe different *physical* spaces (Ericson, Baranek, and Chan 1989). Police are somewhat vulnerable to having their behaviour broadcast in public locations, such as the roadside where the Rodney King beating occurred or the downtown streets that featured the Stanley Cup riot. In more private locations – for example, the police cruisers where much *Cops* footage is recorded – police still maintain almost complete control over what is made visible by TV.

In *No Sense of Place*, Meyrowitz (1985) argued that electronic media, especially TV, diminish hierarchy based on spatial relations – that because of TV, people are no longer are kept in their 'place.' However, police are still able to keep many physical locations (for example, in buildings or police cars) as private back regions, concealed from TV or open to TV only on police terms. The fact is most often police maintain control by keeping the media and others in their place, both literally and metaphorically.[2]

What biases might there be in the social information conveyed by TV, and why?

Even when TV is allowed to broadcast selected criminal justice situations, these situations are not simply 'made visible' or 'unveiled.' My case studies show that TV does not simply reveal social information from these settings. Although TV broadcasts new situations, the biases described by much previous research[3] still remain: biases in how these situations are presented or packaged, biases towards official sources like police.

One key form of power is the ability to define a situation so that others act on that definition as reality (Altheide and Snow 1991: 4). The definition of these criminal justice situations is not self-evident, even if they are recorded directly by cameras. Instead their meaning is negotiated between the key players: television journalists, police, criminal suspects, and TV audiences. This is an interaction in which power relations are usually unequal. Police most often give the authorized definition to these televised situations. Of course, audiences may subvert this definition and make their own sense of what is televised (Fiske 1987). Yet the authorized definition is the one that carries the most force: it is the definition that is actually presented on TV, and the definition that carries the official stamp of the police. Police define the situation for those in front of the TV set, but also for those in front of the camera. Indeed, it is the authorized definition of police that actually constitutes particular televised behaviour as criminal.

What role does the broader cultural context play in television's influences?

My four studies reveal a third factor that limits any potential liberating, levelling, or democratizing influence of TV. This third factor is the broader cultural context. The new information systems created by television on the front lines of criminal justice are not solitary entities, isolated from this broader culture. Instead, these new information systems derive their meanings in part from interaction with the wider culture, which provides the symbolic resources audiences use to make sense of these glimpses into the world of criminal justice. People draw on their pre-existing understandings of crime and its control. Of course, audiences give their own interpretations to what they see on TV, but the cultural context will be a key influence on these interpretations. The wider culture also influences TV production, for example, by shaping the choices producers make in deciding what videotaped activity constitutes a 'story' for *Cops*, and how such a story is packaged interpretively. This broader cultural context has many diverse currents, but more often than not it tends to support what I have called the ideology of law and order (see also Scheingold 1984, 1995). To give one example, with the Stanley Cup riot, the authorized version of events that emerged meshed with dominant cultural understandings of criminal justice, understandings in which such a riot must have been caused by 'punks'; in this way of thinking, police are the solution, never part of the problem.

The studies in this book show how the new cultural logic of mass media interacts with older, more deeply rooted cultural understandings or templates about crime and punishment (Sparks 1992). In the situations I have studied, television tells crime stories in new forms and using new technologies. However, these are often the same old stories, following enduring cultural scripts that were around long before the advent of TV and contemporary media culture.

How much do the formal properties of television as a medium have a liberating influence? To what extent do they tend to reproduce the status quo?

After thinking about my case studies for a long time, I observed that another factor also seems to be at work in reproducing the status quo: the properties of television itself as a medium. Meyrowitz (1985) argued that the formal properties of TV tend to reduce inequality, because TV is more capable than print of revealing new types of social information to wide audiences in ways that reduce social distance. My studies have led me to the opposite conclusions. TV as a medium actually has particular properties that make it more prone than other media to support and strengthen existing power relations.

My case studies demonstrate that Meyrowitz, like many other people, exaggerates the importance of the visual aspect of television in determining the meanings of what is broadcast, for example, by his analogies with a 'one-way mirror,' 'lifting a veil,' and 'peeking behind a curtain.'[4] In my case studies, TV is clearly not dominated so much by its visual component. TV does not simply provide the audience with windows into criminal justice. What is revealed instead is more often what the most powerful players in each situation want us to believe we are seeing. One of the key reasons is that these players often provide the dominant verbal interpretation of the visual material. Television's images certainly have a force. Yet these TV images most often rely to varying degrees on verbal interpretation for their meanings. The words are often more important than the visuals.

For practical reasons as well, when TV producers broadcast video footage of 'real' events, they must rely heavily on oral interpretation of the footage. Producers must make the best of whatever visuals are available, regardless of their quality. Real footage of crime and policing incidents in particular presents practical obstacles to record – it is often of quickly unfolding, chaotic incidents recorded in difficult locations, further limiting the quality of available visuals. This makes such TV footage even more reliant on accompanying oral interpretation.

Countless social scientific and popular understandings of TV heavily emphasize its visual aspect. This emphasis on the visual is even shown in the word 'television' itself, and the fact that TV is commonly understood as something we 'watch' as 'viewers.' However, particularly in my first three case studies, I have found that it is very often largely the words, not the pictures, which give meaning to these various televised events. Rather than revealing the 'truth' of these situations, the fact that there is an actual TV record of the events often serves instead simply to give added legitimacy and force to the chosen verbal account of the most influential players.

Thus, the most important formal property of TV is not its ability to provide audiences with new types of social information. Instead, the most important formal property of television may be its ability, compared to other media, to make more forceful truth claims. In these studies, TV does not have greater ability than other media to let viewers see the 'truth' of institutional life; TV instead has greater power to validate the ideological stories it tells about what happens in other institutions.

Different forms of media like TV have different epistemologies linked with them. Television often relies on the particular epistemology that 'seeing is believing.' Thus, for example, the anchor of television's news magazine *Inside Edition* (5 June 1999) described the video camera as 'the truth machine' and stated, 'It never lies.'

Why can television make such potent truth claims? Through its presentation of visual material, TV invokes a strong tendency in Western culture to understand that 'seeing is believing' (Fetveit 1999). 'Who are you going to believe?' went an old line from comedian Richard Pryor. 'Me or your own lying eyes?' The ironic intent of course relies on the supposedly evident point that, while Pryor presented himself as a fast-talking rogue who would in fact lie to us, our eyes, of course, could not.

This cultural notion that 'seeing is believing' is so ingrained as to be present in the roots, or etymology, of our language, for example in the word 'evidence.' This tendency may be tied in large part to a strong Western bias towards an objectivist notion of truth as something 'out there' in the material world that can be captured through sense evidence, rather than truth as being fundamentally shaped by words and language which are heard.

This Western cultural tendency to rely on the visual for evidence was reinforced by the development of still photography and then video, technologies that were purported to offer an indexical relation to the real. In these technologies, the truth-telling power of visual evidence was paired with the truth-telling power of science. For example, when photography was first developed, it was conceived partly as a tool with both scientific and legal evidentiary uses (Fetveit 1999: 789–90).

Because we think 'seeing is believing,' TV tends to validate the words of those who hold the upper hand. The widely held understanding that 'seeing is believing' might even lead some to think that TV displays a relatively unmediated 'reality.' Consider the notion of 'reality TV' itself, and that the promoters of *Cops* can conceivably sell claims that such TV programs represent 'raw reality' or 'unfiltered reality.' It is difficult to imagine a parallel 'reality book.' Similarly, TV news has greater powers of validation than does radio or newspapers (Ericson, Baranek, and Chan 1991: 23). These increased powers of validation account for the consistent research finding that TV is the most trusted and relied-on source of news, in comparison with print media and radio (Ericson

1991: 24). Ericson, Baranek, and Chan suggest that TV news derives these powers of validation from its ability to present sources making their statements directly to the camera in social contexts that convey those sources' authority. Situations where TV actually records the events in question offer it even greater powers of validation, because they show 'the real thing.'[5] TV is the most trusted news medium because seeing is believing.

Thus, we should invert the meaning of the quotation above from the anchor on *Inside Edition*. TV might indeed be termed the 'truth machine,' but this is not because, as he put it, TV 'never lies.' It is because TV, more strongly than other media, *seems* to be presenting the truth.

I am certainly not claiming that the verbal component is all-important in determining TV's meanings. Words and images interact, and vary in importance in each situation. What I am arguing is that the balance needs to be shifted somewhat: TV is simply not as much a medium dominated by visuals as many suggest.

If TV's powers of truth telling or validation help reproduce established power relations, other formal properties of TV as a medium also have this influence. My data on Greenpeace fit with earlier research suggesting that TV's limited capacity for complex communication inhibits political discourse, and in particular critique of the status quo (Postman 1985; Herman and Chomsky 1988; Gamson and Wolfsfeld 1993; Gitlin 2002).

With the above arguments in mind, I will move on to discuss the question: How does television influence the situations in front of the camera, and, more broadly, the institutions it records? Clearly, TV does indeed alter or reconstitute these four types of criminal justice situations when they are broadcast, essentially creating new social situations. Furthermore, in doing so, television has various broader ripple effects on the institutions studied.

How much does televising these situations have a liberating effect?

I have outlined four factors that, together, mean that TV does not simply expose or reveal these situations, but instead tends to give ideological visions of them that support the established order. These four factors tend greatly to limit the levelling or liberating effects predicted by medium theory, although such effects may still occur in certain instances. There are some examples that do support Meyrowitz's arguments, such as the reported increase in police brutality complaints following the Rodney King incident, or the move to gentler protest policing tactics with some kinds of protesters.

If *Cops* offered a more rounded portrait of front-line police behaviour – if it did reveal 'back stage behaviour' that police wished to keep secret – it might lead police to modify their behaviour. Instead, it selects and presents its 'real' footage to portray crime and policing in ways that legitimate the status quo. Similarly, the televising of surveillance footage and home video footage of crime will tend mostly to reproduce established power relations. It probably does not help create social levelling, or what celebrants of the home video camera called, optimistically, 'video democracy.' Home video is a limited tool in comparison to the expansion of police power that comes with the surveillance camera. My study of the Stanley Cup riot shows that with more marginal, less organized, and less powerful groups of rioters, police can still crack down hard and get away with it, despite the presence of news cameras. The story of violent police suppression of a crowd can sometimes be retrospectively silenced, even if the whole thing is recorded on television.

How might TV audiences apply new pressure for reform in these situations?

TV creates new social situations on the front lines of criminal justice by involving the TV audience in them. TV audiences become not just spectators but players in the situations now broadcast to them. For example, audiences can identify criminal suspects shown in video wanted posters, submit their own home videos of criminal justice situations, participate in public enquiries into a televised event like the Stanley Cup riot, or, after watching protests on TV, support the law-breaking environmental activism by joining Greenpeace and sending in money.

Yet involving audiences in these ways does not seem to produce political pressure for equality. This is because audiences become involved largely through institutional mechanisms and channels. The key institutional players define audiences' roles, and this highly constrains these roles. This is partly because TV is a one-way medium: watching TV does not itself create a vehicle for active involvement,[6] and so audiences tend to wind up being used by powerful institutions in ways that reproduce the status quo. For example, Chapters 4 and 5 show how TV creates new ways that audiences can be used in surveillance of each other, expanding police surveillance power. The Stanley

Cup riot reviews I discussed in Chapter 4 were swathed in rhetoric about the importance of the 'public' and the 'community.' However, public input into the review process was structured in a way that preordained the desired outcome for police and their political allies. When the public account that emerged was not the desired one, as in Dr. Rulka's questioning of the official story, the public voice was quickly stifled. The fact that TV audiences saw the whole thing made little difference.

Ironically, as the example of Greenpeace reveals, even purported resistance to authority, occurs in ways that actually reproduce institutional authority rather than empowering the TV audience. Chapter 6 shows how reliance on television means Greenpeace constitutes its membership, its public, as passive: instead of a protesting crowd, Greenpeace members remain a TV audience of 'couch potato activists.'

The passive television public constituted by Greenpeace's form of activism is analogous to that which emerged in earlier studies: an audience that may be stirred by watching its criminal justice passion play, but is only able to act in narrow and preselected ways through authorized institutional channels.

To sum up, my studies have found a number of limitations to arguments about the liberating potential of TV. Now I will move on to consider the media logic perspective.

How do the activities of the televised institutions come to be shaped by media logic?

When TV broadcasts situations from the front lines of criminal justice, new types of influence are revealed. Televising these situations affects day-to-day practices of criminal justice. TV singles out particular cases as important or 'bigger than life' for the justice system, and the system treats them as such. Televising these situations promotes dramatic, spectacular, simplistic approaches to criminal justice. These kinds of influences are accounted for best by the media logic perspective (Altheide and Snow 1979). Even so, these influences seem largely to take forms, and occur within parameters, set by police.

Through *Cops* and numerous similar programs and initiatives, television feeds into the day-to-day practices of policing. Policing is converted into informal media shaming rituals. Television considerations not only shape the situations before the cameras, but feed back in broader ways into the source institutions I have examined. For example, police-in-training learn from watching *Cops*. 'Video wanted posters' extend police surveillance capability but also spectacularize crime. This may intensify the formal criminal justice process. Media logic influences not only police but prosecutors, judges, and policy makers, promoting dramatic, spectacular, sometimes simplistic forms of criminal justice: media shaming rituals by police like the 'perp walk' (Doyle and Ericson 1996), more vigourous prosecution (Young 1996), spectacular sentences tailored for the media (Altheide 1995), and media-friendly crime policies such as 'three strikes, you're out' (Surette 1996).

Police are often able to maintain a great deal of room to manoeuvre vis-à-vis the media, even when police behaviour is directly recorded on camera. On the other hand, Greenpeace is much more wholly a creature of the media, particularly of television. Greenpeace is the most striking example among my four case studies of how media logic can fundamentally alter organizational activity that TV broadcasts, and in doing so shape the institution itself.

What is the balance of power between media and source institutions?

Even given their great power, media have not become the dominant institution. Police create their own new uses of television for their own purposes, such as the development of video wanted posters or the alternative uses of television made after the Stanley Cup riot. In these cases, it probably makes more sense to speak of television being shaped by 'police logic,' rather than vice versa.

This finding is most consistent with the institutional perspective of Ericson, Baranek, and Chan (1989). Television as a technology, or the influences of media culture more broadly, do not in isolation cause changes in policing and criminal justice, or in other institutions. Police often use broadcast TV to their own ends, centrally as a means of legitimation, but also for other institutional purposes (for example, to assist in identifying and criminalizing suspects). In the case of the Stanley Cup riot, television was even constructed itself as a convenient scapegoat, as blame was deflected from police after they came under fire for heavy-handed crowd policing. In most cases where TV threatens to alter the situation in ways the police do not want, sooner or later police manage to gain control of TV's influences. Police exert control in part through various mechanisms of censoring or of controlling the definition of the situation in the televised account. Alternatively, the status quo is maintained as police simply accommodate – making small adjustments or going along when it costs them relatively little to do so (the softening of crowd police tactics in some circumstances; playing along with Greenpeace media stunts). In short, the introduction of TV does reshape these criminal justice situations – but largely in ways controlled and managed by police.

Do situations directly before the cameras create more vulnerability for police?

Research on the sociology of the news media has long demonstrated the dominance of police over media influences (e.g., Davis 1951; Chibnall 1977; Hall et al. 1978; Fishman 1978, 1980, 1981; Ericson, Baranek, and Chan 1989; Schlesinger and Tumber 1994; Sacco 1995). My research extends this previous work to new contexts involving TV news and reality television. My studies show how police dominate in new ways, not only managing media messages, but mostly controlling how media considerations feed back into the practice of criminal justice itself. Ironically, in these situations where policing is recorded directly, police sometimes are even less vulnerable.

A central aspect of the dominance of key source institutions like police is the power of such institutions and their players to provide the authorized definition of what is televised. This fits with the arguments of Hall et al. (1978), who conceived key news sources like police as 'primary definers,' or those of Ericson, Baranek, and Chan (1989), who conceived institutional news sources as 'authorized knowers.' However, these ways of thinking about the definitional role of official sources need to be extended, to include how official definitions shape the situation in front of the camera. Indeed, the power to provide the authorized definition of the televised situation is the power largely to shape and control all of the institutional influences of television.

A New Model of How Television Influences Other Institutions

Building on this previous work, I can outline some key propositions of a new, synthesized model of how television influences other institutions as it broadcasts their operations. I have focused on situations where television broadcasts crime and policing directly, but these propositions might be extended to a variety of other contexts.

My four case studies have provided substantial evidence supporting each of the following propositions:

1 When television broadcasts situations in other institutions, it re-shapes or reconstitutes them. The presence of television introduces audiences into the social situations, but also changes the meaning of the situations for the various institutional players, thereby altering the experience and behaviour of these players.

2 When television broadcasts front-line situations in institutions, this feeds back into those institutions, resulting in wider changes beyond the front lines.

3 These changes include the institution's becoming more pro-active with the news media and restricting or concealing particular operations. Particular institutional phenomena that are televised will also tend to become more important, tightly managed, dramatic, spectacular, and simplified; to occur in narrative form; and to be shaped to fit more with conventional or dominant values.[7]

4 The more dependent an institution is on television audience support, the more broadly TV reshapes that institution as it televises it.

5 When television records a situation directly, it will be reshaped more fundamentally in the ways stated than if media report on the situation indirectly.

6 Even though television creates new social situations and reshapes institutions more broadly as it televises them, the various changes that result tend simply to reproduce existing power relations, for the following reasons:

- The more powerful players tend to dictate which institutional situations are broadcast.
- The more powerful players tend to be able to produce the authorized definition of the broadcast situations.
- Through its power to invoke the notion that seeing is believing, the medium of TV is uniquely effective at warranting and naturalizing the authorized definition of a situation put forth by the more powerful players.
- The meanings of particular institutional episodes that are broadcast are produced and understood in the context of a broader culture that tends to support the established order.
- Television interacts with other institutions to create new institutional roles for audiences, as they become part of the social situations that are broadcast. However, these institutionally created roles tend to limit the TV audiences to types of involvement that simply reproduce institutional power.
- The more powerful players have more ability to introduce various

changes in institutional practices made possible by TV that are beneficial to those players and reproduce or strengthen their power.
* The more powerful players have greater ability to adapt their operations to avoid negative publicity without substantial harm to themselves, or simply to withstand negative publicity.

We need to move beyond a narrow understanding of media influence as simply affecting the attitudes, beliefs, and behaviour of individual audience members. In the first instance, these propositions I have just outlined apply to situations in which television broadcasts life in other institutions. Our media landscape constantly evolves, and television in its current form is already in the process of being superseded. Yet only in hindsight may we realize just how important TV has been in shaping our society over the last fifty years. As we look forward, I hope the ways of thinking about TV I have suggested here may be extended in various ways to help us understand how media shape institutional life more generally, and how we must be wary that the most powerful players in any context tend to shape the forms this media influence takes.

CHAPTER EIGHT

Postscript: Television and Theorizing the Evolution of Criminal Justice

All this raises important further questions. My case studies have shown that, in recording situations on the front lines of criminal justice, television has wider effects on criminal justice institutions. I began analyzing these effects in order to think about television's influences. But we should also think about its theoretical implications concerning criminal justice. This leads us to another body of theory, one I have not so far touched on very much, one that looks at the nature of contemporary criminal justice and how it came to be. Because television reshapes institutional practices, we need to think about TV when theorizing how criminal justice institutions have evolved. In telling the history of criminal justice, we may need to be a little more sensitive to the historical role of television.

Theorizing a Schism in Contemporary Criminal Justice

Let us first consider the analysis of David Garland (2000, 2001). Garland suggests that a kind of schism or bifurcation has developed in modes of contemporary criminal justice. He argues that in the justice systems of Western democracies (using the examples of the United States and Britain) there are currently two ways of thinking about crime control, and correspondingly, two quite different types of strategies for dealing with crime: on the one hand, a collection of dispassionate, preventive, technical, and managerial strategies (see also Feeley and Simon 1994), and, on the other hand, a set of more expressive, emotionally charged, retributive, vengeance-oriented responses to crime. The latter way of thinking about crime that Garland identifies as an alternative, conflicting current in contemporary Western criminal justice, fits very well with what I described in Chapter 3 as 'law-and-order ideology.'

Garland argues that the punitive public sentiments that fuel this retributive form of criminal justice are especially strong now in Britain and the United States for various historically specific reasons (2000: 11). These reasons include the current media situation and particularly the rise of television:

> Television viewing emerged as a mass phenomenon at much the same time that high crime rates began to become a normal social fact i.e. between about 1950 and 1970. TV's ... affinity for crime as a theme, its sympathetic portrayal of individual victims who have suffered at the hands of criminals and been let down by an uncaring system, have transformed perceptions of crime and further reduced the sense of distance from the problem that the middle classes once enjoyed ... This is not to say that the media has *produced* our interest in crime, nor that it has *produced* the popular punitiveness that appears as such a strong political current today ... My point is rather that the mass media has tapped into, then dramatized and reinforced a new public experience – an experience with profound psychological resonance – and in doing so it has institutionalized that experience. [TV] has surrounded us with images of crime, pursuit and punishment, and provided us with regular, everyday occasions in which to express and play out the emotions of fear, anger and resentment and fascination that crime provokes ... Public knowledge and opinion about criminal justice are based upon collective representations rather than accurate information; upon a culturally given experience of crime rather than the thing itself. (28–30)

Garland thus emphasizes how television has contributed to this schism in criminal justice by fostering more punitive public attitudes towards crime. In effect, he suggests that television promotes ways of thinking about crime by the public that fit with law-and-order ideology. Indeed, three of my case studies offer good examples of TV representations of crime that might well fuel such public punitiveness.

However, I am more concerned with another type of television influence: on criminal justice institutions. I argue that television has contributed to this alternative, more expressive mode in contemporary criminal justice, not just by influencing individual audience members, but also by directly influencing the justice system in a variety of other ways. Thus, TV's role in promoting the schism in criminal justice Garland describes goes far beyond affecting public views of crime.

These alternative, more vengeance-oriented currents within contemporary criminal justice are reflected in some increasingly punitive formal policies (Scheingold 1995; Garland 1996). In the United States, for example, these policies have included 'three strikes, you're out' legislation, boot camps, the rebirth of chain gangs, and the renewed rise of capital punishment. Surette (1996) analyses how media coverage of the murder of a young girl, Polly Klaas, was instrumental in kick-starting a campaign to support 'three strikes' in California in 1993 and 1994. As Surette wrote: 'In an electronic-dominated, visual media society, the massive emotional coverage of heinous crimes overwhelms any analytical coverage' (1996: 198).

But this is not a simple case of television influencing the public who in turn influence criminal justice policy. The news media play an important role in promoting these kinds of policies by creating direct political pressure on politicians and policy makers (Roberts 1992; Surette 1997). In fact, as Surette notes, 'the public is frequently excluded from the process' (1996: 181). With the 'three strikes' legislation there was public pressure for the new law, but this arose only after the Klaas case became a media spectacle, and after electronic media commentators began promoting 'three strikes' specifically as the appropriate response to the Klaas case, putting a good deal of direct pressure on state politicians. David Altheide (1995) describes another type of direct media influence on the justice system, what he calls 'gonzo justice' in the criminal courts, spectacular criminal sentences apparently aimed at getting media attention.

I want to add to these earlier accounts by pointing out that the television culture of crime also feeds back into the day-to-day practices of criminal justice in smaller, more individualized ways. The influences of television both intensify the formal prosecution of individual cases (see the examples in Chapter 4) and affect informal practices in the justice system. Examples of the latter include the unofficial shaming rituals on *Cops* discussed in Chapter 3, and the 'perp walk,' a similar media shaming ritual in which police parade suspects in handcuffs so they can be recorded by news cameras (Doyle and Ericson 1996).

Television and other media do not simply influence the public's views of criminal justice, but feed into the system at numerous points, influencing policy makers, prosecutors, sentencing judges, and frontline police. Media considerations even help shape the operations of organizations that collect crime statistics (Haggerty 2002). And these punitive tendencies fueled by TV and other media in turn feed back into the public culture, further strengthening the element of punitiveness in the wider culture and widening the schism described by Garland (2000, 2001).

Theorizing Spectacle and Surveillance

A second, analogous way of thinking about a split between different modes of criminal justice has been in terms of 'spectacle' and 'surveillance.' Students of the evolution of criminal justice – and social control more broadly – have described a long-term historical shift from 'spectacle' to 'surveillance' as the predominant mechanism of control (Foucault 1977).

In *Discipline and Punish* (1977) Michel Foucault posited that the rise of the modern prison marked a shift from 'spectacle' to 'surveillance.' This shift in predominant mode of control, he thought, began in the early nineteenth century. Prior to this, the predominant mode was the spectacular exercise of 'sovereign power,' in rituals of public punishment and torture directed against the body of the criminal (for example, public hangings). Foucault argued that sovereign power was displaced by a new type of control exemplified by the prison. Foucault famously adopted the metaphor of Jeremy Bentham's proposed Panopticon, an imagined building in which one individual at a central viewpoint might watch many prisoners, each in a different cell, while the prisoners never knew at any time whether they were being watched. For Foucault, the prison was the archetype of modern 'Panoptical' institutions that enable surveillance. Thus, according to Foucault, there was a move from spectacles of criminal justice in which the 'many' saw the 'few,' to surveillance in which the 'few' saw the 'many.' Thus, Foucault concluded, 'our society is not one of spectacle, but of surveillance' (1977: 217).[1]

It is clear that this tendency towards surveillance as a mode of control has been dramatically enhanced in contemporary society (Marx 1988; Dandeker 1990; Staples 1997; Norris and Armstrong 1999). Describing this shift from spectacle to surveillance, and the massive expansion of surveillance, other authors see a move from a highly passionately charged mode of control to a more dispassionate, technical, and instrumental one, a shift from moral outrage to a more utilitarian morality (Shearing and Stenning 1984; Lyon 1993; Feeley and Simon 1994).

In some very broad ways, spectacle and surveillance as modes of control are analogous to the two ways of thinking described by Garland, one of which is spectacular and vengeful and the other, secretive, technical, and instrumental.[1] The Foucauldian account, however, takes a longer term historical view, in which spectacle is superseded by surveillance. Can the history of social control thus be told broadly as a transition from spectacle to surveillance? A number of authors argue against this narrative. They say that the analyses of Foucault and others neglect the persistence of somewhat similar spectacles of punishment in contemporary society. For example, in critiquing the Foucauldian account, Thomas Mathiesen (1997) sets up an opposition between Foucauldian Panopticism – in which 'the few see the many' – and what Mathiesen calls 'Synopticism,' in which 'the many see the few.' Mathiesen argues that Foucault neglects the persistence of Synopticism: Foucault ignores how spectacles persist in contemporary society as a complement to the kind of control in which 'the few see the many.' (For similar arguments about the persistence of spectacle, see Garland 1990: 61, 163; Hatty 1991; Ericson, Baranek, and Chan 1991: 107; Shearing 1992: 428; Sparks 1992: 134; Thompson 1994: 42-3; Garland 1996; Donovan 1998). These alternative accounts that describe the persistence of spectacle fit more closely in a broad way with Garland's analysis of two competing approaches still current in criminal justice, rather than the displacement of one by the other.

The nature of the periodization Foucault actually intended in his account is somewhat unclear, and ultimately beside the point. Regarding interpretation of Foucault's work, Garland argues, 'there is no phased historical progression from "sovereign punishment" to "discipline" ... nor is there an easy or coherent relationship between these different conceptions and practices of crime control. In any concrete conjuncture the field of crime control will manifest an uneven ... combination of these modes of action' (1997: 188). In short, according to Garland, subsequent interpreters of Foucault have read too much periodization into his work. However, whether this neglect of contemporary spectacles of control is attributable to Foucault himself or a fault introduced by his legion of interpreters is moot, ultimately irrelevant. The question is: How we are to take into account the persistence in contemporary society of spectacles of criminal justice that are at least somewhat similar to those back in the eighteenth century? Clearly, a shift has occurred in the profile of *formal* penal practices, which are now largely invisible to the public (Garland 1990). However, one might argue that spectacular power, rather than disappearing, has simply shifted in form and location. Spectacle remains present in contemporary modes of control, but is much less focused on the formal administration of punishment. Thus, in *Wayward Puritans* (1966), Kai Erikson wrote that the contemporary news media 'offer much the same kind of entertainment as public hangings ... A considerable portion of what we call "news" is devoted to reports about deviant behaviour and its consequences' (1966: 12).

A second problem concerns how we theorize exactly what 'surveillance' means in contemporary society. As a number of analysts point out, surveillance is expanding, yet it also seems to be shifting qualitatively. In a second way, these qualitative shifts again lead us to rethink the relationship of surveillance to spectacle.

Surveillance is certainly a central part of the contemporary institutional order (Giddens 1985, 1990), but it is neither the sole nor the defining part. Surveillance and spectacle in contemporary criminal justice have been transformed in part because of the advent of broadcast television. An analogous kind of spectacular power continues, but it is now sometimes intertwined with surveillance in complex ways, so that these two forms of control sometimes converge rather than exist in opposition.

Foucault's neglect of contemporary spectacles of control derives in part from the empirical focus of his analysis: the rise of the modern prison, in which punishment was increasingly made private and invisible. However, another crucial shift took place in Western criminal justice systems around the same time: the birth of the modern police institution. The police have always been a much more public and visible institution than the prison. (See Doyle and Ericson, 1996, for a detailed examination of contrasting attitudes to publicity in these different institutions.) As Garland (1990) has observed, the locus of publicity in the criminal justice system has moved since the eighteenth century from the formal administration of punishment to earlier in the criminal justice process. Ian Loader (1997) argues that sociologists have neglected the broader cultural and communicative aspects of the police institution. For example, the RCMP are a central symbol in Canadian culture (Walden 1982).

As opposed to the dramatization of pre-modern sovereign power described by Foucault (1977), however, police came to symbolize a new kind of power and authority. If spectacle persists in criminal justice, it is now much more the property of the police as well as occurring in the courts; the connection between spectacle and the formal administration of punishment has been severed. As policing and broadcast television come together, spectacle becomes bound up with surveillance. The interaction of surveillance cameras and home camcorders with broadcast TV discussed in the fourth chapter, or the use of TV news footage broadcast to identify rioters described in the fifth, marks not just an expansion of surveillance, but a new kind of surveillance, one that is qualitatively different in significant respects. Previous research has argued that the widespread introduction of surveillance cameras or CCTV may be seen as part of a broad trend towards dispassionate, managerial, technical approaches to crime (Feeley and Simon 1994; Norris and Armstrong 1998; McCahill 1998). More generally, David Lyon (1993) argues that the advent of contemporary electronic surveillance marks a shift to an increasingly rational, dispassionate, instrumental mode of social control.

There has, however, been little scholarly attention to the secondary role of surveillance cameras described in Chapter 4: that of spectacularizing criminal justice through the media. In this situation, the cameras also facilitate a very different form of criminal justice. Their stark visuals add emotional or visceral impact to the media spectacularization of certain crimes. These visuals are anything but dispassionate, rational, and technical when broadcast to audiences in their living rooms. Indeed, police often release footage from surveillance cameras to television as 'promotional footage' even when it serves no rational crime-fighting goal. As Alison Young (1996) describes, the highly passionate and morally charged atmosphere surrounding the Bulger case in Britain, culminating in a massive public call for harsher punishment for the ten-year-old perpetrators, was partly a consequence of the repeated TV broadcast of surveillance camera images. 'Mrs. Bulger's panicked flight from the shop, as she realized her son was gone, was recorded on the security cameras and replayed over and over, on the television news, before and after her son had been found, and then to the jury at the trial' (Young 1996: 118). This use of footage is clearly at odds with the notion that the cameras are simply part of an emerging form of control that is instrumental, technicist, and dispassionate. This type of surveillance is also a spectacle, a media spectacle that fits with the alternative tendency described by Garland towards emotionally charged, retributive criminal justice.

As Pamela Donovan argues, 'The relationship between surveillance and spectacle, 20 years after Foucault's book [*Discipline and Punish*], seems no longer one of competing images or supersession, but mutual dependence. Specifically, the surveillance and spectacle aspects of [reality TV] programming share a technological, ideological and emotional foundation' (1998: 119). Certainly, surveillance is often invisible rather than spectacular, and there are myriad forms of secret surveillance. But surveillance can also now become public spectacle as it occurs through broadcast television, as we saw in Chapters 3 and 4.

The examples in my case studies raise other questions about the properties of surveillance. Some analysts (e.g., Hatty 1991; Thompson 1994; Mathiesen 1997) read Foucault (1977) as describing a shift from a situation in which 'the many see the few' to one in which 'the few see the many.' However, whether or not the notion of surveillance can be captured by the idea that the 'few' see the 'many' is highly debatable. In fact, the Panoptical metaphor did not imply that the few were even actually watching the many. It simply conveyed that the many did not know whether or not they were being watched, and understood they might be watched at any time. In this way, Foucault's use of the Panopticon metaphor thus suggests surveillance was something that was built into a system rather than being conducted by individuals. Indeed, in contemporary surveillance, most often there are no few capable of monitoring the many. It is impossible for a small number of watchers to be so omniscient and all-knowing. Surveillance is often embedded in systems themselves, as Foucault's original reading of the Panopticon suggests, rather than conducted by individuals. There is, however, an alternative solution to the problem of how only a few may monitor a large population: through broadcast television, the many may be enlisted to watch each other. In this situation, to paraphrase William Staples (1997), Big Brother is us.

The metaphor of the Panopticon suggests that each individual is watched in isolation. In contrast, as surveillance has become greatly elaborated as one aspect of the increasing complexification of modern social relations across time and space (Giddens 1990, 1991; McCahill 1998), surveillance has also sometimes become a more public and collective phenomenon. Old-style spectacles of punishment featured an assembled crowd of onlookers; the new forms of surveillance through broadcast TV create a new type of watching collective or public, one that greatly extends the reach of surveillance by enlisting all the knowledge of audiences to identify those whom authorities cannot.

The change has other significance. Like punishment (Garland 1990) and the police (Loader 1997), surveillance has a neglected broader cultural importance beyond its immediate instrumental function. The omnipresent symbolism of surveillance communicates to audiences about late modern life and society more broadly. Another way of looking at the Panopticon metaphor is that it shows how surveillance may centrally involve communication – surveillance is communicated to the subject, and internalized. The Panopticon, like the camera in the corner of the convenience store, doesn't just watch the public; perhaps more importantly, it communicates to them. But it communicates much more than simply that one is being watched. As technologies of surveillance pervade our society, so too do the cultural implications of surveillance (Staples 1997): that crime is everywhere; that others among us are not to be trusted, especially those who are visibly different; that technology rather than community is our safeguard; and that the answer is to surreptitiously monitor all others and report them to authorities, specifically police, who are the only ones authorized to act in order to deal with the crime problem.

The concept of surveillance uses a visual metaphor and visual language to encapsulate a variety of other activities that often do not involve literally watching the subject; instead surveillance often involves other, non-visual ways of gathering knowledge for control action. However, medium theory calls attention to the point that, with the advent of the video camera, and even more so with the broadcast of surveillance footage on television, surveillance has not only expanded its reach; it has also become more literally visual again. With this development, surveillance has also become more intertwined with spectacle, for television is a highly emotive medium (Meyrowitz 1985). Because surveillance moves back into the literally visual realm through the advent of television, it is also more emotionally and morally charged, less dispassionate and instrumental. Other authors have described contemporary surveillance as becoming increasingly instrumental, rational, and technical (e.g., Shearing and Stenning 1984; Lyon 1993). It may be that such more literally visual surveillance – and surveillance using broadcast television in particular – runs counter to this trend.

Conclusions

Like the examples I gave earlier in this chapter, televised spectacles of surveillance contribute to the schism described by Garland: alongside contemporary rational and technical approaches to crime, television influences criminal justice institutions in ways that perpetuate another, age-old, way of understanding criminal justice, one in which crime and punishment become an emotionally charged drama of vengeance. This latter way of thinking about crime fits with what I have called 'law-and-order ideology.'

Television promotes not only this way of thinking about crime by the public, as Garland suggests, but also helps push police, prosecutors, judges, and policy makers towards this mode of criminal justice. Television expands surveillance, but in ways that are qualitatively different from earlier forms and that fuel a passionately charged retributive way of thinking about criminal justice. As it operates through broadcast TV, surveillance is neither embedded in a system independent of human agency, nor a situation where the few see the many. Contemporary theories of surveillance must incorporate the novel way in which instead through broadcast TV the many watch the many, and how this combines surveillance and spectacle. We need to examine how, thanks to television's influences on criminal justice, Big Brother is becoming us.

The spread of surveillance is in part a gradual, almost invisible accretion in which surveillance technology and habits of surveillance slowly penetrate into everyday life, resulting in a 'quiet revolution' (Staples 1997: 128). On the other hand, surveillance is often also a highly visible, shared public cultural phenomenon. If, as Staples suggests, surveillance is gradually expanding through the discreet introduction of innocuous-seeming technologies and habits, consider the alternative example of the reality TV program *America's Most Wanted* (Cavender and Bond-Maupin 1993). After presenting dramatic, highly charged television re-enactments of crimes, the program's host enlists the audience's help in identifying the suspects and announces that criminals will be 'hunted down by millions of viewers.' With the involvement of broadcast television, the 'culture of surveillance' also includes such massive spectacles.

Notes

1. Introduction

1 Ericson (1991, 1994) advocates examining media influence on organizations or institutions as audiences rather than studying its influence on individual audience members. In the same way, Altheide and Snow (1979, 1991) focus on how media considerations shape other institutions. Meyrowitz (1985) is less explicitly focused on institutions, but he does incorporate into his broader theory some particular arguments concerning how TV and other electronic media reshape institutions.

2. Three Alternative Ways of Thinking about Television's Influences

1 Altheide and Snow argue that media logic is often to a great degree constitutive of current realities. Media logic is so fundamental at the micro level as to be 'folded in' to the 'daily routines and expectations of everyday life' in ways taken for granted (1991: 244). At the macro level, media logic is central to questions of historical change (1979: 245–7) as historical events take on their meanings through media logic. Altheide and Snow's work thus anticipates later efforts by others, for example, John Thompson (1990, 1994, 1995), to move the study of media to the heart of general social theory.
2 Meyrowitz used the terms 'front region' and 'back region' to talk about 'informational systems,' whereas Ericson, Baranek, and Chan retained Goffman's original sense of the term as referring to actual physical spaces.

3. Reality Television and Policing: The Case of *Cops*

1 For more analysis of how such documentaries were aesthetic ancestors to *Cops*, see Corner 1996.

2 The interplay and mutual influence between fictional representations and
the criminal justice system itself has not been given enough scholarly
attention, despite all the research on 'crime in the media.' For example,
fictional crime programs like *NYPD Blue* are very influenced by police
advisers. Conversely, as I discuss in the postscript to this work, all of these
different representations in public culture feed back into the criminal justice
system itself in various ways, so it could be said that even fictional representations influence the justice system. As Oscar Wilde observed, life
imitates art.

5. Television and the Policing of Vancouver's Stanley Cup Riot

1 For example, the role of the media is largely neglected in the literature on
protest policing (e.g., Della Porta and Reiter 1998a). Similarly, the research
literature on social movements and the media tends to ignore the police-
movement interaction. Peter Waddington (1994: chap. 1) argues more
broadly that social movement theory has neglected the influence of policing
on movements.
2 Most of the research literature cited here on 'public-order policing' (i.e.,
crowd policing) focuses on political demonstrations or political riots, as
opposed to riots in other contexts, such as those associated with sports
events. One factor enabling less coercive approaches in these situations
is the opportunity for 'negotiated management' (P. Waddington 1994)
through dealings with protest organizers, an opportunity that is not available with sports riots, which are more spontaneous. In other ways, however,
sports riots are very similar to disorderly political protests. Certainly, in
each case, police face a choice about the degree to which they will use
violence to control a crowd, and thus television cameras might be a restraining influence in both contexts.
3 These included not only changes in crowd-policing methods, but also 'a
reorientation of police thinking on a wide front' (Reiner 2000: 205), involving, for example, introduction of a multiagency approach that diffused
responsibility from police, and adoption of new corporate management
techniques.
4 One exception is an analysis by Masterman (1985) of footage of a violent
conflict between police and striking coalminers. Masterman is critical of one
British television news outlet for not airing images of a policeman beating
a miner on the head with a truncheon, when the program did show the
immediate retaliatory attack on police by another miner. Masterman criti-
cizes another television news outlet even though the second outlet did

actually air the very footage in question, of the policeman clubbing the miner. The other TV outlet is also criticized by Masterman because this footage of the police attack was 'not accompanied by spoken commentary, as if the reporter was reluctant to condemn such action' (see D. Waddington 1992: 170). Of course, a journalist cannot simply 'condemn' police actions in any footage, as Masterman called for; this would run afoul of journalistic canons of objectivity. Here again the premise seems to be that it is the words, not the images, that are central to understanding how television portrays riots and their control.

5 I was not present at the riot, but like many thousands of Vancouverites, watched on local television. I monitored television and radio news coverage extensively, collected dozens of news clippings, many from the file on the riot in the Vancouver Public Library, and obtained television transcripts from the Canada News Disc. I attended four community meetings as part of the riot review process. At that time, I spoke or exchanged e-mail with members of the public who had been present that night, and with many people involved in the riot reviews. I obtained and examined in depth various reports on the riot, visited the riot display installed at the Vancouver Public Library, and repeatedly viewed a tape of the Rogers television special on the riot and review.

6 I was unable to obtain a complete set of videotapes from the three local TV stations at that time (CBC, BCTV, UTV). My analysis focuses most heavily on CBC news coverage, as this was the outlet from which the most footage was available, thanks to the CBC's Archive Project. I obtained videotape of all local CBC coverage from the day following the riot through to the end of the reviews in early 1995. I eventually accessed a twenty-five-minute tape of BCTV coverage from the day immediately following the riot, by ordering a copy from the National Archive in Ottawa. I could not obtain any UTV footage. Given these practical constraints, it is fortunate that the CBC represents the best test case among local broadcasters. Of the main Cana-dian television outlets, the CBC is the most likely to be accused of a left-wing bias (see, for example, Cooper 1994). It was CBC coverage of APEC 1997 that was most damaging to police. In contrast, BCTV news, at the time the most-watched Vancouver television news outlet, was apparently cozier with police. Of the three stations, the CBC was the least co-operative with police in the riot aftermath, the only station that did not voluntarily hand over its videotape to police. In sum, of the three local broadcasters, the CBC was the one most likely to offer critical coverage of policing of the Stanley Cup riot. It thus represented the best test case of the power of television to provide such critical coverage.

7 Tumber (1982) and P. Waddington (1998) describe similar processes in the
wake of British riots, in which various political players gave competing
accounts of the riots framed in terms of their own ideological positions.
Similarly in the case of the Stanley Cup riot, for example, *Vancouver Sun*
columnist Trevor Lautens (23 June 1994, p. A17) blamed the riot on a 'small-
ish class' that was nevertheless a 'powerful elite' he called 'the New
Freedomites.' Lautens' New Freedomites ranged from 'grunge rocker
groupies, television zombies and loud noise and violence fans through
drifters, druggies and certified criminals.' In contrast, *Adbusters* magazine
used a photograph of the Robson Street rioters to accompany an article
entitled 'The Age of Info-Toxin' (Winter issue, 1995, 52). This linked the riot
to 'the pollution of the mental environment' by the mass media. The caption
asked whether the rioters were 'drunk on info-toxin or beer?' Diverse other
narratives were voiced following the riot, blaming, for example, the media
for causing 'copycat' behaviour, or violence in professional sports, or
parents for not adequately controlling their young. The *Vancouver Sun*
sports section kept things in perspective with the headline 'Life is still good.
After all, we beat Toronto' (16 June 1994: p. F1).

8 In addition to footage from the rooftop cameras, material came from TV
news crews who mingled with the crowd below and recorded hours worth
of action. In fact, only a small portion of the extensive video television
crews recorded that night was ever aired. A CBC archivist told me the CBC
made forty field-tapes that night. Police also had two of their own video
cameras recording the action. Finally, in-store surveillance cameras captured activity when looters broke into stores, and external security cameras
on some buildings also caught some of the activity.

Analysts have commented that the impact of media imagery of riots
is often dictated by the fact that it is visualized from behind police lines
(Halloran, Elliott, and Murdock 1970; Wren-Lewis 1981; Murdock 1984). In
fact, much of the coverage of the Stanley Cup riot was from other vantage
points. The rooftop cameras looked down on both police and crowd, while
other close-up footage was taken amidst the mêlée. One photograph that
was published several times and was used in the *Vancouver Sun*'s year-end
review (31 December 1994, p. B1) offered quite a different viewpoint from
the one described in earlier research. It showed a lone rioter – from behind
– dwarfed by an oncoming army of police in armour and brandishing
batons.

9 BCTV did not record footage of either victim being shot by the Arwen gun.
Perhaps for this reason, BCTV gave this aspect of the riot less play on the
following day. It did not offer the same kind of unitary narrative; reporter

John Daly simply said he had heard two stories, one in which the man who lay near death as a result of the shooting had been wielding a screwdriver and threatening police, another in which he was an innocent victim.

10 Before that term, the NDP had since 1952 only been in power in B.C. for three years. For the rest of that period, the right-wing Social Credit party had controlled the B.C. legislature. The B.C. attorney-general of the time, Colin Gabelmann, when he announced the riot review, said in the legislature, 'The people of British Columbia need to learn how such an event could unfold, where some individuals behaved with such disrespect and disregard for the law of this province, law enforcement officials, and indeed, common decency.' However, the attorney general 'refused to say if he was also concerned about police conduct' (*Vancouver Sun*, 16 June 1994, p. A1). As we shall see below, Vancouver city council similarly avoided answering difficult questions about police behaviour.

11 The Vancouver police maintained an interesting state of quasi-independence from council. The police were ostensibly administered by the Vancouver Police Board, which was appointed partially by city council and partially by the province. During the review process, city councillors and staff repeatedly denied responsibility for police problems and passed them off to the Police Board instead.

At the final public meeting, one member of Vancouver council spoke about how the city had an arms-length relationship with police and the board. Thus, he said, the public should take concerns about policing the riot to the Police Board, not to council. Afterwards, the councillor told me his role in policing matters was as a 'a lobbyist, trying to persuade the department of a particular course of action, rather than saying, this is what you're going to do.' The examples he gave were lobbying for community policing and for 'Cops on Bikes.' It seemed city councillors such as this man would take credit for this more positive political involvement with the police. Yet this 'lobbying' relationship meant councillors could also deny ownership of police issues when things got politically sensitive, as with the riot.

Similarly, in the case of the city's review, but it was not policing questions per se that were outside the mandate of the review, only awkward questions regarding the police response to the riot. In fact, the city's review did deal with a number of other, less politically dangerous, facets of policing.

A lone city councillor, Jenny Kwan, at that time the sole representative of the left-wing Committee of Progressive Electors (COPE), pushed in vain to get council to take a different approach. She wanted council to look at the role of the police, or alternatively wanted a full, independent inquiry into all aspects of the riot. However, the rest of council sought to distance themselves from the sensitive issue of police misbehaviour during the riot.

12 Not only did the city avoid talking about the police response in their own review, city council didn't want to talk about the police reviews either. Councillor Kwan, the lone left-winger, tried to move that the public should bring comments about the police reviews to city council. The other councillors defeated this motion, and moved that the public should take their comments to the Police Board instead. In the view of most councillors, the city just didn't want to hear about the police reviews.

13 The Oppal Report, the conclusion of the two-year, four-million-dollar Royal Commission Inquiry into Policing in British Columbia (RCIPBC), recommended that the Police Commission be scrapped. Justice Wally Oppal, who headed the inquiry, stated that an independent ombudsman was needed instead to look into suspected cases of police wrongdoing. According to the Oppal Report, 'There are a number of problems with the current mandate and operations of the [B.C. Police] Commission, which raise questions about its ability to carry out the function [of supervising municipal police forces] ... although the commission's mission statement describes it as 'a public accountability body,' the nature of that accountability and mechanisms for enforcing it are poorly defined.

'Since its inception the commission has been staffed primarily by police officers ... the complaint commissioner is deputy chair of the commission, a relationship that was widely criticized in submissions to this Inquiry. The complaint commissioner and the chair of the commission defend their inter-relationship on the basis that they work together to resolve the problems that give rise to complaints. The Inquiry, however, found ample reason to believe this is not, in fact, what is occurring' (RCIPBC 1994: pp. B-46–B-47).

14 Although TV and other media were constructed as partly to blame for the riot, media accounts of the riot were also selectively relied on as evidence for the review. For example, the Police Commission report listed an extensive selection of newspaper articles, yet only one of these more than eighty articles concerned the riot itself. The rest were stories about previous riots. The only article included in the Police Commission's bibliography concerning the current riot was a column by Denny Boyd condemning the rioters as 'Pusillanimous Punks: Classic Non-Achievers with No Class' (*Vancouver Sun*, 17 June 1994). Thus the Police Commission's bibliography included none of the newspaper articles that I quote from above which repeatedly highlighted alleged examples of possible police misconduct.

15 Journalists also experienced interesting confusion or role strain about their role in the review: were they reporting on it or participating in it? For example, one local journalist, asking questions about crowd control at the meeting on police behaviour, directed camera people from other organizations not to record her, saying, 'Don't show me, I'm a journalist.' Another journalist from a prominent national outlet attended the meeting on the media's role on the riot but, despite repeated prompting from the moderators, said he could not participate in the meeting as he was doing a story on it.

16 For example, to quote from the background paper, 'The media has also been blamed for advertising the party on Robson St. at the end of the game.' However, no mention was made of news sources' role in advertising the party. According to several sources, a Vancouver police officer, apparently Constable Drennan, appeared on television shortly before the riot dressed in a Canucks sweater and telling people to come downtown and celebrate! This embarrassing situation was not mentioned at all in the city review. It was, however, acknowledged by the B.C. Police Commission review: 'We have been told that a police spokesperson came on television in the early evening and invited the public to join the party after the game. It is particularly surprising to us that this happened, in view of police intelligence prior to the 14th that there might be trouble' (p. 42).

17 A police inspector said that although police deployed two of their own hand-held video cameras at the scene of the Stanley Cup riot, the news media cameras used to record the riot were superior for surveillance purposes.

6. The Media Logic of Greenpeace

1 Greenpeace has national offices in more than two dozen countries. Greenpeace International's 2001 annual report showed a budget of over $100 million. As of March 2002, the organization claimed 100,000 members in Canada and 2.5 million worldwide, according to the Greenpeace Canada website.

2 Greenpeace documents and texts I obtained include the following: websites, a consumer survey form, a feature-length video, a book-length history by the organization's first president, a photographic history of the organization's protest actions, and a media handbook written by a veteran campaigner. I have analysed examples of Greenpeace news coverage from videotaped television news items and from Greenpeace press releases and TV news transcripts of reports of Greenpeace actions, as well as from

archived newspaper and magazine clippings. I subscribed to a Greenpeace media mailing list and was e-mailed hundreds of press releases over a ten-month period. My interviews also included one with the communications manager of the B.C. Forest Alliance, a pro-logging organization in conflict with Greenpeace. (These interviews were conducted as part of a broader, ongoing research project on media and activism being carried out at the University of British Columbia by Professor David Tindall and myself.)

3 Eyerman and Jamison (1989) analyse the process of rationalization that Greenpeace underwent as it grew from a small band of activists into a massive international institution. However, they neglect how Green-peace's focus on television is a central factor in this rationalization. Indeed, Greenpeace's orientation to television is barely discussed in Eyerman and Jamison's account of the evolution of the organization. This is a crucial missing element that must be considered to understand fully how and why Greenpeace has evolved.

4 Dale's book (1996) makes an analogous argument in non-academic terms that comes closer than any previous social scientific effort, although it only engages in passing with social science research or theory. I am indebted to his outstanding book for some key data in this chapter.

5 Tarrow's argument is of course very analogous to the medium theory argument made by Meyrowitz (1985), although Tarrow makes no mention of medium theory or Meyrowitz's work.

6 These specialized bodies of literature on social movements thus mirror the split described in Chapter 2 between the medium theory account of Meyrowitz and the body of research on the sociology of news production.

7 To quote the official history of Greenpeace: 'Journalists and a cameraman among the crew would play a crucial role, recording the events of the journey and sending reports to radio stations and newspapers back home. A key figure among the journalists was Robert Hunter, a columnist on the Vancouver Sun. There were also Ben Metcalfe, a veteran of radio, politics and public relations, who was the theatre critic for the CBC, and Bob Cummings, a former private detective now on the staff of the Georgia Straight.' (Brown and May 1989: 11). As Robert Hunter, who later became Greenpeace's president, writes in his history of the early years of Green-peace: 'Metcalfe had been in the newspaper business 25 years longer than me. We both had gone through the same hoops in the peculiar small world of western Canadian journalism ... We saw it as a media war. We had studied Marshall McLuhan. Metcalfe had a street fighter's understanding of public relations: "It doesn't matter what they say about you, as long as they spell your name right." ... For Metcalfe, the voyage of the Greenpeace

was a campaign like others he had run in the past when he had been paid by politicians to apply his knowledge of the day-to-day mechanics of journalism to get them elected. Image was everything. He knew exactly how to grab headlines, how to drop catchy phrases that would be re-printed, how to play on the reflexes of bored editors ... Madison Avenue and Hitler had changed the face of the world through application of the tactic of image projection and we could hardly attempt to do less' (1979: 60–1).

8 The official history *The Greenpeace Story* (Brown and May 1989) provides numerous capsule accounts of direct actions throughout the 1980s and repeatedly draws attention to the number of Greenpeace activists arrested. Similarly, the Greenpeace photographic history of its direct actions, *Witness: Twenty-Five Years on the Environmental Front Line* (Warford 1997), features seventeen different photographs of law enforcement officers, such as police, military, and coast guard personnel, arresting or beating Greenpeace demonstrators.

9 Indeed, as the former Greenpeace campaigner describes, a criminal com-ponent to a media stunt may be crucial to obtaining television coverage: 'In Chicago once, I was on a cell phone explaining to a television assign-ment editor at a local TV station that Greenpeace had two activists holding a banner on the side of a major hotel where nuclear power promoters were meeting. I said that the fire department was about to extract the activists from the side of the hotel ... I asked the assignment editor if she was going to send anyone down. She said, "Call me if there is any blood or any signs of police brutality"' (Salzman 1998: 129).

The former Greenpeace staff member advises on how to capitalize on media interest in such arrests: 'If you do get arrested, call journalists from jail. Talk-radio shows, in particular, are receptive to putting you on the air live from jail. (Plan for this by writing the phone number of media outlets on your body in case your clothes and belongings are taken from you.) (130).

10 I obtained a copy of such a survey conducted in the Victoria, B.C., area several years ago. People were asked about their patterns of donating money to Greenpeace and other organizations, and about their level of support for various Greenpeace campaigns and tactics. Then they were asked questions such as 'In the past few months have you seen, heard or read anything about Greenpeace in newspapers, on television, on radio or in any other medium? Please tell me what you recall. Was what you read or heard favourable or unfavourable to Greenpeace? What impressions did these articles give you about Greenpeace?' There were other questions

on people's media consumption, asking how many hours a week they spend watching television, listening to the radio, or reading magazines, whether they watch particular television stations or read certain newspapers on a regular basis, and so on.

11 Chris Rose of the environmental public relations organization Media Natura suggested: 'What Greenpeace are very good at is they've invented, if you like, a sort of morality play ... that takes Greenpeace straight out of the editorial system of gate-keepers ... It puts them into that sort of tabloid news and that's what headline news in television is about because it has to be thirty-second subjects, thirty second-visuals ... So I mean they're using the media in that way, deliberately restricting most of their input using that one visible bit that you can see, using television news, basically and, newspaper photographs' (Anderson 1991: 470).

Rose said some environmental correspondents may dislike Greenpeace for this reason: 'They don't like Greenpeace because Greenpeace goes past them. It gets straight on to the front page of the newspaper because the news editor will say I don't care whether you think this is news or not, that they're blocking this ship up the Thames, it looks like news as far as I'm concerned and the public will think it's news' (Anderson 1991: 471).

12 The former Greenpeace president's daughter is now also a journalist. In this capacity, she spent an extended period living on a Greenpeace vessel and reporting during an ocean-going environmental campaign. She later became a reporter for the *Vancouver Sun*. Similarly to Hunter, the former media director of Greenpeace later became head of the environmental reporting unit at CNN (Motavalli 1995: 37). Today Greenpeace still has numerous journalists in key positions among its staff. For example, Blair Palese, former head of the Greenpeace media unit in Washington, D.C., previously worked as a journalist for a number of years (Dale 1996: 26). In Britain, former Fleet Street journalist John May has been another key Greenpeace communications expert. All of this illustrates not only how Greenpeace may be able to draw on good will from sympathetic journalists, but also how the organization has consistently, from its birth, internalized news media logic and considerations by utilizing journalists as key personnel. Indeed, another former journalist was actually running Greenpeace's training camp in Florida, teaching Greenpeace activists how to break the law for television (Dale 1996: 62). One may see this particular ex-journalist as the very personification of the argument that media do not simply stand back and report the news, but help to shape it.

13 Stephen Dale (1996) found that Greenpeace's Communications Department, or 'Coms,' based in London, England, had a budget of over

$1 million a year by the early 1990s. This department mediates between the campaigners and television news agencies. Because Greenpeace provides its own video footage, it can overcome the problem, discussed earlier, that many environmental problems are focused in geographically isolated spots.

14 Greenpeace members shielded the seals with their bodies or sprayed the live baby seals with a harmless green dye to render their pelts commercially useless. Mother seals barked helplessly and followed pathetically as sealers skulked off with the corpses of their babies (these images feature prominently in the *Greenpeace's Greatest Hits* video). As Draper argues, 'Greenpeace was never able to establish that there was a threat to the seal population at all. They justified the call for preservation with statistics of severe population declines from the 1950s – before the Canadian government had imposed limits restricting the number killed. Today Atlantic coast fishermen complain that seal overpopulation is playing havoc with fish stocks' (1987: 9). While the campaign was a media hit, the indigenous economy of forty Native communities was devastated (Ostertag 1991: 84). The Inuit fishery of adult seals, which includes different methods and which Greenpeace had not meant to shut down, was crushed as a by-product of the publicity. 'Unfortunately, anybody who took any seals was painted the same way in the media ... our attempts to differentiate between the commercial slaughter and other types of sealing didn't make it into the media,' said Greenpeace campaigner David Garrick (Dale 1996: 93).

15 A question that is beyond the scope of this book but a subject for future research is the extent to which the rise of the Internet is creating a new, more active role for the Greenpeace membership: 'cyberactivism.' As James Carey (1989) has argued, the rise of each new medium interacts with and resituates older media. It may be that the Internet will transform the television politics of Greenpeace.

7. Conclusion

1 John Thompson (1990, 1994, 1995) has put forth a somewhat similar argument that we need to integrate medium theory into critical social theory, and has begun to synthesize the work of medium theorists with the critical theory of Habermas. His analysis focuses almost entirely on the increased spatial and temporal reach of media in modernity. Here I focus much more on the distinctive properties of particular media forms, such as television as opposed to print media. Secondly, like most critical analysts, Thompson

focuses only on power relations concerning the *ideological* role of the media, looking solely at their enhanced ability to disseminate ideological messages widely.

2 In this respect my findings in the four case studies thus fit more with the analysis of Ericson, Baranek, and Chan (1989). They also retained Goffman's conception of 'front regions' and 'back regions' as physical spaces. Ericson et al. also found that police control of news media knowledge was in part linked to the ability to keep various physical spaces as private back regions.

3 Meyrowitz (1985) is critical of much previous research on media for focusing overly on content. He charges that such research neglects the question of medium form in analysing media influences. The examples in this book, however, show that these questions are very difficult to separate. In the end, Meyrowitz's analysis itself relies on an argument about content: that TV makes available revealing new types of information from the situations it records. The evidence from my research does not support Meyrowitz's arguments, fitting instead fits with other research showing that, in practice, TV tends to present a worldview that supports established power.

4 One might respond that Meyrowitz is simply using visual metaphors as a way to speak about the knowledge transmitted by TV more generally. However, his various examples also focus very much on the visual.

5 Altheide and Snow (1979: 98–9) offer a similar explanation of the force of TV visuals and how they are open to manipulation. They argue that visual information depends to a large degree on context for its meaning. TV takes its visuals and places them in a new context. The viewer may not be aware of the extent to which visual information depends on context for its validity, and the extent to which, in the absence of such context, the viewer is heavily dependent on verbal interpretation of the visual information.

6 This unidirectional quality is another key way TV differs from a face-to-face interaction, and creates another problem for Meyrowitz's attempt to transpose Goffman's analysis (1959) to mass-mediated situations.

7 This process is much broader than what previous authors have referred to as 'mediatization.' The latter term is used mostly to refer to professionalization of news media relations, only one component of the shifts analyzed here.

8. Postscript: Television and Theorizing the Evolution of Criminal Justice

1 Some authors influenced by Foucault theorize the more recent trend towards increased surveillance in contemporary society as an extension of

Foucault's notion of 'disciplinary' power (e.g., Cohen 1985); others situate it using another Foucauldian formulation, in terms of the strategies of 'government at a distance' (Garland 1997). These differences need not concern us here. Either way, there is a contrast with the old-style spectacular, vengeful approach to punishment.

Works Cited

Acland, Charles. 1995. *Youth, Murder Spectacle: The Cultural Politics of Youth in Crisis*. Boulder, CO.: Westview.

'The Age of Info-Toxin.' 1995. *Adbusters* (Winter).

Altheide, David. 1993. 'Electronic Media and State Control: The Case of Azscam.' *Sociological Quarterly* 34: 53–69.

– 1995. *An Ecology of Communication: Cultural Formats of Control*. New York: Aldine de Gruyter.

– 2002. *Creating Fear: News and the Construction of Crisis*. New York: Aldine de Gruyter.

Altheide, David, and Robert Snow. 1979. *Media Logic*. Beverly Hills: Sage.

– 1991. *Media Worlds in the Post-Journalism Era*. New York: Aldine de Gruyter.

Andersen, Robin. 1996. *Consumer Culture and TV Programming*. Boulder, CO.: Westview.

Anderson, Alison. 1991. 'Source Strategies and the Communication of Environmental Affairs.' *Media, Culture and Society* 13 (4): 459–76.

– 1993. 'Source-Media Relations: The Production of the Environmental Agenda.' In A. Hansen, ed., *The Mass Media and Environmental Issues*. Leicester: University of Leicester Press.

– 1997. *Media, Culture and the Environment*. London: University College of London Press.

Anderson, Carolyn, and Thomas Benton. 1991. *Documentary Dilemmas*. Carbondale, IL: Southern Illinois University Press.

Appleby, Timothy. 1996. 'Publicity-loving Sheriff Plays Tough.' *Globe and Mail* (31 January 1996): A1.

Baker, William F., and George Dessart. 1998. *Down the Tube: An Inside Account of the Failure of American Television*. New York: Basic Books.

Barthes, Roland. 1975. *S/Z*. London: Cape.

Baudrillard, Jean. 1988. *Selected Writings*. Cambridge: Polity Press.

B.C. Police Commission. 1994. *Report on the Riot that Occurred in Vancouver on June 14–15, 1994*. Vancouver: B.C. Police Commission.

Beck, A., and Willis, A. 1995. *Crime and Security: Managing the Risk to Safe Shopping*. Leicester: Perpetuity Press.

Beck, Ulrich. 1992. 'From Industrial Society to the Risk Society: Questions of Survival, Social Structure and Enlightenment.' *Theory, Culture and Society* 9: 97–123.

Benton, Thomas, and Carolyn Anderson. 1989. *Reality Fictions: The Films of Frederick Wiseman*. Carbondale, IL: Southern Illinois University Press.

Bernstein, Sharon. 1992. 'The Force Is with Her.' *Los Angeles Times* (6 October 1992): F1.

Best, Joel. 1999. *Random Violence: How We Talk about New Crimes and New Victims*. Berkeley: University of California Press.

Bird, Roger. 1997. *The End of News*. Toronto: Irwin.

Block, Alex Ben. 1990. *Outfoxed: Marvin Davis, Barry Diller, Rupert Murdoch, Joan Rivers and the Inside Story of America's Fourth Television Network*. New York: St. Martin's Press.

Blumler, Jay G., and Michael Gurevitch. 1995. *The Crisis of Public Communication*. London: Routledge.

Bok, Sissela. 1998. *Mayhem: Violence as Public Entertainment*. Reading, MA: Perseus Books.

Bondebjerg, Ib. 1996. 'Public Discourse/Private Fascination: Hybridization in "True-Life-Story Genres."' *Media, Culture and Society* 18: 27–45.

Brogden, Mike, Tony Jefferson, and Sandra Walklate. 1988. *Introducing Police Work*. London: Unwin Hyman.

Brown, Michael, and John May. 1989. *The Greenpeace Story*. Scarborough: Prentice-Hall.

Carey, James. 1989. *Communication as Culture: Essays on Media and Society*. Boston: Unwin Hyman.

Carroll, William, and Robert S. Ratner. 1999. 'Media Strategies and Political Projects: A Comparative Study of Social Movements.' *Canadian Journal of Sociology* 24 (1): 1–34.

Cassidy, Sean. 1992. 'The Environment and the Media: Two Strategies for Challenging Hegemony.' In Janet Wasko and Vincent Mosco, eds., *Democratic Communications in the Information Age*. Toronto: Garamond.

Cavender, Gray, and Lisa Bond-Maupin. 1993. 'Fear and Loathing on Reality Television: An Analysis of "America's Most Wanted" and "Unsolved Mysteries."' *Sociological Inquiry* 63 (3): 305–17.

Chibnall, Steve. 1977. *Law and Order News: An Analysis of Crime Reporting in the British Press*. London: Tavistock.

City of Vancouver Review of Major Events. 1994. *Riots: A Background Paper*. Vancouver: City of Vancouver.

City of Vancouver Review of Major Events. 1994. *Final Report*. Vancouver: City of Vancouver.

Cleveland, John. 1999. 'Is Repression of Protest Increasing in Canada?' Paper presented at the 34th Annual Canadian Sociology and Anthropology Association Meetings, Sherbrooke, Quebec, June.

Coe, Steve. 1996. 'The Reality of Realities: Lower Numbers.' *Broadcasting and Cable* (15 January 1996): 00–00.

Cohen, Stanley. 1985. *Visions of Social Control*. Cambridge: Polity Press.

Cooper, Barry. 1994. *Sins of Omission: Shaping the News at CBC TV*. Toronto: University of Toronto Press.

Corner, John. 1996. *The Art of Record: A Critical Introduction to Documentary*. Manchester: Manchester University Press.

Couldry, Nick. 1999. 'Disrupting the Media at Greenham Common: A New Chapter in the History of Mediations.' *Media, Culture and Society* 21 (3): 337–58.

Cracknell, Jon. 1993. 'Issue Arenas, Pressure Groups and Environmental Agendas.' In A. Hansen, ed., *The Mass Media and Environmental Issues*. Leicester: University of Leicester Press.

Cumberbatch, Guy, and Dennis Howitt. 1989. *A Measure of Uncertainty: The Effects of the Mass Media*. London: John Libbey and Sons.

Curran, James. 1990. 'The New Revisionism in Mass Communication Research: A Reappraisal.' *European Journal of Communication* 5 (2–3): 135–64.

– 1996. 'Rethinking Mass Communications.' In J. Curran, D. Morley, and V. Walkerdine, eds., *Cultural Studies and Communications*. London: Arnold.

Dale, Stephen. 1996. *McLuhan's Children: The Greenpeace Message and the Media*. Toronto: Between the Lines.

Dandeker, C. 1990. *Surveillance, Power and Modernity: Bureaucracy and Discipline from 1700 to the Present Day*. New York: St. Martin's Press.

Davies, Simon. 1998. 'CCTV: A New Battleground for Privacy.' In Clive Norris, Jade Moran, and Gary Armstrong, eds., *Surveillance, Closed Circuit Television and Social Control*. Aldershot, U.K.: Ashgate.

Davis, James. 1951. 'Crime News in Colorado Newspapers.' *American Journal of Sociology* 57 (1): 325–30.

Della Porta, Donatella. 1998. 'Police Knowledge, Public Order and the Media.' Paper presented to conference, 'Protest, the Public Sphere and Public Order,' University of Geneva, October.

Della Porta, D., and Reiter, H., eds. 1998a. *Policing Protest: The Control of Mass Demonstrations in Western Democracies*, Minneapolis, MN: University of Minnesota Press.

– 1998b. 'Introduction: The Policing of Protest in Western Democracies.' In D. Della Porta and H. Reiter, eds., *Policing Protest: The Control of Mass Demonstrations in Western Democracies*. Minneapolis, MN: University of Minnesota Press.

Donovan, Pamela. 1998. 'Armed with the Power of Television: Reality Crime Programming and the Reconstruction of Law and Order in the United States.' In Mark Fishman and Gray Cavender, eds., *Entertaining Crime: Television Reality Programs*. New York: Aldine de Gruyter.

Doyle, Aaron, and Richard Ericson. 1996. 'Breaking into Prison: News Sources and Correctional Institutions.' *Canadian Journal of Criminology* 38 (2): 155–90.

Doyle, Aaron, Brian Elliott, and David Tindall. 1997. 'Framing the Forests: Corporations, the B.C. Forest Alliance and the Media.' In W. Carroll, ed., *Organizing Dissent: Contemporary Social Movements in Theory and Practise*. 2nd ed. Montreal: Garamond.

Draper, Eric. 1987. 'The Greenpeace Media Machine.' *New Internationalist*, May 1987: 8–9.

Dreschel, R.E. 1983. *News-Making in the Trial Courts*. New York: Longman.

Entman, Robert M., and Andrew Rojecki. 1993. 'Freezing Out the Public: Elite and Media Framing of the Anti-Nuclear Movement.' *Political Communication* 10 (1): 155–73.

Ericson, Richard. 1982. *Reproducing Order: A Study of Police Patrol Work*. Toronto: University of Toronto Press.

– 1991. 'Mass Media, Crime, Law and Justice: An Institutional Approach.' *British Journal of Criminology*, 31 (3): 219–49.

– 1993. *Making Crime: A Study of Detective Work*. 2nd ed. Toronto: University of Toronto Press.

– 1994. 'An Institutional Perspective on News Media Access and Control.' In N. Hewitt and M. Aldridge, eds., *Controlling Broadcasting*. Manchester: University of Manchester Press.

– 1995. 'The News Media and Account Ability in Criminal Justice.' In P. Stenning, ed., *Accountability for Criminal Justice*. Toronto: University of Toronto Press.

– 1998. 'How Journalists Visualize Fact.' *Annals*, AAPSS 560 (November 1998): 83–95.

Ericson, Richard, Patricia Baranek, and Janet Chan. 1987. *Visualizing Deviance: A Study of News Organization*. Toronto: University of Toronto Press/ Milton Keynes: Open University Press.

– 1989. *Negotiating Control: A Study of News Sources*. Toronto: University of Toronto Press/ Milton Keynes: Open University Press.

– 1991. *Representing Order: Crime, Law and Justice in the News Media*. Buckingham: Open University Press/ Toronto: University of Toronto Press.

Ericson, Richard, and Aaron Doyle. 1999. 'Globalization and the Policing of Protest: The Case of APEC 1997.' *British Journal of Sociology* 50 (4): 589–608.

Ericson, Richard, and Kevin Haggerty. 1997. *Policing the Risk Society*. Toronto: University of Toronto Press/Oxford: Oxford University Press.

Ericson, Richard, Kevin Haggerty, and Kevin Carriere. 1993. 'Community Policing as Communications Policing.' In Dieter Dolling and Thomas Feltes, eds., *Community Policing: Comparative Aspects of Community-Oriented Police Work*. Holzkirchen: Felix-Verlag.

Erikson, Kai. 1966. *Wayward Puritans: A Study in the Sociology of Deviance*. New York: John Wiley and Sons.

Etzioni, Amitai. 1970. *Demonstration Democracy*. New York: Gordon and Breach.

Eyerman, Ron, and Andrew Jamison. 1989. 'Environmental Knowledge as an Organizational Weapon: The Case of Greenpeace.' *Social Science Information* 28 (1): 99–119.

Feeley, Malcolm, and Jonathan Simon. 1994. 'Actuarial Justice: The Emerging New Criminal Law.' In D. Nelken, ed., *The Futures of Criminology*. London: Sage.

Fetveit, Arild. 1999. 'Reality TV in the Digital Era: A Paradox in Visual Culture.' *Media, Culture and Society* 21: 787–804.

Fillieule, Olivier. 1998. 'The Police and the Media: Dangerous Liaisons.' Paper presented to conference, 'Protest, the Public Sphere and Public Order,' University of Geneva, October.

Fishman, Mark. 1978. 'Crime Waves as Ideology.' *Social Problems* 25: 531–43.
– 1980. *Manufacturing the News*. Austin, TX: University of Texas Press.
– 1981. 'Police News: Constructing an Image of Crime.' *Urban Life* 9: 371–94.
– 1998. 'Ratings and Reality: The Persistence of the Reality Crime Genre.' In Mark Fishman and Gray Cavender, eds., *Entertaining Crime: Television Reality Programs*. New York: Aldine de Gruyter.

Fiske, John. 1987. *Television Culture*. London: Methuen.
– 1996. *Media Matters: Everyday Culture and Political Change*. rev. ed. Minneapolis, MN: University of Minnesota Press.
– 1998. 'Surveilling the City: Whiteness, the Black Man and Democratic Totalitarianism.' *Theory, Culture and Society* 15 (2): 67–88.

Fiske, John, and John Hartley. 1978. *Reading Television*. London: Methuen.

Flanagan, Timothy, and Dennis Longmire, eds., 1996. *Americans View Crime and Justice: A National Public Opinion Survey*. Thousand Oaks, CA: Sage.

Foucault, Michel. 1977. *Discipline and Punish*. New York: Vintage.

Freedman, Jonathan. 2002. *Media Violence and Its Effect on Aggression: Assessing the Scientific Evidence*. Toronto: University of Toronto Press.

Freeman, Alan. 1999. 'Closed Circuit TV Cameras Have Invaded Great Britain.' *Globe and Mail* (25 May 1999).

Freeman, Mike. 1993. 'Ratings are Reality for Off-Net.' *Broadcasting and Cable* (12 April 1993): 30.

Gamson, William. 1995. 'Foreword.' In *Crime Talk: How Citizens Construct a Social Problem*, by T. Sasson. New York: Aldine de Gruyter.

Gamson, William, and Andre Modigliani. 1989. 'Media Discourse and Public Opinion: A Constructionist Approach.' *American Journal of Sociology* 95 (1): 1–37.

Gamson, William, and Gadi Wolfsfeld. 1993. 'Movements and Media as Interacting Systems.' *Annals*, AAPSS, 528 (July 1993): 114–25.

Gans, Herbert. 1979. *Deciding What's News: A Study of CBS Evening News, NBC Nightly News, Newsweek and Time*. New York: Pantheon.

Garland, David. 1990. *Punishment and Modern Society: A Study in Social Theory*. Oxford: Oxford University Press/Chicago, IL: University of Chicago Press.

– 1996. 'The Limits of the Sovereign State: Strategies of Crime Control in Contemporary Society.' *British Journal of Criminology* 36 (4): 445–71

– 1997. 'Governmentality and the Problem of Crime: Foucault, Criminology, Sociology.' *Theoretical Criminology* 1 (2): 173–214.

– 2000. 'The Culture of High Crime Societies: Some Preconditions of Recent Law and Order Policies.' *British Journal of Criminology* 40 (3): 347–75.

– 2001. *The Culture of Control: Crime and Social Order in Contemporary Society*. Chicago: University of Chicago Press.

Garofalo, James. 1981. 'Crime and the Mass Media: A Selective Review of Research.' *Journal of Research in Crime and Delinquency* 18: 319–50.

Geary, R. 1985. *Policing Industrial Disputes*. Cambridge: Cambridge University Press.

Gerbner, G., and L. Gross. 1976. 'Living with Television: The Violence Profile.' *Journal of Communication* 26: 173–99.

Gerbner, G., L. Gross, M. Morgan, and N. Signorelli. 1994. 'Growing Up with Television: The Cultivation Perspective.' In J. Bryant and D. Zillmann, eds., *Media Effects: Advances in Theory and Research*. Hillsdale, NJ: Lawrence Erlbaum Associates.

Getz, Ronald. 1995. 'A COPS Show of Your Own.' *Law and Order* 43 (2): 43–9.

Giddens, Anthony. 1985. *The Nation-State and Violence*. Cambridge: Polity.

– 1990. *The Consequences of Modernity*. Cambridge: Polity.

– 1991. *Modernity and Self-Identity: Self and Society in the Late Modern Age*. Stanford: Stanford University Press.

Gitlin, Todd. 1980. *The Whole World Is Watching: Mass Media and the Making and Unmaking of the New Left*. Berkeley, CA: University of California Press.

– 2002. *Media Unlimited: How the Torrent of Images and Sounds Overwhelms Our Lives.* New York: Metropolitan.

Goffman, Erving. 1959. *The Presentation of Self in Everyday Life.* New York: Doubleday.

– 1972. *Behaviour in Public Places.* Pelican: Hammondsworth.

Goldstein, Jeffrey, ed. 1998. *Why We Watch: The Attractions of Violent Entertainment.* Oxford: Oxford University Press.

Gooding-Williams, Robert, ed. 1993. *Reading Rodney King, Reading Urban Uprising.* New York: Routledge.

Goodwin, Charles. 1994. 'Professional Vision.' *American Anthropologist* 96 (3): 606–33.

Gorrie, Peter. 1991. 'Greenpeace Grows Up.' *World Press Review* (December 1991): 50.

Graber, Doris. 1980. *Crime News and the Public.* New York: Praeger.

Graham, Stephen. 1998. 'Towards the Fifth Utility? On the Extension and Normalization of Public CCTV?' In Clive Norris, Jade Moran, and Gary Armstrong, eds., *Surveillance, Closed Circuit Television and Social Control.* Aldershot, U.K.: Ashgate.

Grant, Wyn. 1989. *Pressure Groups, Politics and Democracy in Britain.* London: Phillip Allan.

Gunter, Barrie. 1987. *Television and the Fear of Crime.* London: John Libbey.

Hackett, Robert. 1991. *News and Dissent: The Press and the Politics of Peace in Canada.* New Jersey: Ablex.

Haggerty, Kevin. 2002. *Making Crime Count.* Toronto: University of Toronto Press.

Haggerty, Kevin, and Richard Ericson. 2000. 'The Surveillant Assemblage.' *British Journal of Sociology* 51: 605–22.

Haghighi, Bahram, and Jon Sorensen. 1996. 'America's Fear of Crime.' In T. Flanagan and D. Longmire, eds., *Americans View Crime and Justice: A National Public Opinion Survey.* Thousand Oaks, CA: Sage.

Hale, C. 1996. 'Fear of Crime: A Review of the Literature.' *International Review of Victimology* 4: 79–150.

Hall, Stuart, Chas Critcher, Tony Jefferson, John Clarke, and Brian Roberts. 1978. *Policing the Crisis: Mugging, the State and Law and Order.* London: Macmillan.

Hallett, Michael, and Dennis Powell. 1995. 'Backstage with "Cops": The Dramaturgical Reification of Police Subculture in American Crime "Infotainment."' *American Journal of Police* 14 (1): 101–29.

Halloran, James, Philip Elliott, and Graham Murdock. 1970. *Demonstrations and Communication: A Case Study.* Hammondsworth, U.K.: Penguin.

Haney, Craig, and John Manzolati. 1988. 'Television Criminology: Network Illusions of Criminal Justice Realities.' In E. Aronson, ed., *Readings about the Social Animal*. 5th ed. New York: W.H. Freeman.

Hannah-Moffat, Kelly. 2001. *Punishment in Disguise: Penal Governance and the Federal Imprisonment of Women in Canada*. Toronto: University of Toronto Press.

Hannigan, John. 1995. *Environmental Sociology: A Social Constructionist Perspective*. London: Routledge.

Hansen, Anders. 1991. 'The Media and the Social Construction of the Environment.' *Media, Culture and Society* 13 (4): 443–58.

– 1993. 'Greenpeace and Press Coverage of Environmental Issues.' In A. Hansen, ed., *The Mass Media and Environmental Issues*. Leicester: University of Leicester Press.

Harris, Scott. 1991. 'Rape Case Raises Privacy Issue.' *Los Angeles Times* (20 April 1991): B3.

Hatty, Suzanne. 1991. 'Police, Crime and the Media: An Australian Tale.' *International Journal of the Sociology of Law* 19: 171–91.

Hawkins, Keith. 1984. *Environment and Enforcement: Regulation and the Social Definition of Pollution*. Oxford: Oxford University Press.

Heath, Linda, and Kevin Gilbert. 1996. 'Mass Media and Fear of Crime.' *American Behavioral Scientist* 39 (4): 379–86.

Herman, Edward S., and Noam Chomsky. 1988. *Manufacturing Consent: The Political Economy of the Mass Media*. New York: Pantheon.

Human Rights Watch. 1998. *Human Rights Watch World Report 1998*. New York: Human Rights Watch.

Hunter, Robert. 1970. *The Enemies of Anarchy*. Toronto: McLelland and Stewart.

– 1971. *The Storming of the Mind*. Toronto: McLelland and Stewart.

– 1979. *Warriors of the Rainbow: A Chronicle of the Greenpeace Movement*. New York: Holt, Rinehart and Winston.

Innis, Harold. 1950. *Empire and Communications*. London: Oxford University Press.

– 1951. *The Bias of Communication*. Toronto: University of Toronto Press.

Jamieson, Kathleen. 1992. *Dirty Politics: Deception, Distraction and Democracy*. Oxford: Oxford University Press.

Jones, J.B. 1978. 'Prosectors and the Dispositions of Criminal Cases: An Analysis of Plea Bargaining Rates.' *Journal of Criminal Law and Criminology* 69: 402–12.

Kaminer, Wendy. 1995. *It's All the Rage: Crime and Culture*. Reading, MA: Addison-Wesley.

Katz, Jon. 1993. 'Covering the Cops: A TV Show Moves In Where Journalists Fear to Tread.' *Columbia Journalism Review* (January/February): 25–30.

Kielbowicz, Richard B., and Clifford Scherer, 1986. 'The Role of the Press in the Dynamics of Social Movements.' *Research in Social Movements, Conflict and Change* 9: 71–96.

Kimball, Penn. 1994. *Downsizing the News*. Baltimore: Johns Hopkins University Press.

Kriesi, Hanspeter. 1989. 'New Social Movements and the New Class in the Netherlands.' *American Journal of Sociology* 94 (5): 1078–1116.

Lacombe, Dany. 1994. *Blue Politics: Pornography and the Law in the Age of Feminism*. Toronto: University of Toronto Press.

Law Commission of Canada. 2002. *In Search of Security: The Roles of Public Police and Private Agencies*. Discussion Paper. Ottawa: Law Commission of Canada.

Lawrence, R. 2000. *The Politics of Force: Media and the Construction of Police Brutality*. Berkeley, CA: University of California Press.

Lichty, Lawrence, and Douglas Gomery. 1992. 'More Is Less.' In P. Cook, D. Gomery, and L. Lichty, eds., *The Future of News*. Washington, DC: Woodrow Wilson Center Press/Baltimore: Johns Hopkins University Press.

Lippmann, Walter. 1925. *The Phantom Public*. New York: Macmillan.

Livingstone, Sonia. 1994. *Making Sense of Television: The Psychology of Audience Interpretation*. Oxford: Pergamon.

– 1996. 'On the Continuing Problem of Media Effects.' In J. Curran and M. Gurevitch, eds., *Mass Media and Society*. 2nd ed. London: Arnold.

Loader, Ian. 1997. 'Policing and the Social: Questions of Symbolic Power.' *British Journal of Sociology* 48 (1): 1–18.

Luft, Greg. 1991. 'Camcorders: When Amateurs Go after the News.' *Columbia Journalism Review* (September/October): 35–7.

Lyon, David. 1993. 'An Electronic Panopticon? A Sociological Critique of Surveillance Theory.' *Sociological Review* 41 (4): 653–78.

McAdam, Doug. 1996. 'The Framing Function of Movement Tactics: Strategic Dramaturgy in the American Civil Rights Movement.' In D. McAdam, J. McCarthy, and M. Zald, eds., *Comparative Perspectives on Social Movements*. Cambridge: Cambridge University Press.

McCahill, Michael. 1998. 'Beyond Foucault: Towards a Contemporary Theory of Surveillance.' In Clive Norris, Jade Moran, and Gary Armstrong, eds., *Surveillance, Closed Circuit Television and Social Control*. Aldershot, England: Ashgate.

McCarthy, John D., and Clark McPhail. 1998. 'The Institutionalization of Protest in the United States.' In David S. Meyer and S. Tarrow, eds., *The Social Movement Society: Contentious Politics for a New Century*. Lanham, MD: Rowman Littlefield.

McCarthy, John D., Clark McPhail, and Jackie Smith.1996. 'Images of Selection Bias in Media Coverage of Washington Demonstrations, 1982 and 1991.' *American Journal of Sociology*, 61: 478–99.

McCarthy, John D., Clark McPhail, Jackie Smith, and Louis J. Crishock. 1998. 'Electronic and Print Media Representations of Washington, DC Demonstrations, 1982 and 1991: A Demography of Description Bias'. In Dieter Rucht, Ruud Koopmans, and Friedhelm Neidhardt, eds., *Acts of Dissent: New Developments in the Study of Protest*. Lanham, MD: Rowman Littlefield.

McConville, M., A. Sanders, and R. Leng. 1991. *The Case for the Prosecution*. London: Routledge.

McLeod, Douglas M., and James K. Hertog. 1992. 'The Manufacture of "Public Opinion" by Reporters: Informal Cues for Public Perceptions of Protest Groups.' *Discourse and Society* 3 (3): 259–75.

McLuhan, Marshall. 1964. *Understanding Media*. New York: McGraw-Hill.

McMahon, Maeve. 1988. 'Police Accountability: The Situation of Complaints in Toronto.' *Contemporary Crises* 12: 301–27.

McMahon, Maeve, and Richard Ericson. 1987. 'Reforming the Police and Policing Reform.' In R.S. Ratner and John L. McMullan, eds., *State Control: Criminal Justice Politics in Canada*. Vancouver: University of British Columbia Press.

McPhail, C., D. Schweingruber, and J. McCarthy. 1998. 'Policing Protest in the United States: 1960–1995.' In D. Della Porta and H. Reiter, eds., *Policing Protest: The Control of Mass Demonstrations in Western Democracies*. Minneapolis, MN: University of Minnesota Press.

Manning, Peter. 1978. 'The Police: Mandate, Strategies and Appearances.' In P. Manning and J. Van Maanen, eds., *Policing: A View From the Street*. Santa Monica, CA: Goodyear.

Marx, Gary T. 1981. 'Ironies of Social Control: Authorities as Contributors to Deviance through Escalation, Non-Enforcement and Covert Facilitation.' *Social Problems* 28 (3): 221–33.

– 1988. *Undercover: Police Surveillance in America*. Berkeley, CA: University of California Press.

– 1998. 'Afterword: Some Reflections on the Democratic Policing of Demonstrations.' In D. Della Porta and H. Reiter, eds., *Policing Protest: The Control of Mass Demonstrations in Western Democracies*. Minneapolis, MN: University of Minnesota Press.

Masterman, Len. 1985. 'The Battle of Orgreave.' In L. Masterman, ed., *Television Mythologies*. London: Comedia.

Mathiesen, Thomas. 1997. 'The Viewer Society: Michel Foucault's "Panopticon" Revisited.' *Theoretical Criminology* 1 (2): 215–33.

Medler, Jerry F., and Medler, Michael. 1993. 'Media Images as Environmental Policy.' In Robert J. Spitzer, ed., *Media and Public Policy*. Westport, CT: Praeger.

Meyer, David S., and Sidney Tarrow. 1998. 'A Movement Society: Contentious Politics for a New Society.' In D.S. Meyer and S. Tarrow, eds., *The Social Movement Society*. Lanham, MD: Rowman Littlefield.

Meyrowitz, Joshua. 1985. *No Sense of Place: The Impact of Electronic Media on Social Behaviour*. New York: Oxford University Press.

– 1990. 'Television: The Shared Arena.' *The World and I* 5 (7): 464–81.

– 1994. 'Medium Theory.' In David Crowley and David Mitchell, eds., *Communication Theory Today*. Stanford: Stanford University Press.

Moran, Jade. 1998. 'A Brief Chronology of Photographic and Video Surveillance.' In Clive Norris, Jade Moran, and Gary Armstrong, eds., *Surveillance, Closed Circuit Television and Social Control*. Aldershot, U.K.: Ashgate.

Morley, David. 1996. 'Populism, Revisionism and the "New Audience Research."' In J. Curran, D. Morley, and V. Walkerdine, eds., *Cultural Studies and Communications*. London: Arnold.

Motavalli, Jim. 1995. 'In Harm's Way.' *E: The Environmental Magazine* 6 (6): 28–37.

Murdock, Graham. 1984. 'Reporting the Riots: Images and Impact.' In J. Benyon, ed., *Scarman and After: Essays Reflecting on Lord Scarman's Report, the Riots and their Aftermath*. Oxford: Pergamon.

Neugebauer, Robynne, ed., 2000. *Criminal Injustice: Racism in the Criminal Justice System*. Toronto: Canadian Scholar's Press.

Nichol, Bill. 1994. *Blurred Boundaries: Questions of Meaning in Contemporary Culture*. Bloomington, IN: Indiana University Press.

Norris, Clive, and Gary Armstrong. 1998. 'Introduction: Power and Vision.' In Clive Norris, Jade Moran, and Gary Armstrong, eds., *Surveillance, Closed Circuit Television and Social Control*. Aldershot, U.K.: Ashgate.

– 1999. *Maximum Surveillance Society: The Rise of CCTV*. New York: Berg.

Norris, C., C. Kemp, N. Fielding, and J. Fielding. 1992. 'Black and Blue: An Analysis of the Effect of Race on Police Stops'. *British Journal of Sociology* 43 (2): 207–24.

O'Heffernan, Patrick. 1992. 'The L.A. Riots: A Story Made for and by TV.' *Television Quarterly* 26 (1): 5–11.

Oliver, Mary Beth. 1994. 'Portrayals of Crime, Race and Aggression in "Reality-Based" Police Shows: A Content Analysis.' *Journal of Broadcasting and Electronic Media* 38 (2): 179–92.

Oliver, Mary Beth, and G. Blake Armstrong. 1995. 'Predictors of Viewing and Enjoyment of Reality-Based and Fictional Crime Shows.' *Journalism and Mass Communication Quarterly* 72 (3): 559–70.

Ontario. 1995. *Report of the Commission on Systemic Racism in the Ontario Criminal Justice System*. Toronto: Queen's Printer.

Ostertag, Bob. 1991. 'Greenpeace takes over the world.' *Mother Jones* 16 (2): p. 32

Perigard, Mark. 1995. 'The Reality Is, Cop Shows Fuel Bias and Fear of Crime.' *Boston Herald* (25 April 1995): 41.

Perlmutter, D. 2000. *Policing the Media: Street Cops and Public Perceptions of Law Enforcement*. Thousand Oaks, CA: Sage.

Porritt, Jonathan, and David Winner. 1988. *The Coming of the Greens*. London: Fontana.

Poster, Mark. 1990. *The Mode of Information: Post-Structuralism and Social Context*. Cambridge: Polity Press.

– 1995. *The Second Media Age*. Cambridge: Polity Press.

Postman, Neil. 1985. *Amusing Ourselves to Death: Public Discourse in the Age of Show Business*. New York: Penguin.

Potter, Gary W., and Victor E. Kappeler. 1998. Constructing Crime: Perspectives on Making News and Social Problems. Prospect Heights, IL: Waveland.

Pritchard, David. 1986. 'Homicide and Bargained Justice: The Agenda-Setting Effect of Crime News on Prosecutors.' *Public Opinion Quarterly* 50: 143–59.

Pue, W. Wesley, ed. 2000. *Pepper in Our Eyes: The APEC Affair*. Vancouver: University of British Columbia Press.

Reiner, Robert. 2000. *The Politics of the Police*. 3rd ed. Oxford: Oxford University Press.

Robbins, Bruce. 1993. 'Introduction: The Public as Phantom.' In B. Robbins, ed., *The Phantom Public Sphere*. Minneapolis, MN: University of Minnesota Press.

Roberts, Julian, and Anthony Doob. 1990. 'News Media Influences on Public Views of Sentencing.' *Law and Human Behaviour* 14 (5): 451–68.

Robins, Max. 1989. 'Camcorder Assault.' *Channels* 9 (1): 30–1.

Rogers, Everett M., and James W. Dearing. 1994. 'Agenda-Setting Research: Where Has It Been, Where Is It Going?' In Doris A. Graber, ed., *Media Power in Politics*. 3rd ed. Washington, DC.: Congressional Quarterly.

Royal Commmission Inquiry into Policing in British Columbia. 1994. *Closing The Gap: Policing and The Community – The Report*. Vol. 1. Vancouver: Queen's Printer.

Rucht, Dieter. 1995. 'Ecological Protest as Calculated Law-Breaking.' In W. Rudig, ed., *Green Politics Three*. Edinburgh: Edinburgh University Press.

Rutherford, Paul. 1989. *When Television Was Young: Primetime Canada 1952–1967*. Toronto: University of Toronto Press.

Ryan, Charlotte. 1991. *Prime Time Activism: Media Strategies for Grass Roots Organizing*. Boston: South End Press.

Sacco, Vincent. 1995. 'Media Constructions of Crime.' *Annals*, AAAPS, 539: 141–54.

Salzman, Jason. 1998. *Making the News: A Guide for Non-Profits and Activists*. Boulder, CO: Westview.

Sasson, Theodore. 1995. *Crime Talk: How Citizens Construct a Social Problem*. New York: Aldine de Gruyter.

Scattarella, Christy. 1992. 'Wrong Raid Captured for Cops Show.' *Seattle Times* (24 May 1992): A1.

Scheingold, Stuart. 1984. *The Politics of Law and Order*. New York: Longman.

– 1995. 'Politics, Public Policy and Street Crime.' *Annals*, AAPSS, 539: 155–68.

Schlesinger, Philip, Graham Murdock, and Philip Elliott. 1983. *Televising 'Terrorism': Political Violence in Popular Culture*. London: Comedia.

Schlesinger, Philip, and Howard Tumber. 1993. 'Fighting the War against Crime: Television, Police and Audience.' *British Journal of Criminology* 33 (1): 19–33.

Schlesinger, Philip, and Howard Tumber. 1994. *Reporting Crime: The Media Politics of Criminal Justice*. Oxford: Clarendon Press.

Seagal, Debra. 1993. 'Tales from the Cutting Room Floor: The Reality of "Reality-Based" Television.' *Harper's* (November): 50–7.

Seaman, William R. 1992. 'Active Audience Theory: Pointless Populism.' *Media, Culture and Society*, 14: 301–11.

Shaiko, Ronald G. 1993. 'Greenpeace U.S.A.: Something Old, New, Borrowed.' *Annals*, AAPPS, 528: 88–100.

Shanahan, James, and Michael Morgan. 1999. *Television and Its Viewers: Cultivation Theory and Research*. Cambridge: Cambridge University Press.

Shearing, Clifford. 1992. 'The Relation between Public and Private Policing.' In Michael Tonry and Norval Morris, eds., *Modern Policing*. Chicago: University of Chicago Press.

Shearing, Clifford, and P. Stenning. 1984. 'From the Panopticon to Disneyworld: The Development of Discipline.' In A. Doob and E. Greenspan, eds., *Perspectives in Criminal Law*. Toronto: Canada Law Book.

Sherizen, Sanford. 1978. 'Social Creation of Crime News: All the News Fitted to Print.' In C. Winick, ed., *Deviance and Mass Media*. Beverly Hills, CA: Sage.

Simon, Jonathan, and Malcolm Feeley. 1995. 'True Crime: The New Penology and Public Discourse on Crime.' In Thomas G. Blomberg and Stanley Cohen, eds., *Punishment and Social Control*. Hawthorne, NY: Aldine de Gruyter.

Silverstone, Roger. 1988. 'Television Myth and Culture.' In J.W. Carey, ed.,
    Media, Myths and Narratives: Television and the Press. Beverly Hills, CA: Sage.
Smith, Dorothy. 1984. 'Textually-Mediated Social Organization.' *International
    Social Science Journal* 36: 59–75.
Smith, Steven Cole. 1993. 'COPS File Bulges with Rules Broken, Viewers
    Captured.' *Chicago Tribune* (18 February 1993).
Sparks, Richard. 1992. *Television and the Drama of Crime: Moral Tales and the
    Place of Crime in Public Life*. Buckingham, U.K.: Open University Press.
Staples, William. 1997. *The Culture of Surveillance: Discipline and Social Control
    in the United States*. New York: St. Martin's Press.
Stark, Rodney. 1972. *Police Riots*. Belmont, CA: Wadsworth.
Stehr, Nico, and Richard Ericson, eds., 1992. *The Culture and Power of Knowl-
    edge*. Berlin: de Gruyter.
Surette, Ray. 1997. *Media, Crime and Criminal Justice: Images and Realities*. 2nd
    ed. Pacific Grove, CA: Brooks/Cole.
– 1996. 'News from Nowhere, Policy to Follow: The Media and the Social
    Construction of "Three Strikes, You're Out."' In David Schichor, and Dale K.
    Sechrest, eds., *Three Strikes and You're Out: Vengeance as Public Policy*. Thou-
    sand Oaks, CA: Sage.
Tarrow, Sidney. 1994. *Power In Movement: Social Movements, Collective Action
    and Politics*. Cambridge: Cambridge University Press
Thompson, John B. 1990. *Ideology and Modern Culture: Critical Social Theory in
    the Era of Mass Communication*. Stanford, CA: Stanford University Press.
– 1994. 'Social Theory and the Media.' In David Crowley and David Mitchell,
    eds., *Communication Theory Today*. Stanford: Stanford University Press.
– 1995. *The Media and Modernity: A Social Theory of the Media*. Stanford, CA:
    Stanford University Press.
Tindall, David, and Aaron Doyle. 1999. 'Getting into the Media or Getting
    out the Message: Evaluating Mass-Mediated Protest Actions as a Tool for
    Social Movement Framing.' Paper presented at the 34th Annual Canadian
    Sociology and Anthropology Association Meetings, Sherbrooke, Quebec,
    June.
Tuchman, Gaye. 1972. 'Objectivity as Strategic Ritual.' *American Journal of
    Sociology* 77 (January): 660–79.
– 1978. *Making News: A Study in the Construction of Reality*. New York: Free
    Press.
Tumber, Howard.1982. *Television and the Riots*. London: British Film Institute
    Publishing.
Utz, P.J. 1976. *Settling the Facts: Discretion and Negotiation in Criminal Court*.
    Lexington, MA: Lexington Books.

Vick, Karl. 1997. 'Fatal Crash Puts Reality-TV on Trial.' *Toronto Star* 19 December 1997: D16.

Waddington, D. 1992. *Contemporary Issues in Public Disorder: A Comparative and Historical Approach*. London: Routledge.

Waddington, D., K. Jones, and C. Critcher. 1989. *Flashpoints: Studies in Public Disorder*. London: Routledge.

Waddington, Peter. 1994. *Liberty and Order: Public Order Policing in a Capital City*. London: UCL Press.

– 1998. 'Constructing Riots.' Paper presented to the conference 'Protest, the Public Sphere and Public Order' University of Geneva, October.

Walden, Keith. 1982. *Vision of Order: The Canadian Mounties in Symbol and Myth*. Toronto: Butterworths.

Warford, Mark, ed., 1997. *Witness: Twenty Five Years on the Environmental Front-Line*. London: Andre Deutsch.

Wisler, Dominique, and Marco Giugni. 1999. 'Under the Spotlight: The Impact of Media Attention on Protest Policing.' *Mobilization* 4 (2): 171–87.

Wren-Lewis, Justin. 1981. 'The Story of a Riot: The Television Coverage of Civil Unrest in 1981.' *Screen Education* 40 (1/2): 15–34.

Yearley, Steven. 1991. *The Green Case: A Sociology of Environmental Issues, Arguments and Politics*. London: Harper Collins.

Young, Alison. 1996. *Imagining Crime: Textual Outlaws and Criminal Conversations*. London: Thousand Oaks/New Delhi: Sage.

Young, Jock. 1999. *The Exclusive Society: Social Exclusion, Crime and Difference in Late Modernity*. London: Sage.

Young, Kevin. 1986. '"The Killing Field": Themes in Mass Media Responses to the Heysel Stadium Riot.' *International Review for the Sociology of Sport* 21 (2/3): 253–65.

Zoglin, Richard. 1992. 'The Cops and the Cameras.' *Time* 139 (14): 62–3.

Index

Acland, Charles, 5
agenda-setting by the media, 10
Altheide, David, 8, 9, 20–3, 27, 57, 63, 69, 70, 72, 73, 123, 131, 135, 148, 168n. 5
amateur video: arrests initiated by civilians for, 76; authenticity questioned, 79–80; boom in home camcorders, 5, 73; encouraged for local news, 74; explicit narration on, 78; influence on crime and policing, 81; and media logic, 76; stimulated by Rodney King video, 74; versus surveillance video, 77–81, 140; on TV news, 73–6
American Detective, 33, 51, 52, 60, 61
America's Funniest Home Videos, 5
America's Most Wanted, 49, 54, 155
Andersen, Robin, 41, 44, 56
Anderson, Alison, 112, 124, 127
Anderson, Carolyn, 34, 42
APEC 1997, 84, 95, 107, 110
Appleby, Timothy, 70, 71
Armstrong, Gary, 40, 44, 53, 56, 62, 65, 72, 149, 152
Arpaio, Sheriff Joe, 70–1
audiences: as active interpreters, 9,

56, 135; and 'authorized definitions,' 135; and *Cops*, 56; influenced by crime in the media, 56–7; influenced by media, 9–10, 157n. 1; influenced by TV content, 4; and Greenpeace, 127–30; role of, 82, 140–1, 144; as surveillance participants, 66
audience surveys by Greenpeace, 122, 165n. 10
'authorized definition': 46, 47, 63, 80, 84, 109–10, 135, 143, 144; as concept expanding notion of primary definers, 143
Azscam (Arizona), 23, 73

back-region information, 15, 19, 134–5, 157n. 2
back region (physical space), 19, 26–7, 62, 134, 157n. 2
Baker, William F., 16, 26, 73, 112, 124
Baranek, Patricia, 8–9, 23, 24–8, 32, 36, 81, 112, 113, 120, 125, 131, 134, 139, 143, 150
Barbour, Malcolm, 32
Barthes, Roland, 53
Baudrillard, Jean, 11, 14